ESSENTIAL GUIDE TO dBASE III+ IN LIBRARIES

ESSENTIAL GUIDE TO dBASE III+ IN LIBRARIES

Karl Beiser

Meckler Publishing Corporation

Supplement to *Small Computers in Libraries*, no. 1

Library of Congress Cataloging-in-Publication Data

Beiser, Karl.
    Essential guide to dBase III+ in libraries.

    Bibliography: p.
    Includes index.
    1. Libraries--Automation. 2. dBase III+ (Computer
program) 3. Library science--Data processing.
4. Microcomputers--Library applications. I. Title.
Z678.93.D33B44 1986 025'.0028'5536 86-23877
ISBN 0-88736-064-5

Meckler Publishing Corporation, 11 Ferry Lane West, Westport, CT
    06880.
Meckler Publishing, 3 Henrietta Street, London WC2E 8LU, UK.

Printed and bound in the United States of America.

CONTENTS

INTRODUCTION

Libraries make lists--lots of them. Lists of materials in the collection, lists of library users, lists of statistics of library operation. Bibliographies, abstracts, and local newspaper indexes are all variations on the theme. If there is one thing computers are good for, it is keeping track of lists. Whether widgets or patent abstracts, a mailing list or a serials check-in file, the right software and a small computer on which to run it can make operating a library a good deal easier and more efficient.

The key is software, the program or programs that provide instructions to a computer as to how to manipulate the information presented to it. One highly versatile software package for general purpose data manipulation is *dBase III+*, manufactured by Ashton-Tate, Inc. It is the most popular of the "high-powered" database management programs on the market at this time. Whether it is *the* best in all respects is immaterial. *dBase III+* is indisputably one of the best at a wide range of tasks and since it, more than any other program of its type, is likely to be known and used already within a library or its parent organization, it is the focus of this book.

The program enjoys its dominant position for three major reasons. First, in its initial incarnation as *dBase II* (there never was a *dBase I*, nor was there an Ashton, only a Tate), the product was the first capable database manager for microcomputers. The many experienced and satisfied users of the product influenced would-be purchasers ("It's all I know and it works just great.") and were able to provide advice and support to new users. Second, the firm improved the product and effectively promoted it to maintain a lead in sales, if not always in technical specifications, over commercial rivals. Finally, the wealth of commands, functions, operating modes, and miscellaneous facilities provided ensure that whatever *dBase*'s apparent limitations, it contains somewhere within it the capabilities to surmount them. Some of the work-arounds are imaginative and elegant, others just plain ugly. Their availability sustains a significant popularity among both long-time and first-time users of database management software.

Who Should Read This Book?

This book is meant primarily for those who already have acquired a general familiarity with *dBase III+*. Well-written introductions are provided in the manuals that come with the program and in scores of books available at any good bookstore and, one would hope, of books available at any good bookstore and, one would hope, library. In particular, it is for those just starting to apply the facilities of *dBase III+* to the real-life and often frustrating demands of library applications.

Those completely unfamiliar with *dBase* may use the introductory material in each section and the Blitz course section as guides to learning enough about the program to consider applying it to library tasks later on.

This book is also for the general user of *dBase III+* with an interest in learning more about text and bibliographic applications and/or more about the potential of *dBase III+* for library applications.

Library Use of dBase

dBase III+ is a "database manager." Without entering too deeply into the terminological debate on which features differentiate this more capable and more expensive genre from less sophisticated file managers (e.g., *PFS-File* and *PFS-Report* from Software Publishing and their successors), one major feature usually marks part of the dividing line: the ability to work with information stored in more than one computer disk file, and to define, maintain, and produce reports based on the relationship between elements in the various files.

Much of the information libraries might like to manipulate with a computer exhibits characteristics that make it difficult to encompass in a single-file database. As you will see, there are many useful ways in which several files can work together to store information efficiently and retrieve it quickly.

Needless to say, library-specific examples are not plentiful in the literature on *dBase III+*. In addition, the very commands and functions of *dBase* that are most necessary to doing some library jobs are not well explained in the manuals provided. This book demonstrates a variety of ways of using *dBase III+* in libraries. Many of the techniques are generally applicable to a variety of working environments where text information is important and/or one-to-one relationships between data elements are the exception rather than the rule.

It should be kept in mind, however, that not everything that can be done in *dBase* should be done in *dBase*. The program can be bent and twisted to almost any purpose, though with varying results. The section on keyword indexing of abstracts is a case in point. If abstracts are a small, subsidiary application, and *dBase* is readily available, then maybe the approach is worth the effort. If, however, abstracting large numbers of documents is a major concern, there are several programs on the market that will do the job faster, easier, with less wasted disk storage space, and more in keeping with library expectations for quick and flexible retrieval.

Of Silver Bullets, Text Data Managers and dBase

There are three major strategies for applying the speed and power of a computer to library tasks. The first is to buy an arsenal of silver bullets (narrowly defined, special purpose software packages), one per task. To handle overdues, buy *Overdue Writer* (Follett Library Software). To produce bibliographies get *Bibliography Writer* from the same company, or *Pro-Cite* from Personal Bibliographic Software. The chief advantage of the silver bullet approach is ease of learning (usually). Because such programs possess a limited number of options, and because the program designer could focus on just one or two patterns of use, choices available to the user are usually fewer and better documented.

Disadvantages of the silver bullet system include high cost (only if many programs are purchased, each for a particular task); probable incompatibility between file formats, especially if programs come from different vendors; and inability to adapt to local requirements unanticipated by the program designer.

The second alternative is a library-oriented or at least a text-oriented data management package. *INMAGIC* (Inmagic, Inc.) is a good example of this type of program. It allows the user considerable flexibility in defining a data structure appropriate to each of a variety of text-oriented library tasks. Long and variable length fields are no problem. Many-to-one relationships (e.g., multiple subject terms referring to a single bibliographic entity) are easily accommodated through the device of subfields (multivalued fields). Filing order options make a librarian feel right at home.

Yet, such programs are typically weak in numeric manipulation, in generating a wide variety of reports with relatively little effort, and in faciliting fast, easy data entry. A new, recently issued version of *INMAGIC* should make things easier for users of that product at least. Cost is also a concern. Many of the best library-oriented text managers cost $1,000 or more. If text storage and retrieval are the major jobs to be done, files are large, and search capabilities following the style of online systems are desired, then this type of program is the way to go. If a wide variety of list maintenance tasks must be accomplished, sometimes including substantial numeric calculation, another solution is needed.

The third option, and the one upon which this book is founded, is the use of a general-purpose database manager for library-specific applications--in particular *dBase III+*, the most popular product in that class. The advantages are low cost, especially if the cost is spread across a wide variety of uses, and the program is purchased mail-order at the typical thirty to forty percent discount from list price ($695 at this writing); great flexibility in setting things up just the way they should be for local requirements; a community of individuals in the organization or the vicinity ready and willing to help out; and a flood of books, magazine articles, and course materials to help learn how to use the program.

The disadvantages of *dBase III+* include: a longer learning curve than the alternatives because of the multiplicity of commands, functions, and facilities it offers; limited text-handling capabilities, albeit remediable ones; and little information available on how to apply it to individual library needs. Journal articles have appeared with increasing frequency, however, and this book is also meant to help the situation.

A Note on Content

The examples given here are almost all bits and pieces to illustrate a point, rather than full-blown, comprehensive, and polished solutions. It is expected that readers with a special interest in one area or another will examine the outlines and segments of program files included here and build upon them to meet specific local needs. In some cases, an example may offer negative evidence, demonstrating the impracticality of an approach in a particular situation. That's fine, insofar as it steers one in a different, more promising direction.

What You Will Find

Often, there is no "best way" to do a particular job. For that reason, a variety of approaches have been used in the applications sections of this book where perhaps one or two might have sufficed in most of them. In developing any of the applications demonstrated here, it pays to be as consistent as possible in the use of a single set of techniques. Not only does consistency make it easier to understand later what one has done and why, but it also makes it simpler to combine routines as they develop over time.

There are many "tricks of the trade" in using *dBase III+* that are learned over a period of time. I have avoided the more obscure short-cuts that I know of. There are doubtless ways of doing a particular task that are a bit slicker or a good deal more elegant than the way I've presented. Like everyone else working with software of this level of capability, I am still on the "learning curve." Think of the techniques presented here as a workable starting point upon which you can base you own refinements as you become more proficient.

The fact that the same objective can be realized by so many different methods gives some new and would-be users pause. A program with so many possibilities must be hard, right? Is a workshop that contains 200 tools any harder to work in than one that contains a dozen? Laying hands on the correct tool for a job may take a bit of extra time at first, but very quickly one comes to appreciate how swiftly and easily things get done when the appropriate tool is immediately at hand for each job. In starting out, remember that it is not necessary to be conversant in more than a few of *dBase III+*'s commands and concepts in order to process impressive volumes of information in ways utterly impossible in a manual environment.

Versions

This book is based on *dBase III+* versions 1.0 and 1.1. The latter was released as this book went to press. It is likely to have a number of quiet bug-fixes (not that I've had any problems with 1.0 in doing work for this book). The major news, however, is Ashton-Tate's decision to do away with copy-protection. Given the eventual mortality of disks (both floppy and hard), and the disinclination of the average user to deal with installation/de-installation hassles in the middle of trying to get a job done, copy-protection was becoming more of a hassle for the vendor than it was worth in piracy protection.

A fair number of commands and facilities unique to *dBase III+* are employed in the discussions that follow. Those with *dBase III* will need to contrive their own work-arounds here and there. The upgrade to *dBase III+* is worth it.

Conventions

Upper-case representation is used to distinguish *dBase* commands and user-defined file and variable names when they occur within normal text. Within program segments, upper-case is used to represent *dBase* command syntax and lower-case to indicate user-defined file and variable names.

dBase command lines are often too long to fit on a single line in this book. Second and succeeding lines of such long commands are indented and prefaced by ^^^^. When they are entered at the dot-prompt, they should be placed on one line (*dBase III+* scrolls horizontally to allow for entry of up to 254 characters). The built-in text editor for producing program files will automatically wrap the line around at a (more or less) appropriate point.

A comment within a program file is preceded by an asterisk (*) in the first character position of a line, or by && if it follows on the same line as a command. *dBase* gives us no choice in this matter.

Illustrations of the appearance of the display screen are usually set off at top and bottom by a line of slashes (///////////). Since the text width of a page in this book is less than that of a standard display screen, some screen displays have been compressed. If a particular screen looks crowded or "busy," it is probably due to this compression.

It isn't possible to exactly replicate on paper the line and double-line graphics that are used in *dBase III+*. These graphics have been simulated with the hyphen, equal sign, and colon.

ESSENTIAL GUIDE TO dBASE III+ IN LIBRARIES

BLITZ COURSE

It takes Ashton-Tate two large manuals (seven pounds or so at last weigh-in) to lay out in general terms the features and operation of its mammoth database management program, *dBase III+*. Despite the bulk of the documentation, however, it barely touches upon some of the features that are pivotal in using the program in libraries.

What follows here is comment on and explanation of matters which are either of special importance in libraries or are poorly covered in the massive Ashton-Tate books. The novice user is reminded that nothing can replace reading the manuals and/or another good, general introduction to *dBase III+*.

What is dBase III+?

That there are few examples in the manual that illuminate everyday library data management problems, or even fully demonstrate the *dBase* commands that can be used to resolve those problems, is regrettable. It is also not surprising, given the nature of the program.

dBase III+ is a language in the broadest sense. Its elements are many and their permutations in everyday usage are huge in number. It is easier to answer the question, "What can't you do with *dBase III+*" than to state definitively what can be done. The very hardest is to delineate, out of context, how to attack a specific problem in a particular business or institutional setting.

Don't expect a manufacturer providing a software tool to be used in thousands of different kinds of organizations to include step-by-step directions on how to do all the major jobs in everyone of them. If we did, we would also expect Smith-Corona to provide us with directions on what to type with a typewriter in a library, or a French instructor to tell us what we should talk about once we become fluent in the language.

This book will make some assumptions and establish a context within which library-specific uses of *dBase III+* can be discussed and demonstrated. The sections of this book dealing with library applications areas fill in the gaps, providing many specific examples of *dBase* features and *dBase* technique.

The Three Faces of dBase

First impressions of software, as of a people, are based on outward appearances. The look and feel of a program is termed its "user interface." The interesting thing here is that the user interface can be good, bad, or indifferent, independent of the relative merits of the rest of the program. A rapidly executing, flexible, and powerful piece of software can be obscured by an unimaginative, nonintuitive system for interacting with the user. Conversely, a poorly performing program can look a great deal better draped in a jazzy, "user-friendly" interface.

Over time, however, the truth will come out. Steady users of a program will see through the pull-down menus, hot-key-activated help screens, macro-editors, and similar bells and whistles. The bottom-line question, "Does this package efficiently handle my data processing requirements?" does get answered eventually.

Comments vary on the ease of use of *dBase III+*. It is one of the hardest or one of the easiest programs of its type. It is quick and convenient or vast and cumbersome. It is or is not appropriate for large/small jobs. Most comments are based on experience with the user interface. After all, you have to learn the user interface before dealing with the larger, underlying concepts of database creation and manipulation. That public perceptions vary so widely is due, at least in part, to the fact that *dBase III+* has three fairly complete and largely divergent user interfaces.

Those who view *dBase III+* as too obscure for words may not have gotten beyond the dot-prompt. Those who find *dBase III+* cumbersome and unwieldy may have simply become frustrated with the protective shell erected around the system by the *dBase* Assistant, a menu-driven interface available at the touch of a key.

"*dBase III+* isn't a program, its a language." Besides being a contradiction in terms (all languages are programs, though they are not application programs), this statement implies that the availability of a programming language *requires* that every user burden himself with learning how to use it. This is silly. It is like saying that a person would be a terrific basketball player if only he weren't so tall and fast.

The three interfaces available to the *dBase III+* user are tools to be called upon in appropriate circumstances and left alone at other times. To enhance the analogy, they are really tool boxes, each with its own special set of capabilities and limitations. The discussion that follows is designed to help you decide under what circumstances each tool box is worth opening up.

The Assistant

As it comes out of the box, *dBase III+* is set up to place the user in ASSIST mode whenever the program is invoked. Most of the program's functions are available by selecting menu options in sequence. Creating, manipulating, maintaining, and deriving reports from a database are all possible using the interface. For simple operations, the main difference between using the program from the dot-prompt and from within ASSIST is the added time required to accomplish an action in the latter mode.

It takes a fair number of separate selections in ASSIST mode to open a file of statistical information about libraries, indexed on library name, and then produce a list of those serving between 5,000 and 8,000 population that have per capita support greater than $10.00 and less than seventy percent of their budget expended on staff. If you know the syntax well enough, it is far simpler to put forth the following on the dot-prompt command line:

```
. USE stats83
. REPORT FORM statrpt TO PRINT FOR totexp/pop>9.99
     ^^^^ .AND. salaries/totexp<.70 .AND. pop>4999
     ^^^^ .AND. pop<8001
```

The ASSIST mode is a good place for new users to start. It should be thought of as a learning tool and not necessarily as a permanent means of using the program. Library-like tasks often involve multiple files and long command line specifications with lots of FOR and WHILE clauses, which many users will find unsatisfactorily slow when invoked from within the Assistant.

Learning how to work from the dot-prompt or with short command files (i.e., programs) will bear fruit in the long run. Meanwhile, pay close attention to the string of commands formed at the bottom of the ASSIST screen. It is based on successive choices from the menus and is exactly the command line you would have to synthesize at the dot-prompt. It is probably pretty close to what would be needed in a command file as well.

Here is as much of the ASSIST menu arrangement as will fit on the page:

///
Set Up Create Update Position Retrieve Organize
```
|=======================|
| Database file         |
|-----------------------|
| Format for Screen     |
| Query                 |
|-----------------------|
| Catalog               |
| View                  |
|-----------------------|
| Quit dBASE III PLUS   |
|=======================|
```

///

You can exit to the dot-prompt level by hitting the escape key when no other ASSIST menu choices are active. Typing ASSIST or pressing the F2 key (assuming the function keys haven't been redefined to have other meanings) puts you back within the comforting (to some) confines of drop-down menus, dialog boxes, and other such eye-catching stuff.

All it takes to get *dBase III+* to wake up in dot-prompt mode is to edit the CONFIG.DB configuration file and delete the line that says COMMAND=ASSIST.

The Infamous Dot-Prompt

The dot-prompt is the single period at the beginning of a line that indicates that *dBase* is ready to accept a command from the keyboard. Depending on your perspective, this may represent an invitation or a threat. If you don't know what the dot-prompt means, or what commands are available and how to use them, the situation may represent, at the least, a snide dare to play "twenty questions."

The dot-prompt was the only way, short of writing programs, that users of *dBase* II had for getting the program to do their bidding. Initially, there was not even an online help facility. The *dBase* Assistant was introduced with *dBase III* and redone and expanded with *III+*, primarily to help the legions of new users jump into the swim more quickly and with fewer of the frustrations of that nearly blank screen with the diminutive, intimidating point of light at its left edge.

The simple truth is that you are not getting full value from *dBase III+* until you learn how to operate from the dot-prompt. Depending on the jobs at hand, it may not be necessary to use it immediately, but the Assistant should be viewed as just the first step toward making use of the full range of data management tools in the *dBase* tool kit. The next step after developing a familiarity with this level of interactive use is storing sequences of commands in a program file. The fact that most of the programming language consists of the commands that also work interactively makes that step fairly easy and natural.

In the meantime, life at the dot-prompt is considerably easier than it used to be. If you need help, type HELP. The following menu appears:

```
/////////////////////////////////////////////////
                   MAIN MENU
                Help Main Menu

          1 - Getting Started
          2 - What Is a ...
          3 - How Do I ...
          4 - Creating a Database File
          5 - Using an Existing Database File
          6 - Commands and Functions

/////////////////////////////////////////////////
```

This is little more than an online version of the quick reference booklet and command summaries that are included with the printed documentation. It is nevertheless handier than digging out the manual, consulting the index, and figuring out the peculiar page-numbering scheme of the manual. To refresh your memory on the set commands, for instance, choose option 6. A second menu offers a choice of several categories of functions and commands. From this menu, choose the option for showing SET commands and you will end up with:

///
SET TO Commands

1 – SET ALTERNATE   9 – SET FIELDS   17 – SET MESSAGE

2 – SET CATALOG   10 – SET FILTER   18 – SET ORDER

3 – SET COLOR   11 – SET FUNCTION 19 – SET PATH

4 – SET DATE   12 – SET FORMAT   20 – SET PRINT

5 – SET DECIMALS   13 – SET HISTORY   21 – SET PROCEDURE

6 – SET DEFAULT   14 – SET INDEX   22 – SET RELATION

7 – SET DELIMITERS 15 – SET MARGIN   23 – SET TYPEAHEAD

8 – SET DEVICE   16 – SET MEMOWIDTH 24 – SET VIEW
///

More to the point is the ability to call up syntax and usage information about particular commands (and a few specific concepts) by typing HELP (command name). The scheme has the virtues and defects of a dictionary. If you have the command right, you get to find out more about it. If the spelling is wrong or a phrase is inverted, you are tossed into the general help menu.

Here's what appears when you enter HELP CREATE VIEW:

///

MODIFY VIEW
=========

Syntax   :   CREATE/MODIFY VIEW <view file>/?
                  CREATE VIEW FROM ENVIRONMENT

Description :

Allows creation and editing of a view file
using standard cursor controls. Use ? to display a list
of view files. If a catalog is in use, the new .vue file
is added.

See also   : SET VIEW

///

If we incorrectly assumed that the command was SELECT VIEW, we would again find ourselves at the main help menu.

The HISTORY feature makes entering commands, particularly long and complex ones, a lot easier than it used to be. When the feature is on, *dBase* records each command as it is entered. The number of commands retained is user-definable from 1 to 16,000. Ten to twenty is usually adequate. In any case, previously executed commands can be brought back to the command line by hitting the up-arrow. Not only will RETURN re-execute them (e.g., make five back-up copies of a data file while just entering file and subdirectory specifications once), but they can be edited with the standard *dBase* editing keys first.

A 150-character string of commands, field names, and logical operators may fail because of a missing period (.AND. instead of AND), but a second try requires just a couple of keystrokes of editing.

To review a list of previous commands, just enter LIST HISTORY. If you have used SET ALTERNATE TO (filename) and SET ALTERNATE ON, LIST HISTORY will put your sequence of interactive commands into a file ready to be edited and turned into a program file. It's like telling *dBase*, "Take some dictation please." Just be sure that the HISTORY=(number of lines to remember) in the CONFIG.DB configuration file is large enough for your purposes. Incidentally, this approach to creating program files works just as well in the ASSIST mode.

Oh! Programming

"Programming" is scary, or at least worrisome, to a lot of people. Designers of database management programs (and electronic spreadsheets and word processing packages for that matter) know that the majority of their prospective users have developed an antiprogramming mind-set. They go to considerable lengths to semantically distance their programming facilities from "programming." Macro facilities, executable command strings, stored instructions are all nothing but special cases of programs and programming.

Forget that awful experience you once had in school with FORTRAN/COBOL/PL1 or whatever. Programming is the contrivance of instructions into a logical sequence that is understandable to a computer and based upon which it can do useful work. It is as much like teaching a specific skill (first do this, then that, then if it's still not right, try this, etc.) as anything else.

The ability to store instructions for use over and over certainly saves typing time! The ability to test several instructions, see the results, and make minor changes before trying again is extremely convenient. Who wants to make a small change and then redo the whole thing from the start each time the intended result isn't realized?

The *dBase III+* programming language is there to be used when it is appropriate. There are usually several ways of accomplishing a task in *dBase III+*. Generally the program approach is the most powerful and flexible, and ASSIST is the slowest and (for the novice at least) the easiest. Those comfortable enough with the dot-prompt or interactive mode will decide between it and the program mode based on the complexity of the task at hand and the likelihood that it will need to be repeated later or redone in a slightly different form.

Commands that can be squeezed onto one line are usually best done from the dot-prompt. Long sequences of commands are more easily done in a short, impromptu command file. When extensive conditional processing must be done (IF, WHILE, FOR), the program mode is the only choice.

As a language, *dBase* has most of the facilities found in BASIC or Pascal. A major omission is an "array" structure. Good practice in handling file input dictates that information is first stored in a memory variable and only replaced (REPLACE) into a corresponding data field after confirmation by the user. When a user must enter a variable and unpredictable number of elements, each to be stored in its own data record, some means must exist to assign those values to temporary variables.

In BASIC, you might define TERM(1), TERM(2) etc. to receive the data elements. The sections on indexing, reference archives, and circulation, among others, demonstrate variations on a scheme to simulate such an array. Despite the fact that memory variable manipulations occur in internal memory, a large number of them in a repeating loop noticeably slow down a *dBase III+* program routine.

There are doubtless other shortcomings to the language as a language. The compensation is in the ease with which data file operations can be handled. Moving data to and from files, displaying it in an unlimited variety of arrangements, rapidly retrieving records based on complex field specifications, and round-about relationships between files are all strengths in comparison with other programming languages with which I am familiar.

Something of an annoyance is the *dBase III* Wordprocessor, the built-in editor that pops up whenever you create or modify a program file. It is activated by typing MODIFY COMMAND (filename). The editor can handle little more than 4,000 characters of text at a time. When you progress beyond that, the disconcerting message "file too long, data will be lost" appears at the top of the screen. It is time to delete a line or two, enough to turn off the warning, save what's left, and get out.

There is no facility for defining and moving blocks of text. Since some programs consist of several blocks of nearly the same statements, the extra typing is a bit frustrating. Word-wrap is awkward and yet the only way to make a long line of commands visible on the screen. Horizontal scrolling is unavailable.

The antidote here is to use another program as a program editor. This can be done in two ways. A word processing program can be run from within *dBase III+* (e.g., RUN WS brings my rusty old *WordStar* into action), providing the computer system has enough memory to support more than the immediate needs of *dBase* itself (256 kilobytes in the current release). The alternative is to designate a word processing or editing program in the CONFIG.DB set-up file that *dBase* looks to everytime it is loaded. The required line in the file is TEDIT=(filename of editor).

Be sure that the alternative editor operates in a "nondocument" or "ASCII" mode. Many word processing programs introduce invisible formatting codes into a text file. The problem is that the codes are only invisible within the word processor. *dBase* sees them and rejects them.

Watch out for even the nondocument mode. *WordStar*'s TAB function gets in even when all other special characters are turned off. It translates into an oval graphics character when typed (TYPE) to the screen or viewed through MODIFY COMMAND. Fortunately, programs ignore the character when they run. The only ill effect is to spoil the hierarchical indention scheme used to show which command lines are within which control loops. Inadvertently hitting paragraph reform (^B) in *WordStar* makes distinctly noticeable (i.e., chaotic) changes in commands destined for *dBase III+*.

By the way, an interesting way to move into the programming area is to use SET ALTERNATE TO (filename) and SET ALTERNATE ON to record commands and responses at the dot-prompt, or within ASSIST. Later, you can come back to the "log" file, edit out errors, modify existing statements for greater effect, and generally tinker. Changing the file extension to .PRG will make it doable.

The Importance of Relationships

One of the most important commands in *dBASE III+* is practically buried in the manual. SET RELATION TO is what differentiates *dBase III+* from a myriad of $100 (and free) file managers. It allows you to link multiple database files together and, for many purposes, pretend they are just one big file.

So why *can't* you put everything in one big file? Many-to-one relationships is one answer. A bibliographic item may have one title and one publisher (then again it may have more, but let's avoid that complexity for the moment), but more than one person may have authorship responsibility for it. Subject access may be required by one or two terms in the first instance and eight or ten in the next. You could construct a data structure with fields like AUTHOR1, AUTHOR2 and SUBJECT7, SUBJECT8, etc. Yet, sooner or later, a bibliographic item will come along that exceeds whatever arbitrary limits we've defined. And in the meantime, the defined but unused fields will be wasting substantial amounts of storage capacity.

One answer is to place those elements that occur in unpredictable numbers in a separate file, along with a value that can be used to maintain a link to the corresponding record holding all the nonmultiple elements. Thus, a bibliographic database might have a file for unitary information like publisher and publication date, and one or more files for subjects, authors and editors, series, and perhaps titles (consider multiple alternative titles). The sections on bibliographies and on a *dBase III* online catalog go into this matter further.

A typical series of commands to set up file relationships might be:
```
. SELECT 3

. USE register INDEX reglast
. SELECT 2
. USE reserves INDEX rsvbibno
. SET RELATION TO borrowerno INTO register
. SELECT 1
. USE bib INDEX bibttl
. SET RELATION TO bibno INTO reserves
```

Each time a record in BIB.DBF becomes the new current record, the record pointer in RESERVES.DBF moves to a record having the same BIBNO. If there is no match, the pointer is positioned at the end of RESERVES.DBF. At the same time, the record pointer in REGISTER.DBF is moved in concert with moves in RESERVES.DBF, but based on the contents of the field BORROWERNO. To make a list of books on reserve, you could say:

```
. LIST title, register->firstname, register->lastname
    ^^^^ FOR reserved
```

We've created a list of titles and who is waiting for each. The only problem is that this is a noninclusive list. Only the first person in line for a book is listed. Some books are likely to be on reserve for more than one library user. Additional program logic will make use of the SET RELATION command to make the list we want in a more adequate fashion. See the section on reserves for more discussion on this point.

If you plan to work from the dot-prompt, the SET FIELDS TO and SET FIELDS ON/OFF commands are related and equally under-appreciated. By including them in a fields list after SET FIELDS TO, you can eliminate the need to refer to fields in noncurrent work areas by their aliases (i.e., "register->"). You can also exclude extraneous fields from display and from use in FOR and WHILE clauses by not naming them in the field list. Don't assume too much, however. As in the example above, you may get only one

of several matches. And don't forget to type SET FIELDS ON.
Until it is issued, the fields list means nothing.

If a working environment like the one established above is often
required while at the dot-prompt, a view file can be used to capture
it once and to invoke it in the future with a single command. To
create a view file reflecting the current file set-up:

. CREATE VIEW <view name> FROM ENVIRONMENT

A file with the extension .VUE will be created. To open files,
invoke indexes, and redefine RELATIONs, next time around, just
enter:

. SET VIEW TO <view name>

Though I have used view files in some acquisitions programs
further on in this book, they probably are best avoided unless there
is a great deal of opening and closing of files within the program.
Generally, it is easier to just open everything and set up
RELATIONs at the beginning.

Watch out for the fifteen-file limit, though. No more than
fifteen files may be open at any one time. This includes program,
format, and index files along with database and memo files. See the
section on circulation for an example of opening and closing several
files works in getting around this limitation.

There's a useful trick that may come in handy in setting up
relations between files. While there is a limit of one RELATION per
work area, it is not necessary that the relation in any given work
area be based on a field in the file in that work area. Let's look
at another way of producing a list of books on reserve:

. SELECT 3
. USE register INDEX regborno s
. SELECT 2
. USE bib INDEX bibno
. SELECT 1
. USE reserves
. SET RELATION TO bibno INTO bib
. SELECT 2
. SET RELATION TO reserves->borrowerno INTO register
. SELECT 1

The RELATION based in work area 2 resides there because
there's room. It does nothing at all as far as causing the record

pointer in REGISTER.DBF to move in response to changes in BIB.DBF. This trick allows you to effectively circumvent the seeming impossibility of having more than one file move in direct response to movement in a single master file. As far as I can tell, this feature is undocumented in Ashton-Tate literature.

As long as the list of books on reserve doesn't have to appear in alphabetical order, this method of file set-up and a simple interactive command will suffice:

```
. LIST bib->title, register->firstname,
    ^^^^ register->lastname
```

Abbreviation of Commands

Any *dBase III+* command can be abbreviated to its first four or more characters. In some sections of this book you will see SELE 3, in others SELECT 3. CLOSE DATA means the same thing as CLOSE DATABASES. Note, however, that CLOSE DBASES and CLOSED DATABASES won't pass muster.

Documentation--Your Own

If what you do with *dBase* in the library is important enough to spend more than a few minutes on, think about the long-term problem of keeping track of how things work. Which data goes with what report forms? Which index files relate to which program file? Within program files, why was a particular, seemingly unnecessary step included? Here are a couple of sensible practices that, unfortunately, few of us are conscientious enough to follow all the time:

1. Print copies of the structure (LIST STRUCTURE TO PRINT) of all data files involved in a particular application and save them in a notebook or file. Add the text of program files and a list of all other files that are related to the application. If a complex multiple-work area set-up is used, a listing of that would also be helpful (LIST STATUS TO PRINT).
2. Use the comment prefixes * and && to indicate what is happening in parts of a program in which that is likely to be open to question. The program files in this book are not all as well documented in this regard as they should be, but I'm trying to improve.
3. Use the data catalog feature of *dBase III+* to keep track of what files go together.

Naming Conventions

Keeping track of files, fields, formats, and sundry other electromagnetic creations becomes surprisingly difficult as they proliferate on a disk storage device. The logic of naming a certain small program file SUSAN23E.PRG three months ago is likely to be long forgotten when it comes time to dredge up a needed program file and re-use it for some pressing current task.

There is probably no one, best method. The key principles, however, seem to be:

1. Make all file and field names meaningful.
2. Begin the names of related files with the same first and second characters, at least. Doing a directory for files matching the AR*.* specification will bring up all the reference archive files. Copying files is greatly simplified as well. COPY AR*.PRG   B: moves all the program files associated with reference archives to drive B: with a minimum of fuss and muss.
3. Use names that make sense. Eight characters is fairly limiting at first, but a bit of thought will leave you with names like RSVBYLAS.NDX (index based on the lastname of borrowers in the RESERVES.DBF file) that will make more sense later on than LASTNAME.NDX. The same goes for naming memory variables. MFIRSTNAME and MLASTNAME are far preferable to MEMVAR1 and MEMVAR2.
4. If you write programs, and the programs use memory variables to receive data on its way to and from fields, use variable names that are identical to the field names but for an "m" prefix, e.g., the contents of the variable MLASTNAME go into the field LASTNAME.
5. Avoid giving files and fields the same names as *dBase* commands: UPDATE.DBF could cause problems.
6. Give the CATALOG facility a try. After

```
. SET CATALOG TO <catalog file name>
. SET CATALOG ON
```

all database, index, format, report form, query, and view files are "logged" into a catalog of available files for a particular application. USE ? brings up a list of database files currently defined as belonging with the other files in a particular application. I've yet to be convinced it beats my scheme of consistent file name prefixes, but your tastes may be different.

Configuration Basics

CONFIG.DB is the configuration file for *dBase III+*. Every time the program is loaded, it looks to CONFIG.DB for special instructions that change the otherwise expected behavior of *dBase III+*. There are more than forty program defaults that can be changed with a few characters. Want to use *WordStar* to edit memo fields? WP=WS. How about HEADINGS=OFF to turn off column heading display whenever you list (LIST) or display (DISPLAY) information from a file? PATH allows you to specify one or more subdirectories which will be searched for files when they are not found in the current subdirectory. ALTERNATE=(filename) creates a file to receive a log of everything that is sent to the screen in interactive or ASSIST mode, except through "full-screen" operations.

COMMAND=(name of a program file) is powerful indeed. With it, *dBase III+* can be forced to immediately run a particular program or set of programs every time it is loaded. This ought to make things easier for those who will be working entirely from menus put up by command files.

Function Keys

Compared to the DOS function keys, those in *dBase III+* are a snap to redefine. Let's say that every time F3 is pressed, we want to see a directory of all files on drive A:, followed by a directory of all files on C:. From the dot-prompt, enter:

```
. SET FUNCTION 3 TO "DIR A:*.*; DIR C:*.*;"
```

They can also be defined in CONFIG.DB with a line like:

```
F3="DIR A:*.*; DIR C:*.*;"
```

The semicolon is interpreted as a carriage return by *dBase*.

Finding Out about the Fundamentals

This is a book about the fundamentals of applying *dBase III+* in libraries, not the fundamentals of learning *dBase III+* itself. The program is too large and its features too varied and powerful to include a meaningful general summary for the beginner in this book. Others have done it well and at great length in other places.

There is a small industry across America that supplies books, interactive training materials, seminars, and courses designed to help the first-time user gain control of the powerful tools provided by *dBase III+*. Ashton-Tate's manuals improve with every new release. The most recent pair do have a modest amount of tutorial as well as reference material.

Advanced Programmer's Guide (Luis Castro, Jay Hanson, and Tom Rettig. Ashton-Tate, various editions) is well worth its hefty price tag for those doing a fair amount of programming. The edition available as of late 1986 still hadn't fully caught up with the new features unique to *III+*, however.

Databased Advisor is a monthly with lots of useful how-to information for frequent users of *dBase III+*. At least half of each issue focuses on *dBase* usage. Some material is only of interest to programmers, while other material is for the novice. Reviews and commentary regarding other high-end database management software is illuminating.

The *Ashton-Tate Quarterly* is written less for programmers and more for novice and intermediate users. It covers all versions of *dBase* as well as *Framework II*, an integrated, multifunction package from the same firm. Production values, especially arty graphics, make it one of the most handsome yet basic sources of *dBase* information.

Hard-core users will want to consider Ashton-Tate's *Tech Notes* for information on bugs, work-arounds, and general software arcana.

Adam Green, a *Databased Advisor* columnist and author of a number of books on *dBase,* is one writer to seek out. His books on *dBase II* are good, but dated. (*dBase II User's Guide*, Prentice-Hall, 1983; *The Advanced dBase II User's Guide*, Prentice-Hall, 1984.) Should he produce anything on the latest version of *dBase III+*, I'd strongly consider getting it, sight unseen.

Look also for the name Robert Byers. He has written some good introductory books published by Ashton-Tate itself.

Beyond these few recommendations, a visit to a good bookstore is the best way to find a usable introductory book. If ten minutes reading in the store improves your insight into how the program works, it probably is a good book for you. It definitely will be more current with the latest *dBase* version than anything I can recommend here.

Numerous colleges, universities, and adult education evening programs offer courses in *dBase II* and *III+*. Seek out courses that cover the most current versions of the program. *dBase II* is only for masochists and those using computers that won't run the newer version.

The bottom line is that anyone wishing to become proficient in use of *dBase III+* will have to work at it. Learning is best facilitated by applying specific commands to specific tasks. When a new task requires an approach not used before, something new is learned. It might not hurt, after working with The Assistant for a while, to explore the dot-prompt commands using HELP. The two HELP screens below list Ashton-Tate's estimation of the commands most needed by beginners and advanced users. Flipping through them as time and interest dictate can be informative.

///
dBase III PLUS Commands --- Starter Set

1 - ?	12 - DELETE FILE	23 - LABEL	34 - REPORT
2 - APPEND	13 - DIR	24 - LIST	35 - SCREEN
3 - AVERAGE	14 - DISPLAY	25 - LOCATE	36 - SEEK
4 - BROWSE	15 - DO	26 - MODIFY	37 - SET
5 - CHANGE	16 - EDIT	27 - PACK	38 - SKIP
6 - CLEAR	17 - ERASE	28 - QUERY	39 - SORT
7 - CONTINUE	18 - EXPORT	29 - QUIT	40 - STORE
8 - COPY	19 - FIND	30 - RECALL	41 - SUM
9 - COUNT	20 - GO/GOTO	31 - RELEASE	42 - TOTAL
10 - CREATE	21 - IMPORT	32 - RENAME	43 - TYPE
11 - DELETE	22 - INDEX	33 - REPLACE	44 - USE

///

//

dBASE III PLUS Commands --- Advanced Set

1 - @	12 - IF	22 - ON	32 - RETURN
2 - ACCEPT	13 - INPUT	23 -PARAMETERS	33 - RUN/!
3 - CANCEL	14 - INSERT	24 - PRIVATE	34 - SAVE
4 - CALL	15 - JOIN	25 - PROCEDURE	35 - SELECT
5 - CLOSE	16 - LOAD	26 - PUBLIC	36 - SUSPEND
6 - COPY FILE	17 - LIST CMDS	27 - READ	37 - TEXT
7 - DISPLAY CMDS	18 - LOOP	28 - REINDEX	38 - UPDATE
8 - DO CASE	19 - MACRO/&	29 - RESTORE	39 - VIEW
9 - DO WHILE	20 -MODIFY CMDS	30 - RESUME	40 - WAIT
10 - EJECT	21 - NOTE/*	31 - RETRY	41 - ZAP
11 - EXIT			

//

Protecting Files from the User

Interactive use of *dBase* is predicated on users (1) opening files, (2) adding new data, (3) deleting old data, (4) otherwise modifying data, and then setting aside the newly updated files for later use. This approach is all well and good if the job is simple or all users are fully competent in performing the more complex operations that may be necessary.

But what happens if old, erroneous information is entered, or if essential data fields are left blank due to misunderstanding or inattention to detail? Natural disaster could strike, too. A momentary burp in the power from Bangor Hydroelectric Company zapped a page and a half of text destined for this book. Unsaved to disk, it evaporated instantly into the random chaos of unordered electric fields. Had this incident occurred in the process of modifying a database file, considerably greater frustration might have resulted.

The answer to ensuring that required data is entered, and performing checks on its validity (or at least its plausability) is a system of data entry and data modification programs. Examples abound in this book. Security for the integrity of existing data is increased by following these principles in designing data entry programs:

1.   Never allow users to work directly with data fields.

2. Always store information in a temporary location as it is entered or changed, ask the user for confirmation before using it to change a data file, and only then open files, replace (REPLACE) data into them, and quickly close the files again. An alternative is the use of a TEMP.DBF file. After data entry, UPDATE is used to move data from it into the main file.

3. Use the Rule of Bearable Pain to determine how often to make back-up copies of data files. Ask yourself, how painful would it be if this entire file were to disappear right now? Would the hour, the day, the week required to reconstitute the file cause a major headache? How much pain would the worst disaster, occurring right now, cause me?

Importing and Exporting Data

Getting data into *dBase III+* that was entered using another program is generally not too difficult. A number of spreadsheet file types, including *Lotus'* .WKS files, can be imported directly using routines written into *dBase*. Records from *PFS-File* are also imported in a single step. Other data can come in either as comma-and-quotes-delimited ASCII files (e.g., "Karl," "Beiser," "NMLD," "145 Harlow St," "Bangor," "MAINE," "04401") or as system data format (SDF) files. The latter are ASCII files with data elements placed in fixed locations. Most spreadsheet programs produce an SDF file when their print-to-disk option is used to place a copy of a series of rows and columns in a form suitable for use in a word processor.

The command to import ASCII files is:

APPEND FROM <filename> DELIMITED/SDF

In using the DELIMITED approach, be sure that the sequence of data elements in the ASCII file is exactly and invariably the same as that in the data structure designed to receive them. If no values are to be entered in some fields, a comma must still be included in the input file as a place-holder to ensure that the corresponding *dBase* field is skipped.

The same concern applies to SDF files. In addition, remember that most spreadsheet programs include a space or two between columns to keep information in them from running together with that from adjacent columns. *dBase* doesn't know a formatting space from an in-column space. Yet you must compensate somehow to avoid having it look for data in that character position. I prefer to increase the size of each field by the number of spaces between it and the field after it. That way, blanks trail rather than precede imported field contents.

Data can be exported using COPY TO DELIMITED/SDF/TYPE where type indicates whether the *Lotus*, *Multiplan*, or *VisiCalc* format is desired.

Magic of IIF

An interesting and powerful new command is the "immediate if," IIF. The function tests the logical result of the first expression within the parenthesis, then returns the second expression if the first is true, and the third if the first is false. One line saves four or five in the programming fragment below.

```
mtext=IIF(EOF(),"This is the end!", "More to come...")
@ 10,10 SAY mtext
```

It is particularly useful within a REPORT FORM. A list of overdue materials could contain a column with the IIF and a choice of two comments:

```
IIF(date()-datedue>21,"Go after him/her!",
     ^^^^ "Hope for the best")
```

Any book overdue more than twenty-one days will cause "Go after him/her" to be printed.

Check Boxes

Logical fields allow you to economically designate whether a particular record belongs to a particular category. My office mailing list of 700 names contains "check boxes" to indicate whether a particular individual is a director, a librarian, a trustee, a lay person, a media contact, or a legislator. District council representatives, executive board members, and members of the Maine Library Commission are all designated. Their are additional check boxes for public, school, postsecondary, and special libraries, and for whether the individual is interested in computer applications or children's services.

When I need labels for just the directors of school libraries and those interested in children's services, and only in Aroostook County, I type:

```
. USE mlist INDEX mlistzip
. LABEL FORM mlist TO PRINT FOR zip="047" .AND.
    ^^^^ ((director .AND. sch) .OR. kids)
```

Running Programs from the Inside Out

It is easy to run another program from within *dBase III+*. Simply type RUN (program name) at the dot-prompt. This feature will not work with a mere 256 kilobytes of memory, however. The tremendous convenience of being able to jump in and out of a word processor, a telecommunications package, or some other piece of software, and to have full access to DOS commands, is worth the cost of an inexpensive board and some memory chips.

Writing this book would have been considerably harder without *WordStar* immediately on tap. (While I could have designated *WordStar* as my program file editor (TEDIT=WS), I prefer to maintain access to *dBase*'s fast but limited editor for short programs.

Compilers

Sooner or later, anyone who writes or depends on *dBase III+* programs will become interested in compilers. A compiler is a piece of software that takes original program statements and converts them to an independent, stand-alone, machine-language program. That program can be run without the presense of *dBase* itself. It will usually run substantially faster than the original *dBase* program.

Compiling is a good way to produce *dBase* routines that can be sold or given away to large numbers of users without access to *dBase* itself. It is also a useful means of speeding up screen displays and other operations where *dBase* is perceptably (though not unbearably) slow.

The major disadvantages of compilers are:

1. Compatibility: Some are not fully compatible with *dBase* commands. To get top performance, or indeed any performance, you have to change a few commands to those understood by the compiler. The trade-off is usually better performance than with those compilers providing greater language compatibility.
2. Complexity: Rarely is it possible to "just compile it" and walk away. The process may involve a separate "linking" step or

other operations that require you to know more about languages and compilers than you might like.

3. Cost: Compilers cost several hundred dollars. Every time *dBase III+* comes out in a new version, plan to spend money ($50 to $100 often) on an updated version of the compiler.

4. Size: Even a short program can come out of a compiler 100 kilobytes or larger. No matter how small the program, the compiler attaches a certain minimum of machine-language boiler plate to make it functional as an executable program file. Depending on how they are compiled, the small number of compiled modules that can fit on one floppy disk may represent a significant nuisance for some users.

The Curse of Improvability

A *dBase* system for doing any old job in a library can always be improved. Improvement is easy. Improvement is quick. Improvement can be overdone.

It can be overdone in pursuit of an illusory perfection. *dBase III+* is so malleable that it is easy to be seduced by the medium as opposed to its content. Ongoing changes in order to do a job better, to add functions, to give the user new choices, or to make those choices clearer are all legitimate reasons for modifying the *dBase* set-up. Programming elegance is not.

Modular Program Design

Working with program files in *dBase III+* is easier if each one is dedicated to performing just one or two steps in a larger process. KISS (Keep It Simple, Stupid) applies here. Once one program works, you can put together the next and the next. When they are all done, they can be brought together in a single PROCEDURE file. A menu program, perhaps created with the APPSGEN.PRG applications generator, offers the user the means to pick and choose among the files.

It is possible to develop (or to acquire from other sources) a library of standard routines that can be transplanted into whatever program requires them. The DO (filename) WITH (parameter list) construction allows the user to look at a routine as a black box. For example, give the routine the name of a text file and it produces a keyword file from it; give a routine figures for population, collection size and circulation and it will produce a list of libraries within plus or minus twenty percent of all three values.

Other dBase III+ Facilities

Screen Generator

CREATE SCREEN (filename) allows you to paint a screen format for later use whenever APPEND, EDIT, or READ are used. The screen image is stored with a .SCR extension. The format file produced when you save a generated screen bears the FMT extension. You can convert a format file to a PRG file by changing the extension, adding a few lines of commands to open files, and putting the READ command after all @ ... SAY ... GETs.

It is possible to add fields to an existing database, change the characteristics of old fields, or create an entirely new database by manipulating field names onscreen. If you are designing a database around an existing paper form, this may be the most natural way of killing two birds (data structure and data entry format) with one stone.

Report Generator

Columnar reports are the forte of the report generator. Word-wrap within columns suffices for many text-oriented reporting tasks, however. Still, when a paragraph format is required, the report generator can also be of use.

By concatenating fields and interspersing semicolons enclosed in quotes at appropriate points, it is possible to give reports a paragraph look within a single column. For best results, define the entire report as having just one column the width of a page.

The major problem with this approach is that it only works if the concatenated fields together are less than 255 characters in length. *dBase III+* balks at working with character strings longer than that.

Label Generator

Standard mailing labels are quick and easy. Fields separated by a comma are automatically trimmed. To get "Karl Beiser" all I need enter is "FIRSTNAME, LASTNAME". In the report generator, I would have needed to type "TRIM(FIRSTNAME)+' ' +TRIM(LASTNAME)". Unfortunately, "Bangor, ME 04401" can't be done without the TRIM function. All bets are off when a comma is to be inserted between fields.

If ADR3 is alone on a line in the label format, and there is no value in ADR3 for a given address, the label generator will pull up all other lines to avoid a gap. That is usually what you would want. It is an annoyance in doing envelope labels that are larger than standard size, however. If you want blank lines between the last line of the address and "LIBRARY RATE," you cannot get them. Not even "   " will work as contents for a blank line. The trick is instead to enter CHR(255), the ASCII code for a nonblank but nevertheless nonprinting character, on every line that is to be kept blank. Aren't work-arounds wonderful?

Applications Generator

The applications generator can be thought of as an easy route to quick-and-dirty file maintenance programs, or as a menu generator. I take the latter view. The "Advanced Applications Generator" option allows you to specify up to nine choices and a command string associated with each choice. That command string will almost inevitably consist of DO (program file name). Menu programs are desireable from the user's standpoint and boring to write from scratch. APPSGEN.PRG can be a great time saver here.

Since APPSGEN.PRG is just another *dBase* program file, it is possible to go in and change it so that the programs it creates will conform more to your individual preferences. I plan to delete the code that produces the SET STATUS ON line in generated programs.

Query Files

CREATE QUERY (query file name) assists the user in constructing a logical filter that will exclude from display all records but those that meet the filter conditions. It allows you to build a complex filter more easily than could be done with SET FILTER TO (expression). It is appropriate where extensive use will be made of a well-defined subset of a database, with no need for access to records that don't meet the subset definition.

I haven't found a tremendous need for the construct yet, but sooner or later I probably will.

String Functions

A few of the string functions get a big workout in the pages that follow. TRIM trims off the trailing blanks on a character string. It is often necessary to find out whether a field or a variable has any characters in it. LEN((fieldname)) returns thirty, even if there are only thirty spaces. TRIM must be used with it to find out whether it is empty or not.

LTRIM deletes leading blanks. When importing a spreadsheet from outside *dBase* you sometimes end up with leading blanks. They can be dropped by entering:

REPLACE ALL <fieldname> WITH LTRIM(<fieldname>)

MAILING LIST MANAGEMENT

A satisfactory mailing list system should produce labels and lists in various formats. It should allow for direct typing onto tractor-feed postcard stock and individual envelopes. Arrangement by zip code, surname, city, telephone area code, or any other data element should be possible. The user should be able to include or omit any data element and place each just about anywhere on the printed page.

Depending on the nature of the mailing list, it may be necessary to add various category fields that can be used as the basis for outputing information about subsets of those listed in the database. We must also accommodate the need to swiftly locate records by surname, city, and zip code.

Pitfalls

Canadian and other foreign addresses can cause problems. If there are very few instances, you may be able to "fudge" with contractions, using the CITY, STATE, and ZIPCODE fields. Think ahead about where the components of a foreign address will fit in the data structure used to maintain the mailing list.

Structure

Let's create a listing of media contacts to serve the publicity activities of a library. Its structure might look like this:

```
Structure for database: C:mail.dbf
Number of data records:        5
Date of last update    : 05/21/86
Field  Field Name  Type       Width   Dec
    1  FIRSTNAME   Character     15
    2  LASTNAME    Character     20
    3  ADR2        Character     30
    4  ADR3        Character     30
    5  CITY        Character     20
    6  STATE       Character      2
    7  ZIP         Character     10
    8  PHONE       Character     20
    9  AFFILIATE   Character     40
   10  NEWSPAPER   Logical        1
   11  RADIO       Logical        1
   12  TV          Logical        1
```

```
         13   LEADTIME    Numeric        2
      ** Total **                      193
```

FIRSTNAME and LASTNAME have been made separate fields to make it easy to arrange records in alphabetical order by surname (INDEX ON LASTNAME TO MAILLAST), to omit or use the first name at will (LIST LASTNAME, CITY, PHONE), and to display names in inverted form if desired (LIST TRIM(LASTNAME)+', '+TRIM(FIRSTNAME)). Very seldom is it satisfactory to put first name and surname in the same field, despite the small savings in record size.

ADR2 and ADR3 are simply the second and third lines of the typical business address. Anything at all can be entered here. The assumption is that one will not want to sort or locate by a person's title, street address, post office box, etc. Depending on the form of the addresses of the people with whom you normally correspond, you may want to add additional lines, e.g., ADR4, ADR5, etc. The label form generator strips out empty address lines and short *dBase* command files can be written to do the same thing in just about any kind of listing.

Thirty characters for ADR2 and ADR3 is cutting it pretty close, considering the verbose titles and institutional addresses one is likely to encounter in librarydom. The size of label stock and the print pitch in use may allow for longer fields. Standard 3 1/2 inch stock works well with thirty character fields at ten characters per inch (pica) pitch.

An institutional affiliation is often part of an address. Where one needs to arrange or search for records based on that affiliation, problems can develop. Sometimes such an affiliation is absent. Or a person's address may contain an institutional name other than that which you would like indicated as an affiliation in your mailing system; e.g., a stringer for a regional paper may get her mail at the insurance agency where she works. For these and other reasons, it is simplest to include a separate AFFILIATE field if affiliation information is required and not attempt to manipulate the fields that will form the middle lines of the printed address.

If legal residence is important, you might add a field called TOWNSHIP or HOMETOWN. Public libraries with many out-of-town users will be particularly interested in having a handle on where people actually live, rather than through which post office they get their mail.

STATE could just as well be a larger field, allowing for full names rather than two-character abbreviations. A side benefit is additional space for sneaking in the occasional foreign address. Ten digits for ZIP would be enough for the new nine-digit zip code, including the hyphen or space that is often included in it.

Twenty characters may seem like a lot for a phone number. WATS numbers, local extensions, and varying ways of separating the parts of a telephone number from one another demand no less, however.

The PAPER, RADIO, and TV fields are one of the two ways to handle selection categories. A "Y" or "T" (for true) in any one of these fields will cause the entire record to come up in response to a command like LIST LASTNAME, PHONE FOR RADIO .OR. TV. An alternative would have been to include a single field called MEDIA, and to enter a word or several letters into it, depending on which medium was involved. This is less effective because (1) maintaining consistency in spelling and capitalization is more difficult, yet failure to do so will hide some records from a query or report; and (2) it takes a larger field size to enter a meaningful indicator of medium type than to employ three single-character logical fields with readily understandable field names.

LEADTIME stores the number of days ahead of an event that a particular publication needs to be notified. It can be used to perform date arithmetic upon which production of labels and lists may be based, e.g., LABEL FORM MAILALL FOR (event date) - LEADTIME > DATE().

First, the database is indexed:

- INDEX ON lastname TO maillast
  100% indexed   5 Records indexed
- INDEX ON city TO mailcity
  100% indexed   5 Records indexed
- INDEX ON affiliate TO mailaffi
  100% indexed   5 Records indexed
- INDEX ON substr(affiliate,1,15) TO mailaffil
  100% indexed   5 Records indexed

The MAILAFFIL index was generated based on the first fifteen characters of the AFFILIATE field rather than all forty. In most situations, additional characters beyond about fifteen are unnecessary to differentiate between field contents. Considerable reductions in index file size can result from using the substring function SUBSTR in constructing indexes to large data files. In a small file such as this, the difference is trivial.

Since the index by AFFILIATE was the last one generated, the database is still controlled by it when we look at several of its fields:

```
. LIST affiliate, firstname, lastname
Record#  affiliate                 firstname    lastname
      1  Bookcity Sentinel         Fred         Smith

      2  Broadway Broadcasting     Frances      Smith

      4  East County Weekly Sun    Edward       Senter

      5  Endicott Broadcasting     Blakely      Summers

      3  WWME TV                   Sanford      Franklin
```

To make the listing more compact, we can strip off the record numbers with the OFF clause and eliminate the blank spaces between fields with the TRIM function:

```
. LIST TRIM(affiliate)+", "+TRIM(firstname)+" "+TRIM
   ^^^^ (lastname) OFF
trim(affiliate)+", "+trim(firstname)+" "+trim(lastname)
Bookcity Sentinel, Fred Smith
Broadway Broadcasting, Frances Smith
East County Weekly Sun, Edward Senter
Endicott Broadcasting, Blakely Summers
WWME TV, Sanford Franklin
```

A label form can be created with the CREATE LABEL MAILLBL command, where MAILLBL is the name of the file we are creating to contain label specifications. The contents portion of the label format looks like this:

```
firstname,lastname
adr2
adr3
trim(city)+", "+state+"  "+zip
```

The label form generator automatically strips trailing blanks and inserts a single space between fields separated by commas. This differs from conventions within the report generator, where commas leave trailing blanks in place. Unfortunately, the current version of *dBase III+* (1.0), despite manual illustrations to the contrary, does not allow one to place a literal comma directly after city with no intervening space. Thus, for this line only, one must revert to the syntax required elsewhere in *dBase*. The labels are generated with this label format file:

```
. LABEL FORM maillbl
```

```
Fred Smith
52 Evensong Road
Bookcity, ME   04422
```

```
Frances Smith
Parsons Insurance
53 Center St.
Bookcity, ME   04422
```

```
Edward Senter
22 West Ave.
Endicott, ME   04122
```

```
Blakely Summers
Endicott Broadcasting
P.O. Box 55
Endicott, ME   04122
```

```
Sanford Franklin
Director of Community Affairs
WWME TV
Frye, ME   04434
```

To produce labels in order by surname just for those addressees associated with newspapers:

```
. USE mail INDEX maillast
. LABEL FORM maillbl FOR newspaper
```

```
Edward Senter
22 West Ave.
Endicott, ME   04122
```

```
Fred Smith
52 Evensong Road
Bookcity, ME   04422
```

To produce an on-screen list by lead-time, you can issue the following command:

```
. LIST firstname, lastname, phone, affiliate OFF FOR leadtime<12
```

```
firstname lastname  phone        affiliate
Sanford    Franklin  442-2211     WWME TV

Frances    Smith     555-3114 X234 Broadway Broadcasting
Blakely    Summers   222-9934      Endicott Broadcasting
```

To find a record for a person affiliated with a specific media organization:

```
. SET INDEX TO mailaffi
  FIND Bookcity
. DISPLAY TRIM(firstname)+" "+TRIM(lastname)+"  "+phone
Record#  TRIM(firstname)+" "+TRIM(lastname)+"  "+phone
     1  Fred Smith  555-2211
```

Alternative Approaches

A word processing program with mail-merge capability allows one to create and maintain mailing lists and generate mailing labels and lists. Few programs allow for sorting, however. Those that do usually sort only from the first element stored for each addressee. If that is the first name, the sort facility is not terribly useful. A single sort order is maintained "by hand" as the user locates the appropriate spot in the alphabetical sequence and there inserts new information.

Also, few word processing/mail-merge programs allow one to select based on combinations of the contents of the address record. Producing labels only for those addressees who work for radio stations and have a lead time of less than fourteen days is usually not possible.

A word processing program is likely to be most satisfactory in the following situation: labels, lists, and other products generally include all addressees, with no need to select subsets from the whole; the file is relatively small, no more than several hundred names; and arithmetic operations are not required, e.g., calculation of fees owed and paid.

A simple file manager like *PFS-File*, combined with *PFS-Report* would be sufficient for handling mailing list tasks as long as the mailing file need not be related to additional files. *File Express* and *PC-File*, both freeware programs for the IBM PC and compatibles, would be an even more economical choice for a job such as this.

BIBLIOGRAPHIES

Handling bibliographies with a computer consists of three distinct activities: (1) creating and maintaining a data file of bibliographic information; (2) providing interactive access to that information; and (3) producing printed listings in a wide variety of formats. Depending on the materials being entered and the purpose and clientele for whom listings are to be produced, *dBase* may or may not be adequate to the task.

If the final printed format of listings is critical, and if you have neither the time nor the inclination to learn enough about *dBase* programming to perform the necessary string manipulations, you may be better off with a commercial product like *Pro-Cite* from Personal Bibliographic Software. That program's strong suit is formatting output to any one of a wide variety of standards, e.g., *MLA*, *Chicago Manual of Style*, etc.

Other than in the matter of output formatting, however, *dBase* does a bang-up job of handling the kind of information typically found in bibliographies. Its only significant limitation stems from the fact that field lengths are fixed. Dealing with the occasional 300-character title is difficult, given a typical field length of 100 characters or so and the 255-character maximum field capacity.

There are several ways of coping with this limitation. You can (1) truncate, adding ". . ." to the end of the field to indicate something has been dropped; (2) abbreviate, preferably toward the end of the field so that searching won't be impeded; or (3) put any field element likely to be extremely long in a memo type field.

If you follow the last course, the fact that memo fields are unsearchable will be a problem. One answer would be a SHORTTITLE field fifteen or twenty characters in length. Indexing for access by title would actually be done on the SHORTTITLE field instead. Depending on the nature of the listings you wish to print, additional complications may arise from the inability of *dBase* to concatenate memo type fields with character type fields.

We want printed lists of bibliographic references in order by author, title, or other ordering element (subject or category, for instance). We would like to have a wide variety of standard formats at our disposal so that bibliographies matching the requirements of different publications and different functions could be generated from the same data file. We also will want to be able to rapidly search the data file by author, title, publisher, date, and other elements.

Structure

To accommodate both serial and monographic references, we could create separate files, each with its own data structure. I choose not to do that because (1) one more often wants to combine monographic and serial references than to separate them; and (2) the references can be more easily separated than they can be merged, using the "all things for all people" bibliographic data structure below.

```
Structure for database: C:biblio.dbf
Number of data records:        5
Date of last update    : 05/23/86
Field   Field Name   Type        Width   Dec
    1    AUTHFIRST    Character      15
    2    AUTHLAST     Character      20
    3    TITLE        Character     100
    4    JOURNAL      Character      50
    5    PUBLISHER    Character      40
    6    EDITION      Character       5
    7    DATE         Character      20
    8    VOLUME       Character      15
    9    NUMBER       Character      15
   10    PAGES        Character      15
   11    SERIES       Character      50
   12    PERIODICAL   Logical         1
   13    MONOGRAPH    Logical         1
   14    ORDER        Character      15
** Total **                        363
```

All references will usually have data in the AUTHFIRST, AUTHLAST, and TITLE fields. Article citations will also include information in the JOURNAL, DATE, VOLUME, NUMBER, and PAGES fields. Monographic citations will have information in the PUBLISHER, EDITION, and DATE fields and maybe the PAGES and SERIES fields.

PERIODICAL and MONOGRAPH are check boxes to indicate which form of reference is included in the record. ORDER is a field that contains a term to describe a broad subject category. Depending on your needs, additional check boxes and ordering fields could be added to allow for finer discrimination in retrieving groups of citations.

To arrange records for presentation in author, title, and subject category sequence we index:

. INDEX ON authlast+authfirst TO biblast
  100% indexed   5 Records indexed

. INDEX ON substr(title,1,15) TO bibtitle
  100% indexed   5 Records indexed

. INDEX ON order TO biborder
  100% indexed   5 Records indexed

Since TITLE is such a large field (100 characters) and there is little anticipated duplication in titles, indexing was done on the first fifteen characters of TITLE. In a database containing dozens of references that start "Journal of the American ...", you would want to choose a longer substring to keep ambiguity to a minimum.

Here's a quick-and-dirty listing of our database in order by title:

. USE biblio INDEX bibtitle
. LIST TRIM(title)+", "+TRIM(authfirst)+" "+TRIM
  ^^^^ (authlast)

```
Record#  trim(title)+", "+trim(authfirst)+" "+
    ^^^^ trim(authlast)
      2  Advanced Programmer's Guide, Luis Castro
      3  Comprehensive Guide to the IBM Personal
  ^^^^ Computer, George Markowsky
      4  Costs of Copy Protection Hit Software Maker,
  ^^^^ Too, Jim Seymour
      5  Looking at the Future of Local-Area Networks,
  ^^^^ Patricia Keefe
      1  Secret Guide to Computers: Volume 1, Secret
  ^^^^ Skills, Russ Walter
```

This sort of listing is adequate for quick, interactive queries. It can get a bit messy if more than two or three fields are to be listed, both because of the disordered screen created by lines wrapping around and because of the long, complex command line that must be exactly right in order to produce the intended results. Fortunately *dBase III+*, unlike *dBase III*, has the HISTORY feature, whereby the last few commands typed at the dot-prompt are retained in memory. They can be retrieved, edited, and reissued simply by hitting the up-arrow key, making the necessary changes to the command syntax, and striking the return key.

The *dBase III+* report generator provides an easy way to come up with more presentable listings. Unfortunately, its columnar format isn't always the most appropriate for bibliographic information. Here's the sort of thing you can expect from it:

```
. USE biblio
. SET INDEX TO bibtitle
. REPORT FORM bibrpt
```

Page No.   1
05/24/86
          Sample Bibliography of Computer References

Author   Title   Citation

Castro, Luis   Advance Programmer's   Ashton-Tate,
               Guide   1985
Markowsky,   Comprehensive Guide to   Prentice-Hall,
George   the IBM Personal Computer 1984
Seymour, Jim   Costs of Copy Protection PC Week.
               Hit Software Maker, Too   May 20, 1986
                                         Vol 3 No 20
Keefe,   Looking at the Future of Micromarketworld
Patricia   Local-Area Networks   May 12, 1986,
                                         Vol. 9 No. 10
Walter, Russ   Secret Guide to   The Author, 1986
               Computers: Volume 1,
               Secret Skills

By modifying the report form to group references by ORDER, the catch-all subject category field, you can produce a report like this:

```
. USE biblio INDEX biborder
. MODI REPO bibrpt
```

Page No.   1
05/24/86
          Sample Bibliography of Computer References

Author   Title   Citation

** Copy Protection
Seymour, Jim   Costs of Copy Protection PC Week. May 20,
               Hit Software Maker, Too   1986, Vol. 3
                                         No. 20

```
**  Introductory
Walter, Russ  Secret Guide to         The Author,
              Computers: Volume 1,    1986
              Secret Skills
Markowsky,    Comprehensive Guide to  Prentice-Hall,
George        the IBM Personal Computer 1984

**  LAN's
Keefe,        Looking at the Future of  Micromarketworld
Patricia      Local-Area Networks       May 12, 1986,
                                        Vol. 9 No. 10

**  dBase III
Castro, Luis Advanced Programmer's    Ashton-Tate, 1985
              Guide
```

With short fields, you can simulate a paragraph format by defining the report as containing just one column and then concatenating all the fields within that column. The automatic word-wrap feature of the report generator will conveniently control line length without user involvement.

Because of the length of the fields defined here, however, you are likely to come up against the 255-character limit on concatenated character strings.

Here is the first of two program files designed to produce listings closer to those that are generally required in library and research settings:

```
** BIBPROG.PRG -- Program to print simple list of
     ^^^^ items in BIBLIO.DBF

SET TALK OFF
** Arrange by lastname
USE biblio INDEX biblast

DO WHILE .NOT. EOF()
  ? "AUTHOR: "+TRIM(authlast)+", "+TRIM(authfirst)+"."
  ? "TITLE: "+TRIM(title)+"."

** Vary citation format depending on whether a journal
**   article or a monograph is being cited.
  IF periodical
```

```
            citation=TRIM(journal)+".   "+TRIM(date)+",   Vol.   "+
     TRIM(volume) +" No. "+TRIM(number)+", p. "+
         ^^^^ TRIM(pages)+"."
       ELSE
          IF LEN(TRIM(edition))>0
              citation=TRIM(publisher)+", "+TRIM(edition)+
       ^^^^ " ed., "+TRIM(date)
          ELSE
              citation=TRIM(publisher)+", "+TRIM(date)
          ENDIF
          IF LEN(TRIM(pages))>0
              citation=citation+", p. "+TRIM(pages)+"."
          ELSE
              citation=citation+"."
          ENDIF
       ENDIF

       ? "CITATION: "+citation
       ?
       SKIP
     ENDDO
     SET TALK ON
     RETURN
```

Here's what happens when the program is run:

```
. DO bibprog

AUTHOR: Castro, Luis.
TITLE: Advanced Programmer's Guide.
CITATION: Ashton-Tate, 1985.

AUTHOR: Keefe, Patricia.
TITLE: Looking at the Future of Local-Area Networks.
CITATION: Micromarketworld. May 12, 1986, Vol. 9
     ^^^^ No. 10, p. 32-36.

AUTHOR: Markowsky, George.
TITLE: Comprehensive Guide to the IBM Personal
     ^^^^ Computer.
CITATION: Prentice-Hall, 1984.

AUTHOR: Seymour, Jim.
TITLE: Costs of Copy Protection Hit Software Maker,
     ^^^^ Too.
CITATION: PC Week. May 20, 1986, Vol. 3 No. 20, p. 66.
```

AUTHOR: Walter, Russ.
TITLE: Secret Guide to Computers: Volume 1, Secret
    ^^^^ Skills.
CITATION: The Author, 12th ed., 1986, p. 35-76.

A more satisfactory and more sophisticated approach is
represented by the following program. While it is somewhat slow
because of the character manipulations involved, it is a more
generalized method that should work for a wider array of formatting
requirements. You could create a series of modules, one for each of
the major formats used in an institution, and present the user with
a menu from which to pick the particular module to be used in a
given instance.

The *dBase* code here offers a working example of this approach
in action, albeit with a bibliographic format of no particular
pedigree or difficulty.

```
** BIBPROG2.PRG works with BIBLIO.DBF to produce
formated
** bibliograpy.  Line-wrap is provided through
    ^^^^ WRAPFILE.PRG
** procedure file.

** initialize environment
SET TALK OFF
SET CONFIRM ON
SET BELL OFF
USE biblio
SET PROCEDURE TO wrapfile
PUBLIC currline

** ask user for some formatting parameters
flag=0
DO WHILE flag=0
    CLEAR
    linemax=00
    leftmarg=00
    subindent=00
    @ 5,10 SAY "Print Formatting Choices"
    @ 10,10 SAY "Line length? " GET linemax PICTURE
     ^^^^ "99" RANGE 20,80
    @ 12,10 SAY "Left margin? " GET leftmarg PICTURE
     ^^^^ "99" RANGE 0,15
    @ 14,10 SAY "Indention for continuation lines? "
```

```
      ^^^^ GET subindent picture "99" RANGE 0,15

** make sure no line runs longer than 80 columns
    flag=IIF(linemax+leftmarg+subindent<81,1,0)
    READ
ENDDO
CLEAR

** send to printer or only to screen?
answer=.N.
@ 10,10 SAY "Send to Printer? " GET answer PICTURE "L"
READ
IF answer
    SET PRINT ON
ENDIF
CLEAR

** examine each BIBLIO.DBF record in turn
indent1 = SPACE(leftmarg)
indent2 = SPACE(subindent)
DO WHILE .NOT. EOF()
    currline = indent1
    IF LEN(TRIM(authlast))>0
        currline=currline+TRIM(authlast)+",
  ^^^^ "+TRIM(authfirst)+".  "
        DO wrapper
    ENDIF
    currline=currline+TRIM(title)+".  "
    DO wrapper

** processing just for article citations
    IF periodical
        currline=currline+TRIM(journal)+", "
        Do wrapper
        currline=currline+TRIM(date)+", "
        DO wrapper
        currline=currline+"Vol. "+TRIM(volume)+", "
        DO wrapper
        currline=currline+"No. "+TRIM(number)+"."
        IF LEN(TRIM(pages))>0
            currline=currline+" P. "+TRIM(pages)+"."
            DO wrapper
        ENDIF

** processing just for monographic citations
    ELSE
        IF LEN(TRIM(edition))>0
```

```
            currline=currline+TRIM(edition)+" ed., "
            DO wrapper
        ENDIF
        currline=currline+TRIM(publisher)+", "
        DO wrapper
        currline=currline+TRIM(date)+"."
        DO wrapper
        IF LEN(TRIM(pages))>0
            currline=currline+" P. "+TRIM(pages)+"."
            DO wrapper
        ENDIF
    ENDIF

** print remaining characters at the end of the record
    IF LEN(TRIM(currline))>0
        ? currline
    ENDIF
    SKIP
ENDDO

** reset environment to status before program ran
SET PRINT OFF
SET TALK ON
SET BELL ON
SET CONFIRM OFF
SET PROCEDURE TO
RETURN

** WRAPFILE.PRG  works with BIBPROG2.PRG to wrap
**  bibliographic citations at the end of each line.

PROCEDURE wrapper

DO WHILE LEN(TRIM(currline))>linemax+1
    trialpt=linemax

**  if space or period at exact end of allowed line
    IF SUBSTR(currline,trialpt,1)=" " .OR.
     ^^^^ SUBSTR(currline,trialpt,1)="."

**  print line, save rest of characters for next line
        ? SUBSTR(currline,1,trialpt)
        currline=indent1+indent2+LTRIM(SUBSTR(currline,
     ^^^^ trialpt+1))

**  otherwise, look for last blank in CURRLINE
**    before end of allowed line
```

```
    ELSE
        i=0
        DO WHILE SUBSTR(currline,trialpt,1)<>" "
            i=i+1
            trialpt=linemax-i
        ENDDO

** print line, save rest of characters for next line
        ? SUBSTR(currline,1,trialpt-1)
        currline=indent1+indent2+SUBSTR(currline,
    ^^^^ trialpt+1)
    ENDIF
ENDDO
RETURN
```

Here's what happens when BIBPROG2.PRG is run:

```
. USE biblio
. DO bibprog2
```

Walter, Russ.   Secret Guide to Computers: Volume 1,
    Secret Skills.   12th ed., The Author, 1986. P.
    35-76.
Castro, Luis.   Advanced Programmer's Guide.   Ashton-
    Tate, 1985.
Markowsky, George.   Comprehensive Guide to the IBM
    Personal Computer.   Prentice-Hall, 1984.
Seymour, Jim.   Costs of Copy Protection Hit Software
    Maker, Too.   PC Week, May 20, 1986, Vol. 3, No. 20.
    P. 66
Keefe, Patricia.   Looking at the Future of Local-Area
    Networks.   Micromarketworld, May 12, 1986, Vol. 9,
    No. 10. P. 32-36.

Pitfalls

Alphabetization is a problem whenever computers are used to
organize bibliographic information. Leading articles, abbreviations,
numerals to be filed as if spelled out, and filing rules that don't
follow a strict character-by-character sequence can all cause
trouble.

Generally, it is easiest to deal with leading articles by dropping
them at the time of data entry. If that is unacceptable, a separate
sorting field can be added to each record, perhaps called SORTFLD.
The version of the title without leading article or other peculiarity

would go in the SORTFLD field and indexing for title access and sequencing would be done using it (INDEX ON SORTFLD TO BIBTITLE), even though the contents of TITLE would be included in the report.

The same technique will serve with abbreviations and numbers. In a manual system "IBM" comes at the beginning of the "I"s, well before "International Business Machines" and "Individual Retirement Account." *25 Ski Tours in Maine* appears before "America the Beautiful" (or any other alphabetic character). If that is the preferred format, nothing need be done. The sorting field allows for placing the listing anywhere else it is required.

Inconsistent capitalization can throw things off. "America the beautiful" is not the same as "America the Beautiful." One way to ensure that capitalization doesn't make retrieval difficult is to index on the upper- or lower-case equivalents of the fields in question. INDEX ON UPPER(SUBSTR(TITLE,1,15)) TO BIBTITLE puts "IBM" between "Iambic Pentameter" and "Iona," which may or may not be desirable in a given situation. Remember, however, that when the index BIBTITLE.NDX is in effect, you must capitalize search terms as well, e.g., FIND IONA, not FIND Iona.

COMMUNITY RESOURCES FILE

A community resources file contains information about programs, services, and organizations in a community or region. It is designed to put people with a particular interest or need in touch with appropriate services, groups, or individuals. While this would seem to be a public library-oriented affair, corporate and professional institutions also have need for lists of contacts and other resources. Organizing those lists involves the same issues as arise with the community resources file that will be considered here.

The advantages of maintaining a resources directory on a computer are:

1. Ease of adding, deleting, and changing information "at the drop of a hat."
2. Speed and power of computer-aided retrieval from a data file.
3. Convenience and speed with which you can print customized lists of only that information of interest to a particular individual.
4. Savings in staff time as compared with maintaining a comparable or inferior manual file.

The task of maintaining a community resources file has much in common with the indexing task discussed elsewhere in this book. Both require multiple access points that lead a user to a kernel of unitary information, in one case the bibliographic citation, in the other the name, address, phone, and other particulars of a resource.

The resources file is likely to be smaller than an index database, however. It probably won't grow in a linear fashion over time. In many cases, a staff person will be available to assist or to actually do searches in the resource file.

Because of the small size, the availability of a staff person in the typical reference environment in which the file will be used, and because the treatment of indexing elsewhere in this book adequately demonstrates an applicable programmed approach, we will handle this job interactively.

Data Structure

The two data files involved are RESOURCE.DBF, containing information about an organization and its contact person, and RESFOCUS.DBF, which provides access by organizational focus:

```
Structure for database: C:RESFOCUS.DBF
Number of data records:        21
Date of last update    : 08/12/86
Field  Field Name  Type        Width      Dec
    1 >RESNO        Character     5
    2 >INTEREST     Character     40
** Total **                      46
```

```
Structure for database: C:RESOURCE.DBF
Number of data records:        4
Date of last update    : 08/12/86
Field  Field Name  Type        Width      Dec
    1 >RESNO        Character     5
    2 >ORG          Character     50
    3 >FIRSTNAME    Character     12
    4 >LASTNAME     Character     18
    5 >ADR2         Character     35
    6 >ADR3         Character     35
    7 >CITY         Character     15
    8 >STATE        Character     2
    9 >ZIP          Character     9
   10 >PHONE        Character     15
   11 >NARRATIVE    Character     254
** Total **                      451
```

Setting up the Operating Environment

The ">" beside each field indicates that it has been named in a SET FIELDS TO command. The following sequence of commands allows us to address all fields of both data files without having to specify a file name alias. There is one exception: since RESNO is in both files, we need to preface that field name with its alias (e.g., RESOURCE->RESNO) if we seek to gain access to it when it is not in the currently active work area.

The sequence of commands to establish the operating environment for our interactive work, and to preserve that environment for future recall, follows:

```
. SELECT 2
. USE resource INDEX resnum
. SELECT 1
. USE resfocus INDEX resfoint
. SET RELATION TO resno INTO resource
. SET FIELDS TO ALL
```

```
. SELE 2
. SET FIELDS TO ALL
. SET FIELDS ON
. SELE 1
. CREATE VIEW resource FROM ENVIRONMENT
```

The resulting environment appears this way when you display status (DISPLAY STATUS):

```
Currently Selected Database:
Select area:  1, Database in Use: C:RESFOCUS.DBF
     ^^^^ Alias: RESFOCUS
    Master index file:  C:RESFOINT.NDX  Key:
     ^^^^ upper(interest)
    Related into: RESOURCE
    Relation: resno

Select area:  2, Database in Use: C:RESOURCE.DBF
     ^^^^ Alias: RESOURCE
    Master index file:  C:RESNUM.NDX  Key: resno
```

Notice that INTEREST is indexed in upper case. This ensures consistent indexing even if information is entered in unpredictable combinations of upper- and lower-case. When FIND is used to locate a record in the database, the search term will have to be entirely in upper-case, however.

Besides making it easier to refer to fields from multiple databases, SET FIELDS TO makes the designing of report forms more convenient as well. All fields named in a SET FIELDS TO statement appear in the F10 fields menu within CREATE/MODIFY REPORT. It isn't necessary to remember the names of fields in linked files when they have been amalgamated with those in the current work area in this way.

Searching the Resource File

Let's inspect our small test database of imaginary organizations. The crudest retrieval comes with the LIST command:

```
. LIST interest,org, OFF
interest                     org
Apple Macintosh computers Penobscot Valley Computer
     ^^^^ Society
Ballston Business Notes    Greater Ballston Chamber of
```

```
       ^^^^ Commerce
Ballston Corner, Maine   Brandytown Historical Society
Ballston Spa, Maine      Brandytown Historical Society
Brandytown, Maine        Brandytown Historical Society
Brazil                   Greater Ballston Friendship
        ^^^^ Association
*** INTERRUPTED ***
```

A nicer display is pretty easy:

```
. LIST TRIM(interest)+" -- "+TRIM(org) OFF
trim(interest)+" -- "+trim(org)
Apple Macintosh computers -- Penobscot Valley Computer
     ^^^^ Society
Ballston Business Notes -- Greater Ballston Chamber of
     ^^^^ Commerce
Ballston Corner, Maine -- Brandytown Historical Society
Ballston Spa, Maine -- Brandytown Historical Society
Brandytown, Maine -- Brandytown Historical Society
Brazil -- Greater Ballston Friendship Association
Business development -- Greater Ballston Chamber of
     ^^^^ Commerce
computer education -- Penobscot Valley Computer
     ^^^^ Society
computers -- Penobscot Valley Computer Society
economic development -- Greater Ballston Chamber of
     ^^^^ Commerce
*** INTERRUPTED ***
```

Here's part of the output from report form RRPT1.FRM:

```
Page No.       1
08/12/86
                  Community Resource File
                      Report #1


Focus       Organization                    Contact

Apple       Penobscot Valley Computer       Ed Miller
Macintosh   Society                         22 Main St.
computers   Computer club meets monthly at
            Maine National Bank downtown.   Ballston Spa,
            Focus on IBM-compatible,        ME
            Macintosh computers. $12/yr     044322211
            dues.  Visitors welcome at
            meetings.  Sponsors annual
            computer fair.  Speakers,
            user-group workshops.
Ballston    Greater Ballston Chamber of     Franklin Talbot
```

Business Notes	Commerce	Director
	Promotes growth of business and industry in Ballston Spa area. Sponsors Home Show. Publishes Ballston Business Notes. Dues based on size of business. Public sector members welcome.	P.O. Box 567 Ballston Spa, ME 04330
Ballston Corner, Maine	Brandytown Historical Society Concerned with history of Brandytown, Ballston Spa, Ballston Corner, Mulville, and the entire Eduwocatuc river valley.	Frank Gersham 12 Pleasant St. Ballston Corner, ME 04431
Ballston Spa, Maine	Brandytown Historical Society Concerned with history of Brandytown, Ballston Spa, Ballston Corner, Mulville, and the entire Eduwocatuc river valley.	Frank Gersham 12 Pleasant St. Ballston Corner, ME 04431
Brandytown, Maine	Brandytown Historical Society Concerned with history of Brandytown, Ballston Spa, Ballston Corner, Mulville, and the entire Eduwocatuc river valley.	Frank Gersham 12 Pleasant St. Ballston Corner, ME 04431
Brazil	Greater Ballston Friendship Association Sponsors exchange student program, international sister city exchange visits with Sao Hidalgo, Brazil. Meets monthly during the school year. Dues of $20/year.	Mary Heney West Clover High School 56 Mill Rd. Brainerd, ME 04411

*** INTERRUPTED ***

Adding to the Database

Adding data to multiple files can be tricky, and it exposes the database as a whole to possible damage from accident or carelessness. That's why it is usually done under program control. With a small, simple file system like this, however, a fully articulated data entry module may be overkill.

The function keys offer a simple way to streamline data entry. They make flipping from the APPEND mode in one data file into the APPEND mode in the second data file a one-key operation. The ";" is very important. It represents striking the RETURN key. Be sure any index files are in effect so that new entries (and modifications to old ones, for that matter) are immediately reflected in search results.

Here's how to define the function keys:

```
. SET FUNCTION 8 to ";SELE 2;APPEND;"
. SET FUNCTION 7 TO ";SELE 1;APPEND;"
```

To get the ball rolling, you would USE RESOURCE.DBF in work area 1 and RESFOCUS.DBF in work area 2. All indexes used later for searching and listing purposes should be in effect during data entry in order for them to maintain their currency. Prime the pump by typing APPEND.

When the last field in the RESOURCE.DBF record has been dealt with, a blank form will appear for a second record. Having noted the RESNO just entered, the user now switches to entry into RESFOCUS.DBF by hitting F8. The semi-colon is equivalent to a carriage return and kicks the user out of APPEND mode. SELE 2 switches work areas and APPEND puts the user back in APPEND mode again, this time in the RESFOCUS.DBF data file. As many records as necessary are entered, all with the same RESNO. When entry is completed and a blank RESFOCUS.DBF form is on the screen, F7 transfers the user back to appending in the RESOURCE.DBF file again.

This method of data entry is far simpler than this description may make it sound. The need for data entry error-checking and a general concern for database integrity may limit it to smaller operations involving just one or two regular users, but that includes quite a few library applications.

Searching by "Keyword"

Just because we have set up RESFOCUS.DBF as our subject access tool doesn't mean we can't use string searching as well. To find out who is concerned with the communities of Ballston Spa and Ballston Corner:

```
. LIST org FOR "Ballston" $narrative OFF
org
Brandytown Historical Society
Greater Ballston Chamber of Commerce
```

Now let's use the Boolean .OR. operator to find out what organizations are interested either in music or history, as determined from the contents of the narrative field:

```
. LIST org, phone FOR "MUSIC" $(UPPER(narrative)) .OR.
   ^^^^ "HISTORY" $(UPPER(narrative))
Record#  org                                 phone
     3   Brandytown Historical Society       555-9211
```

Boolean operators work with REPORT FORM as well as LIST:

```
. REPO FORM rrpt1 FOR "HISTORY" $UPPER(interest) .OR.
   ^^^^ "HISTORY" $UPPER(narrative) .OR.
   ^^^^ UPPER(interest)="INTERNATIONAL RELATIONS"
```

```
Page No.       1
08/12/86
                    Community Resource File
                         Report #1

Focus          Organization                    Contact

Ballston       Brandytown Historical Society   Frank Gersham
Corner,        Concerned with history of       12 Pleasant
Maine          Brandytown, Ballston Spa,        St.
               Ballston Corner, Mulville, and  Ballston
               the entire Eduwocatuc river      Corner, ME
               valley.                          04431
Ballston       Brandytown Historical Society   Frank Gersham
Spa,           Concerned with history of       12 Pleasant
Maine          Brandytown, Ballston Spa,        St.
               Ballston Corner, Mulville, and  Ballston
               the entire Eduwocatuc river      Corner, ME
               valley.                          04431
Brandytown,    Brandytown Historical Society   Frank Gersham
Maine          Concerned with history of       12 Pleasant
               Brandytown, Ballston Spa,        St.
               Ballston Corner, Mulville, and  Ballston
               the entire Eduwocatuc river      Corner, ME
```

	valley.	04431
history	Brandytown Historical Society	Frank Gersham
	Concerned with history of	12 Pleasant St
	Brandytown, Ballston Spa,	
	Ballston Corner, Mulville, and	Ballston
	the entire Eduwocatuc river	Corner, ME
	valley.	04431
interna	Greater Ballston Friendship	Mary Heney
tional	Association	West Clover
relations	Sponsors exchange student	High School
	program, international sister	56 Mill Rd.
	city exchange visits with Sao	Brainerd, ME
	Hidalgo, Brazil. Meets	04411
	monthly during the school	
	year. Dues of $20/year.	
local	Brandytown Historical Society	Frank Gersham
history	Concerned with history of	12 Pleasant
	Brandytown, Ballston Spa,	St.
	Ballston Corner, Mulville, and	Ballston
	the entire Eduwocatuc river	Corner, ME
	valley.	04431
Penobscot	Brandytown Historical Society	Frank Gersham
River	Concerned with history of	12 Pleasant
	Brandytown, Ballston Spa,	St.
	Ballston Corner, Mulville, and	Ballston
	the entire Eduwocatuc river	Corner, ME
	valley.	04431

NEWSPAPER INDEXING

Newspaper indexing is a special case of periodical indexing, which in turn is a special case of the general task of providing convenient, topical access to any collection of bibliographic materials. Many of the issues that could be raised here are addressed instead in sections on the catalog and on bibliographies.

Fortunately, newspaper indexing is one of the simplest, most straightforward, and unequivocally appropriate uses for *dBase III+*. Once you come to understand the principles at work and the design choices available, indexing of materials considerably more complex than a local newspaper will pose no large obstacles.

At the very least, we want a printed listing of all citations in the database, grouped by subject term. The subject term itself should appear once as a heading followed by references to all articles which are referenced by it.

From the keyboard, we will want to answer questions like:

1. What has been written on a given subject?
2. Is there an article with a term in the title?

The Simple Way

First let's look at a simple approach to indexing that employs a single data file and makes extensive use of the SET CARRY ON command. After the command has been issued, APPEND operations will carry the contents of the previous record over to each new blank record. Those fields that are the same in the both records can be left alone in the new one. Only those that are different need be changed. This data entry feature makes it reasonably satisfactory to use a data structure like this:

```
Structure for database: C:simplndx.dbf
Number of data records:      27
Date of last update   : 06/16/86
Field  Field Name  Type       Width    Dec
    1  SUBJECT     Character     50
    2  TITLE       Character     50
    3  DATE        Date           8
    4  PAGES       Character     10

** Total **                    119
```

INDEX ON SUBJECT TO SIMPLSUB allows us to view the data file as if it were sorted by subject. It also makes it possible to use the FIND command to rapidly locate any reference based on the subject term associated with it. Keyword searches on subject would look like this:

. LIST title, date, pages FOR "tax" $subject

The chief virtues of this approach are its simplicity and ease of data entry. To apply five subject terms to a particular citation, you need only type the citation once and modify the contents of the SUBJECT field each time. PgDn on the PC keyboard takes you from the end of the SUBJECT field in the current record to the beginning of the SUBJECT field in the next record.

A major drawback of this method is that it wastes disk storage capacity. If the citation fields total seventy-eight characters and the subject field runs to fifty, then providing five subject access points requires a commitment of 740 bytes. Add to that the overhead accounted for by indexes by subject, title, and author (even if you index only on a substring of each field) and only a couple of hundred records will fit on a 360 kilobyte floppy disk drive.

An additional shortcoming involves searches on fields other than the SUBJECT field. TITLE is not unique. If three subjects have been assigned to the same article, then the same title exists at least three times. Keyword searches on TITLE would bring up redundant information. Printing an alphabetical listing by TITLE, eliminating identical entries, requires special arrangements. You could do SET UNIQUE ON before indexing (INDEX) on TITLE. That, however, might strip out some frequently repeated titles that don't refer to the same article, e.g., "Court News."

You could write a program routine to compare succeeding records field by field to determine whether they are identical before sending each to the printer or screen. That seems needlessly complicated and slow, however.

A More Effective Way

The best way of handling the job is with two interrelated files, one containing bibliographic citations, the other containing subject terms referring to particular citations. The ability of *dBase III+* to store data in multiple files and specify logical links between them is the origin of the program's designation as a "relational database manager." Use of two files allows us to nearly eliminate the storage of data in more than one place. The only field common to both files is the TITLENO. It serves to maintain the connection between the files below:

```
Structure for database: C:subjects.dbf
Number of data records:      27
Date of last update   : 07/20/86
Field  Field Name  Type       Width    Dec
    1  SUBJECT     Character     50
    2  TITLENO     Character      5
** Total **                      56
```

```
Structure for database: C:bettrndx.dbf
Number of data records:      11
Date of last update   : 07/20/86
Field  Field Name  Type       Width    Dec
    1  TITLENO     Character      5
    2  TITLE       Character     50
    3  DATE        Date           8
    4  PAGES       Character     10
** Total **                      74
```

Assume that the following indexing has already been done:

. USE subjects
. INDEX ON UPPER(subject) TO sub
. USE bettrndx
. INDEX ON titleno TO bettrttl

To create the proper environment for searching by subject, issue the commands below:

. USE subjects INDEX sub
. SELECT 2
. USE bettrndx INDEX bettrttl
. SELECT 1
. SET RELATION TO titleno INTO bettrndx

The resulting status is summarized as:

```
Currently Selected Database:
Select area:  1, Database in Use: C:SUBJECTS.DBF
     ^^^^ Alias: SUBJECTS
    Master INDEX file:  C:SUB.NDX  Key: UPPER(subject)
    Related into: BETTRNDX
    Relation: titleno
```

```
Select area:  2, Database in Use: C:BETTRNDX.DBF
    ^^^^ Alias: BETTRNDX
Master INDEX file:  C:BETTRTTL.NDX  Key: titleno
```

To list references on a given subject, you might enter:

```
LIST TRIM(B->title)+", "+DTOC(B->date)+", p. "+
    ^^^^ TRIM(B->pages) FOR subject="Economic" OFF
```

The result:

```
TRIM(B->title)+", "+DTOC(B->date)+", p. "+TRIM(B->pages)
Magazine publisher considers new plant, 05/16/86, p. 1, 2-3
Bird feeder manufacturer to locate in town, 04/11/86, p. 1
Fish farm folds due to pesticide accident, 06/01/76, p. 3
Tax rates to increase 8%, 06/16/86, p. 1, 12
```

While the simpler indexing approach required 740 bytes to handle the data fields associated with a reference with five subject headings, this one needs only 354, better than a fifty percent savings. The index by title will be smaller as well because there is only one instance of each TITLE to store.

Once you get the hang of the approach and finally become used to having to precede field references not in the currently selected work area with the work area alias and "->", the interactive mode may be sufficient. Others, however, will find it just too demanding. Even with the ability to recall earlier commands by hitting the up-arrow, added in *dBase III+*, there is still too much tedious and precise typing required.

Using Program Files

Entering data first into the citation field and then into multiple subject fields requires a lot of the novice user. The section on a community resource file describes a fairly streamlined technique involving function keys, but they may not meet needs in every situation. Typographical errors in the repetitive entry of the TITLENO can still cause access points to become lost. A more automatic approach would be useful here.

A set of simple programs is needed to guide users at all levels of experience through the processes of adding data and searching the database. What follows is a menu-based system to add citations and related subject headings, to search by subject and by title keyword, and to print a subject index to the entire database.

Doubtless many features and refinements could be added to make this a finished product. Still, what follows serves to outline the approach and to expedite data entry and searching in a useful way.

The NDXMENU.PRG program listed at the end of this chapter puts up a menu of choices from which the user may choose:

//

```
:==========================================:
:                                          :
: N E W S P A P E R   I N D E X I N G   S Y S T E M :
:==========================================:
:                                          :
:                                          :
:       1. Enter citations                 :
:       2. Print subject listing           :
:       3. Search by subject               :
:       4. Search for title keyword        :
:                                          :
:       0. EXIT                            :
:                                          :
:=============== select  0 ================:
```

//

Data entry is done into the screen below. Remember that on a display screen the form is larger than it is possible to show here. Only one subject is on screen at a time during data entry. A more sophisticated approach that displays all subject terms entered and allows you to go back and change them is demonstrated in the section on reference archives:

//

```
:==========================================:
:                                          :
:   TITLENO [55555]                        :
:                                          :
:   TITLE    [Smith gives $5 M to library        ]  :
:                                          :
:   DATE         [8/06/86]                 :
:                                          :
:   PAGES    [1, 7      ]                   :
:                                          :
:==========================================:
```

    SUBJECT   Smith, John Quincy
//

The PRINTNDX.PRG program, called from the main menu when the user makes choice 2, produces this printed index to our fictious local newspaper:

Bird feeders
 Feeding Birds in Winter, 11/05/85, 4
 Bird feeder manufacturer to locate in town, 04/11/86, 1

Bird feeding
 Feeding Birds in Winter, 11/05/85, 4

Birds
 Feeding Birds in Winter, 11/05/85, 4

Court News
 Man bites dog in West Baldwin, 04/01/86, 12
 Computer thieves rob dry goods store, 04/01/86, 1, 4-5

Dogs
 Man bites dog in West Baldwin, 04/01/86, 12

Eastern Publishing Company
 Magazine publisher considers new plant, 05/16/86, 1, 2-3

Economic development
 Magazine publisher considers new plant, 05/16/86, 1, 2-3
 Bird feeder manufacturer to locate in town, 04/11/86, 1
 Fish farm folds due to pesticide accident, 06/01/76, 3
 Tax rates to increase 8%, 06/16/86, 1, 12

Option 3, subject searching, asks for a term in upper- or lower-case:

///

Subject term to be searched?   bird

Enter term, followed by <RETURN> to search

<RETURN> alone ends searching

///

The results are provided on the screen in this fashion (note that to send this display to the printer, you could type Ctrl-PrtSc before specifying the subject to be searched, or Shift-PrtSc once the display stops scrolling):

```
//////////////////////////////////////////////////

        Subject:  BIRD

     Bird feeders
Feeding Birds in Winter, 11/05/85, 4

Bird feeder manufacturer to locate in town, 04/11/86, 1

     Bird feeding
Feeding Birds in Winter, 11/05/85, 4

     Birds
Birds in Winter, 11/05/85, 4

Press any key to continue...

//////////////////////////////////////////////////
```

Searches for keyword in title are handled in the same way on the screen as subject searches:

```
//////////////////////////////////////////////////

     Title keyword to be searched?  [ bird        ]


   Enter term, followed by <RETURN> to search

     <RETURN> alone ends searching

//////////////////////////////////////////////////
```

The results:

```
//////////////////////////////////////////////////

        Keyword:  BIRD

Bird feeder manufacturer to locate in town, 04/11/86, 1

Feeding Birds in Winter, 11/05/85, 4


Press any key to continue...

//////////////////////////////////////////////////
```

Program Listing

Here are the program routines that accomplish the tasks discussed above:

```
* Program..: NDXMENU.PRG  Menu for newspaper indexing
*   Created with APPSGEN.PRG, applications generator
*   supplied with dBase III+
SET TALK OFF
SET BELL OFF
SET ESCAPE OFF
SET CONFIRM ON

DO WHILE .T.

    * ---Display menu options, centered on the screen.
    *     draw menu border and print heading
    CLEAR
    @ 2, 0 TO 14,79 DOUBLE
    @ 3,10 SAY [N E W S P A P E R   I N D E X I N G
    ^^^^ S Y S T E M ]
    @ 4,1 TO 4,78 DOUBLE
    * ---display detail lines
    @  7,26 SAY [1. Enter citations]
    @  8,26 SAY [2. Print subject listing]
    @  9,26 SAY [3. Search by subject]
    @ 10,26 SAY [4. Search for title keyword]
    @ 12, 26 SAY '0. EXIT'
    STORE 0 TO selectnum
    @ 14,33 SAY " select       "
    @ 14,42 GET selectnum PICTURE "9" RANGE 0,4
    READ

    DO CASE
       CASE selectnum = 0
          SET BELL ON
          SET TALK ON
          CLEAR ALL
          RETURN

       CASE selectnum = 1
       *  DO Enter citations

          DO inputndx

          SET CONFIRM OFF
          STORE ' ' TO WAIT_subst
```

```
            @ 23,0 SAY 'Press any key to continue...'
     ^^^^ GET WAIT_subst
            READ
            SET CONFIRM ON

      CASE selectnum = 2
      *   DO Print subject listing

            DO printndx

            SET CONFIRM OFF
            STORE ' ' TO WAIT_subst
            @ 23,0 SAY 'Press any key to continue...'
     ^^^^ GET WAIT_subst
            READ
            SET CONFIRM ON

      CASE selectnum = 3
      *   DO Search by subject

            DO subjndx

            SET CONFIRM OFF
            STORE ' ' TO WAIT_subst
            @ 23,0 SAY 'Press any key to continue...'
     ^^^^ GET WAIT_subst
            READ
            SET CONFIRM ON

      CASE selectnum = 4
      *   DO Search for title keyword

            DO ttlndx

            SET CONFIRM OFF
            STORE ' ' TO WAIT_subst
            @ 23,0 SAY 'Press any key to continue...'
     ^^^^ GET WAIT_subst
            READ
            SET CONFIRM ON
ENDCASE

ENDDO T
RETURN  && end ndxmenu.prg


* INPUTNDX.PRG Guides BETTRNDX.DBF, SUBJECTS.DBF input
```

```
CLEAR
SET TALK OFF
CLOSE DATA
USE bettrndx INDEX bettrttl
SELECT 2
USE subjects INDEX sub
SELECT 1

APPEND BLANK
DO WHILE .T.   && prompt for contents of citation fields
    @ 2,2 TO 12,69 DOUBLE    && draw double-line box
    @  4,  5  SAY "TITLENO"
    @  4, 17  GET  BETTRNDX->TITLENO
    @  6,  5  SAY "TITLE"
    @  6, 17  GET  BETTRNDX->TITLE
    @  8,  5  SAY "DATE"
    @  8, 17  GET  BETTRNDX->DATE
    @ 10,  5  SAY "PAGES"
    @ 10, 17  GET  BETTRNDX->PAGES
    READ
    SELECT 2   && make subjects.dbf the active data file
    flag=1

    DO WHILE flag>0   && accept subject entries until
     ^^^^ done
        msubject=SPACE(50)
        @ 15,  5  SAY "SUBJECT"
        @ 15, 17  GET  msubject
        READ

        IF LEN(TRIM(msubject))=0   && loop exit if
            flag=0          &&  empty field is entered
        ELSE
            APPEND BLANK
            REPLACE subject WITH msubject
            REPLACE titleno WITH bettrndx->titleno
        ENDIF

    ENDDO flag

    SELECT 1
    CLEAR
    answer=" "

    @ 10,10 SAY "Do you wish to add more index
     ^^^^ entries?  " GET answer
    READ
```

```
        IF UPPER(answer)="N"
            EXIT
        ELSE
            CLEAR
            APPEND BLANK
        ENDIF


ENDDO
SET TALK ON
CLOSE DATA
RETURN  && end inputndx.prg


** PRINTNDX.PRG Prints a subject index
*       using SUBJECTS.DBF and BETTRNDX.DBF
SET TALK OFF
CLOSE DATA
USE subjects INDEX sub
SELECT 2
USE bettrndx INDEX bettrttl
SELECT 1
SET RELATION TO titleno INTO bettrndx
CLEAR
msubject=subject
SET PRINT ON
? subject

DO WHILE .NOT. EOF()

    IF subject<>msubject  && Avoid duplicating headings
        ?    &&  by comparing successive subject fields
        ? subject
        msubject=subject
    ENDIF

    ? "   "+TRIM(bettrndx->title)+", "+DTOC
     ^^^^ (bettrndx->date)+", "+TRIM(bettrndx->pages)

    IF PROW()>55
        EJECT
        SKIP
        IF subject=msubject
            ? subject
        ENDIF
    ELSE
        SKIP
    ENDIF
```

```
ENDDO
EJECT
SET TALK ON
SET PRINT OFF
CLOSE DATA
RETURN   && End of printndx.prg


** SUBJNDX.PRG  Subject searching of SUBJECTS.DBF
*              and BETTRNDX.DBF
SET TALK OFF
CLOSE DATA
USE subjects INDEX sub
SELECT 2
USE bettrndx INDEX bettrttl
SELECT 1
SET RELATION TO titleno INTO bettrndx
DO WHILE .t.
    CLEAR
    subterm=SPACE(30)
    @ 10,10 SAY "Subject term to be searched?  "
     ^^^^ GET subterm
    @ 22,5 SAY "Enter term, followed by <RETURN>
     ^^^^ to search"
    @ 23,10 SAY "<RETURN> alone ends searching"
    READ
    subterm=TRIM(UPPER(subterm))
    IF LEN(subterm)=0
        CLEAR
        EXIT
    ENDIF
    FIND &subterm
    IF .NOT. found()
        CLEAR
        @ 10,10 SAY "There are no citations under "+
      ^^^^ subterm
        ?
        ?
        WAIT
        LOOP
    ENDIF
    CLEAR
    @ 5,10 SAY "Subject:  "+subterm
    ?
    ?
    msubject=subject
    ? "      "+subject
```

```
    DO WHILE UPPER(subject)=subterm .and. .NOT. EOF()
    IF subject<>msubject
        ? "        "+subject
        msubject=subject
    ENDIF
    ? TRIM(bettrndx->title)+", "+DTOC(bettrndx->date)+
     ^^^^ ", "+TRIM(bettrndx->pages)
        ?
        IF ROW()>20
            WAIT
        ENDIF
        SKIP
    ENDDO
    ?
    ?
    WAIT
ENDDO
SET TALK ON
CLOSE DATA
RETURN  && subndx.prg


** TTINDX.PRG  Keyword search of title field
SET TALK OFF
CLOSE DATA
USE bettrndx INDEX better
DO WHILE .t.
    GO TOP
    CLEAR
    keyword=SPACE(30)
    @ 10,10 SAY "Title keyword to be searched?  "
     ^^^^ GET keyword
    @ 22,5 SAY "Enter term, followed by <RETURN>
     ^^^^ to search"
    @ 23,10 SAY "<RETURN> alone ends searching"
    READ
    keyword=TRIM(UPPER(keyword))
    IF LEN(keyword)=0
        CLEAR
        EXIT
    ENDIF
    CLEAR
    @ 5,10 SAY "Keyword:  "+keyword
    ?
    ?
    DO WHILE .NOT. EOF()
        IF "&keyword" $ UPPER(TITLE)
```

```
            ? TRIM(title)+", "+TRIM(DTOC(date))+", "+
    ^^^^ TRIM(pages)
            ?
            IF ROW()>20
                WAIT
            ENDIF
        ENDIF
        SKIP
    ENDDO
    ?
    ?
    WAIT
ENDDO
SET TALK ON
CLOSE DATA
RETURN   &&  ttlndx
```

ABSTRACTS

It sometimes falls to the librarian/information specialist to produce abstracts of reports, articles, patents, and other materials of potential use to an organization. While *dBase III+* is not especially well suited to this application, it can nevertheless prove adequate where the database isn't terribly large and limitations on field length can be satisfactorily circumvented. The exercise of dealing with the abstract problem can illustrate some interesting but not widely used text-manipulation capabilities of *dBase III+*.

Text Filing Using MEMO Fields

At first glance, *dBase III+*'s MEMO fields seem to offer an answer. They accommodate variable length data, and, provided that an abstract is more than the 512-character default minimum, take only as much space as is absolutely necessary. Their fatal flaw is that they are not searchable. It is not possible to index (INDEX), sort (SORT), qualify with, search within for an embedded string value, or otherwise use field contents as part of any search specification.

MEMO fields are only useful where filing is more important than retrieval access to the entire MEMO field. Storing lots of text and providing access only through a few descriptors stored in other fields or another file is possible through creative use of a word processor/text editor, however.

It is assumed that the contents of a MEMO file will be entered from the keyboard for each record. To do this, however, *dBase* requires use of an editor. *dBase* calls upon its built-in editor unless a different editor is specified in the CONFIG.DB file. It is that file that *dBase* looks to for changes to system defaults. In either case, once in the editor, you can read in a disk file, delete extraneous material, and modify as needed. The ^KR command does the trick, both in *WordStar* and in *dBase*'s editor.

Be careful. The editor that comes with *dBase* can't handle files larger than four to five kilobytes. Anything longer cannot be saved and will be lost to the MEMO file meant to receive it.

If you use a separate word processing program, be sure that you are producing a straight ASCII text file. Many word processors play special tricks with some of the character code values in a file to control formatting on the screen and the printer. Generally, a plain vanilla ASCII mode is available, often at the price of giving up word-wrap and perhaps other niceties. It may be necessary, with some word processors, to switch to the ASCII mode each time you edit a MEMO field. Others may allow a change in default mode using a configuration routine.

A Simple Abstracting Method

A very small database with brief abstracts that never exceed 254 characters can be handled in a single file with additional fields for elements of the bibliographic citation and a single character field for the abstract. String searching is quite slow but probably workable for a few hundred records:

```
. LIST title FOR "solar" .OR. "thermal" $abstract
```

Keyword Access to Abstracts

A completely satisfactory method of handling abstracts and other large bodies of text ought to provide the following:

1. Accommodation of variable and potentially large amounts of text without wasting disk storage capacity
2. Convenient import of ASCII text files, preferably on a "batch" basis, independent of user involvement with every record
3. Retrieval of abstracts by one or more keywords, with matching keyword(s) highlighted
4. Boolean logic for use in searching
5. Ability to print abstracts in one or more convenient formats
6. Modifiable "stop list" of terms not to be included in a keyword index
7. Ability to totally recreate keyword index should problems with equipment or software make that necessary

This approach will make use of these data files:

CITATION.DBF: Bibliographic details regarding a particular abstract, including a unique citation number, CITENO

ABSTRACT.DBF: The abstract itself, stored one line at a time in the field ABS, with a second field CITENO pointing back to the corresponding citation number for that abstract. ORDERNO indicates which line of the abstract is contained in a particular ABSTRACT.DBF record, allowing for reconstruction of abstracts for display and printing.

TEMP.DBF: Lines of abstract, on their way to ABSTRACT.DBF, are imported to this file first, before being transferred to ABSTRACT.DBF with appropriate citation and order number. This file has just one field, TEMPABS.

KEYWORDS.DBF:Individual keywords, stored in the KW field, accompanied by CITENO and ORDERNO fields that provide direct access to the corresponding CITATION.DBF and ABSTRACT.DBF records

A text file called TEST is prepared with a carriage return/linefeed at the end of each line, short field tags preceding the elements of the citation, and "***" at the end of each citation and abstract.

A utility program that converts nonstandard characters to straight ASCII format may also be needed, depending on the nature of existing word processing files. The syntax for use of FIXWS.COM, a public domain utility for dealing with the peculiarities introduced by *WordStar*'s document mode format is:

```
. RUN FIXWS  test  testasci.txt
```

The results of the conversion are stored in TESTASCI.TXT. A random section of the file looks like this:

```
AIA in New York and SIA in Boston offered a heady insight into the
microcomputer-related developments that will shake library
automation in general for the next several years.
***
CD-ROM (Compact Disc Read-Only Memory) technology is showing up in
lots of places. The most revolutionary application is the scoped
CD-ROM catalog (SCROM Cat?). Storing bibliographic data in their
full MARC II-format splendor is common enough. Vendors
```

This text file first is moved into a temporary *dBase III+* file called TEMP.DBF. It has only one field, called TEMPABS.

```
. USE TEMP
. APPEND FROM testasci.txt SDF
  196 records added
```

The SDF parameter advances to the next TEMP record each time a carriage return/linefeed is encountered. The "196" is the number of lines imported. The first few records of TEMP look like this:

```
. LIST TRIM(TEMPABS)
Record#  TRIM(TEMPABS)
```

```
 1  AU Beiser, Karl
 2  JL Wilson Library Bulletin
 3  DT 9/86
 4  PP 27-28
 5  CD-ROM (Compact Disc Read-Only Memory)
^^^^ technology is showing
 6  up in lots of places.  The most revolutionary
^^^^ application is the
 7  scoped CD-ROM catalog (SCROM Cat?).  Storing
^^^^ bibliographic data
 8  in their full MARC II-format splendor is
^^^^ common enough.  Vendors
 9  such as Library Corporation (Bibliofile) can
^^^^ pack more than
10  500,000 bibliographic records on each disk.
^^^^ A library or library
```
*** INTERRUPTED ***

The TEMP records are next processed to update the CITATION and ABSTRACT files. Citation elements are stripped out based on the short field tags and placed in appropriate CITATION fields. Lines not preceded by a recognized field tag are presumed to be part of the abstract and are replaced (REPLACED) into the ABSTRACT file, along with a reference to the corresponding CITATION record (CITENO). Also stored is ORDERNO, preserving information about the order of lines within an abstract.

The program file to accomplish this transformation is called ABADDBAT (standing, more or less, for adding abstracts in batch mode):

```
** ABADDBAT.PRG
** Move text lines TEMP.DBF to ABSTRACT.DBF, inserting
** CITENO and ORDERNO as required
CLOSE DATA
SET TALK OFF
SELE 3
USE citation INDEX cino
GO BOTTOM
mciteno=STR(VAL(citeno)+1,5)
SELE 2
USE abstract INDEX abcitord
SELE 1
USE temp

DO WHILE .NOT. EOF()
```

```
      IF LEN(TRIM(tempabs))>0
          SELE 3
          APPEND BLANK
          REPLACE citeno with mciteno
          SELE 1
      ENDIF
      mtag=SUBSTR(tempabs,1,2)
      DO WHILE mtag $(AU,JL,DT,PP)
          SELE 3
          REPLACE &mtag WITH LTRIM(SUBSTR(tempabs,3))
          SELE 1
          SKIP
          mtag=SUBSTR(tempabs,1,2)
      ENDDO
      morderno="000"
      DO WHILE tempabs <>"***"
          SELE 2
          APPEND BLANK
          REPLACE abs WITH temp->tempabs
          morderno=STR(VAL(morderno)+1,3)
          REPLACE orderno WITH morderno
          REPLACE citeno WITH mciteno
          SELE 1
          SKIP
      ENDDO    end of citation check
      ? "Citation #"+mciteno+" has been added with "+
       ^^^^ morderno+" lines."
      SKIP      && skips over "***"
      mciteno=STR(VAL(mciteno)+1,5)
ENDDO
CLOSE DATA
SET TALK ON
```

When the routine is run, the screen allows the user to follow what is going on.

```
. DO abaddbat
Citation #  1 has been added with  17 lines.
Citation #  2 has been added with  12 lines.
Citation #  3 has been added with   3 lines.
Citation #  4 has been added with  11 lines.
Citation #  5 has been added with   5 lines.
Citation #  6 has been added with  11 lines.
Citation #  7 has been added with   7 lines.
Citation #  8 has been added with   4 lines.
Citation #  9 has been added with   7 lines.
 etc.
```

This is the data structure for CITATION.DBF:

```
Structure for database: C:citation.dbf
Number of data records:        23
Date of last update   : 08/11/86
Field  Field Name  Type        Width    Dec
    1  CITENO      Character       5
    2  AU          Character      30
    3  TI          Character      50
    4  JL          Character      15
    5  DT          Date            8
    6  PP          Character      10
** Total **                     119
```

Let's look at the structure of ABSTRACT.DBF and the first few records, minus the ends of each line which "fall off" the edge of the screen:

```
Structure for database: C:abstract.dbf
Number of data records:       173
Date of last update   : 08/11/86
Field  Field Name  Type        Width    Dec
    1  CITENO      Character       5
    2  ORDERNO     Character       3
    3  ABS         Character      80
    4  KWDONE      Character       1
** Total **                      90
```

```
. USE abstract
. LIST
Record#  CITENO  ORDERNO  ABS
      1     1       1      Once upon a time, computers wer
      2     1       2      computer, it was by definition
      3     1       3      extremely expensive behemoth.
      4     1       4      smaller computers.  Minicompute
      5     1       5      a lot of folks thought that in
      6     1       6      full-powered computers at all.
      7     1       7      programmed minicomputers develo
      8     1       8      Because they were less expensiv
      9     1       9      could do most of the same thing
     10     1      10      and convenience) they prospered
     11     1      11      when people talked of computers
     12     1      12      minicomputers in mind.  The big
     13     1      13      now the exception and generally

*** INTERRUPTED ***
```

The Light Duty Method

What we've done so far allows us to meet the design requirement that abstracts can be of indefinite and, potentially, great length. We could stop here and rely on string searching for a measure of keyword access. Performance will deteriorate as the file grows, as noted earlier. But a smallish file may be adequately served by this approach:

1. Open CITATION.DBF indexed on citation number (CINO.NDX).
2. Open ABSTRACT.DBF in another work area, indexed on CITENO+ORDERNO.
3. Relate (RELATE) the second file into the first on the contents of the CITENO field.
4. Prompt for the search term.
5. Locate (LOCATE FOR) the search contained in ABS, e.g., LOCATE FOR "CD-ROM" $abs.
6. Print citation information.
7. Do FIND CITENO+"001" to skip to beginning of abstract lines.
8. Print abstract, wait for user to read.
9. Do FIND CITENO+1, skipping additional instances of the search term in the same abstract, and continue search.

Steps 5 through 9 would be enclosed in a DO WHILE .NOT. EOF() loop.

The Heavy Duty Method

In order to avoid the performance penalty for keyword searching in larger files, we need to bring the rapid-access FIND command into play. All we need to do is place all significant words appearing in the abstracts file into a separate KEYWORDS file, along with CITENO and ORDERNO to provide connections to CITATION.DBF. We then index the KW field, giving us alphabetic access by keyword. ABKWGEN.PRG does the job.

A "stop list" of extraneous, "noise" words is checked before a term is accepted for inclusion in KEYWORDS. The file is meant to be maintained interactively. A good way to create one to meet local needs, however, is to run a file through keyword generation with an empty stop list, copy the contents of the resulting keyword file to the stop list file, delete significant, non-noise words, and pack (PACK) what remains.

Here is the stoplist and the first few records in it:

```
Structure for database: C:stopword.dbf
Number of data records:      73
Date of last update  : 08/11/86
Field  Field Name  Type       Width    Dec
   1   WORD        Character    15
** Total **                     16
```

```
. LIST
Record#  WORD
      1  A
     54  AFTER
     38  ALL
     18  AM
      2  AN
     22  AND
     16  ARE
     37  AT
     44  BECAUSE
     61  BIGGER
     42  BUILT
     39  BUT
     67  BUYING
     66  BY
     26  CAME
*** INTERRUPTED ***
```

Unfortunately, better performance in searching is bought at the cost of a time-consuming preprocessing of text information. To produce a keyword index to 196 lines of abstract took about forty-two seconds on a hard disk-equipped Leading Edge Model D. The KWDONE field in ABSTRACT.DBF allows the keyword-generating routine to locate and process only those abstract lines that have not already been added to the KEYWORDS file.

The routine looks like this:

```
** ABKWGEN.PRG
**   Routine to generate a keyword index to ABSTRACT.DBF
**   -- a file of text representing parts of multiple
**   abstracts stored as a series of 80-character lines.

SET TALK OFF
CLOSE DATA
SELE 3
USE stopword INDEX stoppers
SELE 2
USE keywords INDEX keycite,keyalpha
```

```
SELE 1
USE abstract

DO WHILE .NOT. EOF()
    IF kwdone <> "T"
        remainder=UPPER(abs)
        SELECT 2
        DO WHILE LEN(TRIM(remainder))>0
            mkeyword=LEFT(remainder,AT(" ",remainder)-1)
            DO WHILE LEN(TRIM(mkeyword))>0 .AND.
    ^^^^ (ASC(RIGHT(mkeyword,1))>90 .OR.
    ^^^^ ASC(RIGHT(mkeyword,1)) <65)
                mkeyword=LEFT(mkeyword,
    ^^^^ LEN(TRIM(mkeyword))-1)
            ENDDO
            IF LEN(TRIM(mkeyword))=0
                EXIT
            ENDIF
            DO WHILE ASC(LEFT(mkeyword,1))>90 .OR.
    ^^^^ ASC(LEFT(mkeyword,1))<65
                mkeyword=SUBSTR(mkeyword,2)
            ENDDO
**  Check stopword file STOPWORD.DBF
            SELECT 3
            FIND &mkeyword
            IF .NOT. FOUND()
                SELECT 2
                APPEND BLANK
                REPLACE kw WITH mkeyword
                REPLACE citeno WITH A->citeno
                REPLACE orderno WITH A->orderno
            ENDIF
        remainder=LTRIM(SUBSTR(remainder,AT(" ",
    ^^^^ remainder)))
        ENDDO
        SELECT 1
        REPLACE kwdone WITH "T"
    ENDIF
        SKIP

ENDDO
** CLOSE DATA
SET TALK ON
```

Here is the structure of KEYWORDS and the first few records
with KEYALPHA.NDX in effect:

```
Structure for database: C:keywords.dbf
Number of data records:      902
Date of last update    : 08/11/86
Field  Field Name  Type         Width     Dec
   1   CITENO      Character       5
   2   ORDERNO     Character       3
   3   KW          Character      20
** Total **                       29
```

```
Record#  CITENO  ORDERNO  KW
   238      6       2     ABILITY
   366      9       3     ABLE
    46      1      16     ACCESS
   409     11       1     ACCESS
   770     18       5     ACCESS
   332      8       1     ACQUIRED
   446     12       3     ACQUIRING
   813     20       5     ACTIONS
    92      2       8     ADD
   555     15       6     ADDITIONAL
   447     12       4     ADVANTAGES
   645     16       8     AGENCIES
   123      3       1     ALA
*** INTERRUPTED ***
```

Searches are done using ABSEARCH.PRG:

```
** ABSEARCH.PRG
**    Searches abstract files

CLOSE DATA
SELE 3
USE abstract INDEX abcitord
SELE 2
USE citation INDEX cino
SET RELATION TO citeno INTO abstract
SELE 1
USE keywords INDEX kwciteno
SET RELATION TO citeno INTO citation

DO WHILE .T.
    CLEAR
    mkeyword=space(20)
    @ 10, 10 SAY "Keyword to be searched " GET mkeyword
    @ 22, 15 SAY "Type <RETURN> alone to exit"
    READ
    mkeyword=LTRIM(RTRIM(UPPER(mkeyword)))
```

```
    IF LEN(TRIM(mkeyword))=0
        EXIT
    ENDIF


* Look for search word in KEYWORDS.DBF, display message
*  if not there.
    FIND &mkeyword
    CLEAR
    IF .NOT. FOUND()
        @ 10,1
        @ 10,10 SAY "Sorry, this keyword isn't in file"
      * @ 22,1 SAY " "
        WAIT
        LOOP
    ENDIF
        mciteno=citeno
    DO WHILE kw=mkeyword
        ? B->au
        ? B->ti
        ? B->jl, B->dt, "PP. "+B->pp

        SELE 3

***  Display citations and abstracts
        DO WHILE citeno=mciteno
            keystart=AT("&mkeyword", UPPER(abs))
            IF keystart>0
                ? SUBSTR(abs,1,keystart-1)
                SET COLOR TO I
                ?? mkeyword
                SET COLOR TO
                ?? TRIM(SUBSTR(abs,keystart+
    ^^^^ LEN(TRIM(mkeyword))))
                SKIP
            ELSE
                ? TRIM(abs)
                SKIP
            ENDIF
        ENDDO  citeno=mciteno in ABSTRACT
        SELE 1

***  Skip repetitive references to the same citation
        DO WHILE citeno=mciteno
            SKIP
        ENDDO citeno=mciteno in KEYWORDS
        ?
        WAIT
```

```
*  Skip matches on longer terms containing search root
       IF citeno<mciteno
           EXIT
       ENDIF

       mciteno=citeno
    ENDDO kw=mkeyword
ENDDO T
CLOSE DATA
RETURN
```

The result of running ABSEARCH.PRG, looking for the term "CD-ROM," is as follows (note that on-screen the term will be displayed in reverse video wherever it appears):

```
. DO absearch
```

///

Breslin, Thomas
New Library Products
LJ   05/15/86 PP. 22-24+
Evolving in the shadow of the minicomputer, the microcomputer has developed into a potent tool for managing small libraries. But a microcomputer isn't a real computer in the same sense as those sleek but pricey boxes that drive online integrated library systems. Its only place in larger libraries is in word processing, statistical and financial management, list maintenance and such small domesticated applications. Wrong. Add a cheap, reliable mass storage device (CD-ROM for now) and some intelligent local area network links to other computers in the library and its time to redefine "computer" again. It looks like tasks that cannot be done on a micro, rather than those that can be will soon be the exception.

Press any key to continue...

///

//

Pierce, Franklin
The New Catalog
LJ   07/15/86 PP. 12-13+
CD-ROM (Compact Disc Read-Only Memory) technology is showing up in
lots of places. The most revolutionary application is the scoped
CD-ROM catalog (SCROM Cat?). Storing bibliographic data in their
full MARC II-format splendor is common enough. Vendors such as
Library Corporation (BiblioFile) can pack more than 500,000
bibliographic records on each disk. A library or library system
could just as easily have the machine-readable bibliographic
records representing their collection mastered onto CD-ROM. With
the appropriate software, both staff and library users would have
an automated catalog functionally similar to the much more
expensive online version.

Press any key to continue...

/ //

SERIALS UNION LIST

In producing a serials union list with *dBase III+*, we will aim to achieve efficient storage of data, convenient data entry, and a simple, straightforward methodology employing the interactive approach.

Products/Queries

We need to be able to easily find answers to the following queries:

1. What libraries own a particular title and what are the holdings of each?
2. What are the interloan policies of a particular library?

Among the printed products required from a union list database are:

1. A list by title of all the holdings of every participating library
2. A list of addresses and lending policies of participating libraries, in order by library
3. A list by library of the titles held by that library, for editing purposes

Data Structure

These aims can be met by a data structure involving three files: ULBIB.DBF for bibliographic information pertaining to a specific title; HOLDINGS.DBF for the specifics of a given library's holdings of a particular title; and LIBRARY.DBF for the names, addresses, and interloan policies of participating libraries.

The bibliographic file for a real union list system would likely use large, full, and, insofar as possible, MARC-like records for each serial title. The nature and contents of a fully adequate record structure for a particular union list project are highly variable, dependent on local requirements, and generally beyond the scope of this discussion. The abbreviated BIB.DBF below serves solely to demonstrate the manner in which a bibliographic file can be made to interact with other files containing holdings and library data.

The consistent recording of library serial holdings (i.e., volume, number, dates, format, gaps) is a complex topic, also beyond the scope of the current discussion. In the interest of simplicity, holdings statements are accorded one 254-character field in

ULHOLDNG.DBF.   There is no checking for consistency of form or completeness of content.   Such checking could be done under program control but would require substantial analysis of applicable standards and local adaptations thereof.

Statements regarding a particular library's policies on interloan, photocopying charges, and related matters are lumped together in the POLICY field of ULLIBS.DBF. A single text field seems the only alternative, unless a group of libraries can enforce an extremely narrow range of variance in such policies. Only with a narrow range of policy categories could local rules with regard to each category be stored in its own field. The advantage of such a structure would be in making each category independently searchable.

```
Structure for database: C:ulbib.dbf
Number of data records:        8
Date of last update   : 08/09/86
Field  Field Name  Type        Width   Dec
    1   TITLENO     Character      5
    2   TITLE       Character     60
    3   FORMER1     Character     60
    4   FORMER2     Character     60
    5   ISSN        Character     15
    6   COMMENTS    Character     60
** Total **                     261


Structure for database: C:ullibs.dbf
Number of data records:        6
Date of last update   : 08/09/86
Field  Field Name  Type        Width   Dec
    1   LIBRARYNO   Character      5
    2   LIBRARY     Character     50
    3   ADR2        Character     35
    4   ADR3        Character     35
    5   CITY        Character     15
    6   STATE       Character      2
    7   ZIP         Character      9
    8   POLICY      Character    254
** Total **                     406


Structure for database: C:ulholdng.dbf
Number of data records:       22
Date of last update   : 08/09/86
Field  Field Name  Type        Width   Dec
    1   TITLENO     Character      5
    2   LIBRARYNO   Character      5
```

3 HOLDINGS   Character   150

Additions to the Database

Additions to the database are made with APPEND. In order to fill in the LIBRARYNO and TITLENO fields from scratch, the user must have a manual list of these numbers available for convenient consultation. Needless to say, error checking is nonexistent with this approach. Individual circumstances will determine whether this is a problem or not. You must be sure that all indexes are being updated as new entries are made:

```
. USE ulholdng INDEX ulhldttl, ulhldlib, ulhldduo
. APPEND
```

Holdings Queries

Perhaps the most frequent question a union list is called upon to answer is, "Which libraries own Title X, and what time span is covered by their holdings?" It is fairly easy to answer this question with a series of interactive commands from the *dBase III+* dot-prompt.

The first step is to set up the required relationships between files.

```
. SELECT 3
. USE ullibs INDEX ullibno
. SELECT 2
. USE ulholdng INDEX ulhldttl
. SET RELATION TO libraryno INTO ullibs
. SELECT 1
. USE ulbib INDEX ulbibttl
. SET RELATION TO titleno INTO ulholdng
```

The resulting environment is summarized by doing DISPLAY STATUS:

```
. DISPLAY STATUS
Currently Selected Database:
Select area:  1, Database in Use: C:ULBIB.DBF
    ^^^^ Alias: ULBIB
    Master index file:  C:ULBIBTTL.NDX  Key:
    ^^^^ substr(title,1,15)
    Related into: ULHOLDNG
```

Relation: titleno

Select area: 2, Database in Use: C:ULHOLDNG.DBF
    ^^^^ Alias: ULHOLDNG
    Master index file: C:ULHLDTTL.NDX Key: titleno
    Related into: ULLIBS
    Relation: libraryno

Select area: 3, Database in Use: C:ULLIBS.DBF
    ^^^^ Alias: ULLIBS
    Master index file: C:ULLIBNO.NDX Key: libraryno

But we aren't finished setting up the working environment for making inquiries into the union list database. It is extremely convenient to be able to redefine the fields that are to be available (or not available) to interactive commands. The SET FIELDS command is used for this purpose. A by-product of its use is the ability to refer to fields from multiple files without use of an alias ("ULBIB->" or "A->" for instance). It's surprising how much time such a little change can save.

This is the command we enter to specify the fields we wish to use:

. SET FIELDS TO titleno,title,B->titleno,B->holdings,
    ^^^^ C->library,C->policy

These are the only fields that can be displayed or referenced in WHILE and FOR clauses.

If we take a moment to look at the structure of our three database files, we see that those fields currently available because of SET FIELDS TO are indicated by a ">".

Structure for database: C:ULBIB.DBF
Number of data records: 8
Date of last update   : 08/09/86

Field	Field Name	Type	Width	Dec
1	>TITLENO	Character	5	
2	>TITLE	Character	60	
3	FORMER1	Character	60	
4	FORMER2	Character	60	
5	ISSN	Character	15	
6	COMMENTS	Character	60	
** Total **			261	

```
Structure for database: C:ULHOLDNG.DBF
Number of data records:      22
Date of last update   : 08/09/86
Field  Field Name  Type        Width    Dec
    1 >TITLENO     Character       5
    2  LIBRARYNO   Character       5
    3 >HOLDINGS    Character     150
** Total **                      161
```

```
Structure for database: C:ULLIBS.DBF
Number of data records:       6
Date of last update   : 08/09/86
Field  Field Name  Type        Width    Dec
    1  LIBRARYNO   Character       5
    2 >LIBRARY     Character      50
    3  ADR2        Character      35
    4  ADR3        Character      35
    5  CITY        Character      15
    6  STATE       Character       2
    7  ZIP         Character       9
    8 >POLICY      Character     254
** Total **                      406
```

Going through these contortions at the start of every session would be a pain in the neck. Fortunately, it is easy to record the environment we have created for later use. We just enter:

```
. CREATE VIEW ulttlqry FROM ENVIRONMENT
```

All we need do to get things rolling next time is to invoke the appropriate VUE file and proceed with our query. Here is a sample session in which we look for holdings information for the titles *Forestry and Flight* and *Popular Commuting*.

```
. SET VIEW TO ulttlqry
.
.
. FIND Forest
. DISP title
Record#  title
     2  Forestry and Flight

. SELE 2
. LIST library, TRIM(holdings) OFF WHILE
     ^^^^ titleno=a->titleno
library                                   trim(holdings)
```

```
Fleversham Public Library                    V. 12, NO. 5
    ^^^^ TO DATE
Blankenship Oceanographic Products Library v. 23, no. 4
Brittlebone Institute Library                Jan 1985+
 .
 .
. SELE 1
. FIND Popular
. DISP title
Record#  title
     5   Popular Commuting

. SELE 2
. LIST library, TRIM(holdings) OFF WHILE
    ^^^^ titleno=a->titleno
library                                 trim(holdings)
Fleversham Public Library                    v. 3,
    ^^^^ no. 5, May, 1974+; On microfilm 1974-1980.
Franklin College Library                     v. 10+
Beetlebomb Vocational Technical Inst. Library v. 12+
 .
 .
. SET VIEW TO
```

A series of inquiries is made easier by the HISTORY feature introduced with *dBase III+*. The long line beginning with LIST need not be typed more than once. It can be accessed subsequently by hitting the up-arrow until it reappears. In-line editing can be done if desired.

Rather than list (LIST) libraries and holdings, you might prefer that they appear in columnar form. A short REPORT FORM, once created, can subsequently be invoked in place of LIST. The WHILE clause limits retrieval to records meeting only specified criteria.

Another useful enhancement might be to construct a short command file to:

1.   Invoke the view file.
2.   Prompt for the title to be found.
3.   Confirm that it is the correct title.
4.   Select (SELECT) another work area.
5.   Do LIST or REPORT FORM to send output to screen.

Policy Queries

Finding out about a particular library's policies is a straightforward, single-file operation. In outline form:

```
USE ullibs INDEX ulliblib
FIND <libary name>
EDIT
```

To print the current policies of all libraries, a REPORT FORM called ULPOLICY.FRM is created. Its output is shown below:

```
. USE ullibs INDEX ulliblib
. REPORT FORM ulpolicy
```

Page No.   1
08/09/86
    Interloan Policies of Union List Libraries

Lib #	Library	Interloan Policy
20006	Beetlebomb Vocational Technical Inst. Library, Route #3, Box 4556, Backstrom, ME 04111	$.10/page.
20004	Blankenship Oceanographic Products Library, P.O. Box 54, Freeland, ME 048308823	$.10/page for photocopies. Requires use of AIA request forms. Not open to public on walk-in basis.
20003	Brittlebone Institute Library, Brittlebone Institute, P.O. Box 233, Kartoffel, ME 04969	Lends only to academic and research libraries, and regional resource libraries. All other libraries should direct requests to resource libraries.
20005	East Hodgepodge Regional High School Library, P.O. Box 234, Hodgepodge, ME 04000	$.05/page, first 10 pages at no charge.
20001	Fleversham Public Library, 57 Maine Avenue, Tregoria, ME 04333	$.10/page, first 15 pages free.
20002	Franklin College Library, 27	$.15/page. First 30 pages

Riverview St., Skyton, ME   free to NELINET member
04901   libraries.

Complete Holdings of Each Library

It may be necessary to generate a complete list of the current
holdings of each library for editing purposes, for local distribution
to library users, or for incorporation in other local databases. This
is, unfortunately, something that cannot be done easily from the
dot-prompt. If we were willing to copy the TITLE field from
ULBIB.DBF into each corresponding ULHOLDNG.DBF record, the list
we want to generate would be a snap. We could open
ULHOLDNG.DBF, index it on TITLE, and LIST TITLE and
HOLDINGS.

The cost for this simplicity is great, as usual. If fifty libraries
each hold an average of 200 titles, 600,000 extra bytes of storage
capacity (10,000 x 60 characters/title) will be required.

A more economical approach using a short command file is
preferable. For it to work, however, we need to generate a new
index for ULHOLDNG. By concatenating TITLENO and LIBRARYNO
to generate ULHLDDUO.NDX, we will minimize the time required to
jump back and forth between files in generating our list. Doing
SET RELATION is not necessary, as the new index takes the routine
directly to the proper holdings statement in just one step.

The command file to accomplish all this, ULEACH.PRG, looks
like this:

```
** ULEACH.PRG
**    Extracts holdings of a specified library from
**    ULHOLDNG.DBF, ULBIB.DBF and ULLIBS.DBF, prints to
**    the screen and, optionally, a printer.
SET TALK OFF
CLOSE DATA
CLEAR
USE ulbib INDEX ulbibttl
SELE 2
USE ulholdng INDEX ulhldduo
SELE 3
USE ullibs INDEX ullibno
SELE 1

****  Prompt for libraryno
mlibraryno=SPACE(5)
```

```
@ 10,10 SAY "What is the identification number of the
      ^^^^ library"
@ 11,15 SAY "whose holdings are to be printed?"
@ 13,40 GET mlibraryno PICTURE '99999'
READ
answer=" "

****  Ask whether to send list to printer
@ 20,10 SAY "To printer? (Y/N)   " GET answer
READ
IF UPPER(answer)="Y"
    SET PRINT ON
ENDIF
CLEAR
SELE 3
FIND &mlibraryno

****  Check for validlibrary number
IF .NOT. FOUND()
    CLEAR
    @ 10, 10 SAY "This is not a valid library number."
    @ 10, 15 SAY "Please restart program by typing DO
     ^^^^ uleach."
    @ 22,1 SAY " "
    WAIT
    CLEAR
    RETURN
ENDIF

? SPACE(20)+TRIM(library)
?
?
SELE 1

***    Work through whole bibliographic file

DO WHILE .NOT. EOF()
    mtitleno=titleno+mlibraryno
    SELE 2
    FIND &mtitleno

***    Look for holdings that match on libraryno
    IF FOUND()
        ? TRIM(A->title)
        ? "  "+TRIM(holdings)
    ENDIF
    SELE 1
```

```
      SKIP
ENDDO
CLOSE DATA
SET TALK ON
```

The lists that follow were produced as a result of five-digit library numbers given in response to the full-screen prompt resulting from the @ ... SAY ... GET ... sequence near the beginning of the command file. Output will go to the printer as well as the screen if the user answers "Y" when queried about printing.

Fleversham Public Library

Breeder's Digest; Journal of the Cattleman's Association
   July, 1956 to August 1982
Forestry and Flight
   V. 12, NO. 5 TO DATE
Nineteen
   July 1986+
Popular Commuting
   v. 3, no. 5, May, 1974+; On microfilm 1974-1980.
Regional Report
   v.1+
Santayana Commentary
   December, 1983+

Franklin College Library

Journal of Numeric Musicology
   Jan 1967+, microfilm 1967-1985
Popular Commuting
   v. 10+
Regional Report
   Jan 1982+

Beetlebomb Vocational Technical Inst. Library

Breeder's Digest; Journal of the Cattleman's Association
   v. 4-7
Journal of Numeric Musicology
   scattered issues
Popular Commuting
   v. 12+
Regional Report
   v. 12+

Preparing a Printed Union List

As with the previous task, a special command file is necessary to produce a printed union list. There is one interesting trick to producing such a list, using the approach adopted here. A new index file, ULHLDEXP.NDX, is employed to ensure that each library will appear in alphabetical order under the appropriate serial title. The index is composed of fields from two different work areas. The environment within which the command file that follows operates can be summarized by the following status listing:

```
Currently Selected Database:
Select area:  1, Database in Use: C:ulbib.dbf
    ^^^^ Alias: ULBIB
   Master index file:  C:ulbibttl.ndx  Key:
   ^^^^ substr(title,1,15)
   Related into: ULHOLDNG
   Relation: titleno

Select area:  2, Database in Use: C:ulholdng.dbf
    ^^^^ Alias: ULHOLDNG
   Master index file:  C:ulhldexp.ndx  Key: titleno+
   ^^^^ substr(c->library,1,15)
   Related into: ULLIBS
   Relation: libraryno

Select area:  3, Database in Use: C:ullibs.dbf
    ^^^^ Alias: ULLIBS
   Master index file:  C:ullibno.ndx  Key: libraryno
```

The command file that prints the union list is listed here:

```
** ULALL.PRG
SET TALK OFF
CLOSE DATA
CLEAR

SELE 3
USE ullibs INDEX ullibno
SELE 2
USE ulholdng INDEX ulhldexp
SET RELATION TO libraryno INTO ullibs
SELE 1
USE ulbib INDEX ulbibttl
SET RELATION TO titleno INTO ulholdng
CLEAR
```

```
onpaper=" "
@ 15,10 SAY "To printer? (Y/N)  " GET onpaper
READ
onpaper=UPPER(onpaper)
IF onpaper="Y"
    SET PRINT ON
ENDIF

? SPACE(20)+"Union List of Confederated Libraries"
?
?
linect=3
SELE 1

***   Work through whole bibliographic file

DO WHILE .NOT. EOF()
    mtitleno=titleno
    SELE 2
    FIND &mtitleno

    IF FOUND()
       IF linect>=55 .AND. onpaper="Y"
           EJECT
           linect=0
       ENDIF
       ? "-- "+TRIM(A->title)+" --"
       ?
       linect=linect+2
       DO WHILE titleno=mtitleno
           ? TRIM(c->library)
           ? "  "+TRIM(holdings)
           linect=linect+2
           IF linect>=55 .AND. onpaper="Y"
               EJECT
               linect=0
           ENDIF
           SKIP
       ENDDO
       ?
       linect=linect+1
    ENDIF
    SELE 1
    SKIP
ENDDO
CLOSE DATA
SET PRINT OFF
```

```
SET TALK ON
RETURN
```

Notice the LINECT variable in the command file. It ensures that the printer will skip over the perforations in continuous feed paper if the user decides to send output to the printer. What follows is the result of a run with the small database available for demonstration purposes:

```
. DO ulall
```

Union List of Confederated Libraries

-- Appaloosa --

Blankenship Oceanographic Products Library
    v.1, no. 1 Jan 1971+

-- Breeder's Digest; Journal of the Cattleman's
        ^^^^ Association --

Beetlebomb Vocational Technical Inst. Library
    v. 4-7
Fleversham Public Library
    July, 1956 to August 1982

-- Forestry and Flight --

Blankenship Oceanographic Products Library
    v. 23, no. 4
Brittlebone Institute Library
    Jan 1985+
Fleversham Public Library
    V. 12, NO. 5 TO DATE

-- Journal of Numeric Musicology --

Beetlebomb Vocational Technical Inst. Library
    scattered issues
Brittlebone Institute Library
    v. 2, no. 3+
Franklin College Library
    Jan 1967+, microfilm 1967-1985

-- Nineteen --

Blankenship Oceanographic Products Library
    January, 1976- July 1986
East Hodgepodge Regional High School Library
    v.1+
Fleversham Public Library
    July 1986+

-- Popular Commuting --

Beetlebomb Vocational Technical Inst. Library
    v. 12+
Fleversham Public Library
    v. 3, no. 5, May, 1974+; On microfilm 1974-1980.
Franklin College Library
    v. 10+

-- Regional Report --

Beetlebomb Vocational Technical Inst. Library
    v. 12+
East Hodgepodge Regional High School Library
    Microfilm Jan '82-Dec '85
Fleversham Public Library
    v.1+
Franklin College Library
    Jan 1982+

-- Santayana Commentary --

Brittlebone Institute Library
    v. 5, no. 4 + (missing scattered issues)
East Hodgepodge Regional High School Library
    v. 1+
Fleversham Public Library
    December, 1983+

REFERENCE ARCHIVE

A common reference practice is to keep a log of questions asked, the answers found, and where they were found. Should a similar inquiry come up again, the log can save considerable leg-work. As the book gets larger, it gets harder and harder to locate the information so carefully stored there, however. Even if only the "toughies" are recorded, quickly locating the relevant information becomes more difficult over time. The larger the number of staff members who contribute to the log, the more information will be recorded. Much of this information will be unfamiliar to many of the staff members.

Enter *dBase III+*. Though it is not optimized for such text storage and retrieval, the program nevertheless does pretty well in providing quick access to reference archives. And not only is subject retrieval available, but keyword retrieval as well, albeit at a slower pace.

Data Structure

For simplicity, only three fields are contained in ARCHIVE.DBF:

```
Structure for database: C:archive.dbf
Number of data records:      17
Date of last update    : 08/14/86
Field  Field Name  Type       Width    Dec
    1   QUERYNO     Character      6
    2   QUESTION    Character    100
    3   ANSWER      Character    100
** Total **                     207
```

QUERYNO is a unique, sequential number which will form the basis of a link between this file and a subject term file. The data entry routine we will use will automatically assign the next available sequential number to QUERYNO. QUESTION and ANSWER are self-explanatory, although admittedly simple-minded.

A full-fledged reference archive would probably have fields for source, date question was asked, and staff member who dealt with the question. Considerations of patron confidentiality argue against recording patron name, at least in the public library environment. Imagine, though, basing a current awareness service on keywords associated with past reference inquiries by particular individuals.

Searching by Keyword

Subject access is available in two ways. Uncontrolled vocabulary access is afforded by the string search operator $. To find whether anything is in the file regarding former astronaut Deke Slayton:

```
. LIST question, answer FOR "Slayton" $answer .OR.
    ^^^^ "Slayton" $question
Record#  question answer
     7  What were the names of the Mercury astronauts
Alan Shepard, Gus Grissom, John Glenn, Walter Shirra,
    ^^^^ Scott Carpenter, Gordon Cooper, Deke Slayton
```

You could also use LOCATE to find each instance of a match and EDIT to look at the corresponding record:

```
. LOCATE FOR "Slayton" $answer .OR. "Slayton" $question
  RECORD=       7
. EDIT
. CONTINUE
```

Controlled Vocabulary Search

The second way to gain subject access to a reference archive file is through a controlled vocabulary approach. After entering information about a reference transaction, the staff member enters one or more terms by which information may be retrieved in the future. Those terms go in a separate file, ARCHSUBJ.DBF, along with the QUERYNO identical to that in the corresponding ARCHIVE.DBF record. The terms are indexed on their upper case equivalents to provide a true alphabetical list.

```
Structure for database: C:archsubj.dbf
Number of data records:       47
Date of last update   : 08/14/86
Field  Field Name  Type       Width   Dec
    1  QUERYNO     Character      6
    2  TERM        Character     40
** Total **                      47
```

In a sense, "controlled vocabulary" is a misnomer. The approach described below provides no authority control component. Any heading can be entered--the more headings the better. It is assumed that a time-efficient reference archive doesn't allow for a thesaurus-checking step, even if it were to some extent automatic.

Entering Information

But before we can discuss controlled vocabulary searching at greater length, we must have a convenient way to put the data into the appropriate files. The data entry program below has several interesting attributes. As mentioned earlier, it automatically checks the QUERYNOs already assigned and gives the next available number to the next set of ARCHIVE.DBF data entered.

Look carefully at how it enters data into both ARCHIVE.DBF and ARCHSUBJ.DBF. The user's keystrokes are saved in memory variables. A large number (limited to six to keep data entry on one screen--see the section on circulation for ideas on how to do double columns) of subject terms can be entered, and all remain on the screen until RETURN alone is entered. Only then are APPEND BLANK and REPLACE used to put data into records in each database. If the user changes his or her mind anytime prior to hitting RETURN alone, ESC will abandon all data entered without snarling up the two data files.

Let's look at a typical data entry session:

. DO archntry

//

Query Number   000019

Question   [Who discovered radium   ]

Answer   [Madame Curie   ]

//

After entering information for the ANSWER field, the program starts prompting for subject terms. Up to six will be accepted. Changing a value in just two places in the ARCHNTRY.PRG file would raise or lower that limit:

//

Query Number   [000019]

Question   [Who discovered radium   ]

Answer   [Madame Curie   ]

Term(s)
              [radium   ]

              [Curie   ]

              [   ]

//

    Here's the data entry program file:

```
** ARCHNTRY.PRG
** Data entry routine for ARCHIVE.DBF and ARCHSUBJ.DBF
SET TALK OFF
CLOSE DATA
CLEAR
SELECT 1
USE archive INDEX query
GO BOTTOM
mqueryno=queryno
SELE 2
USE archsubj INDEX subjterm
SELE 1
DO WHILE .t.
    mqueryno=STR(VAL(mqueryno)+1,6)
    mquestion=SPACE(100)
    manswer=SPACE(100)
    @  4,0  SAY "Query Number  " + mqueryno
    @  6,0  SAY "Question  " GET mquestion FUNCTION "S40"
    @  8,0  SAY "Answer    " GET manswer FUNCTION "s40"
    @ 22,5 SAY "<ESC> to abandon"
    READ
    IF READKEY()=12 .OR. READKEY()=268 .OR.
     ^^^^ LEN(TRIM(manswer))=0
        EXIT
    ENDIF
    SELECT 2
    counter=1
```

```
DO WHILE counter<10
    mterm="mterm"+STR(counter,1)
    &mterm=SPACE(40)
    counter=counter+1
ENDDO
counter=0
@ 10,0 say "Term(s)"
startpos=ROW()
@ 20,0 SAY REPLICATE("*",79)
@ 22,40 SAY "<RETURN> alone to save, move on"

DO WHILE .t.
    counter=IIF(counter<1,1,counter+1)
    mterm="mterm"+STR(counter,1)
    IF TYPE(mterm)="U"
        &mterm=SPACE(40)
    ENDIF
    @  startpos+counter, 12  GET &mterm
    READ
    @ startpos+counter, 12 SAY &mterm
    IF READKEY()=12 .or. READKEY()=268
        SET TALK ON
        CLOSE DATA
        RETURN
    ENDIF
    IF READKEY() = 4 .OR. READKEY() = 260
        counter = counter - 2
    ELSE
        IF LEN(TRIM(&mterm))=0 .OR. counter=9
            EXIT
        ENDIF
    ENDIF
ENDDO
counter=counter-1
DO WHILE counter>0
    APPEND BLANK
    mterm="mterm"+STR(counter,1)
    REPLACE queryno WITH mqueryno
    REPLACE term WITH &mterm
    counter=counter-1
ENDDO
SELECT 1
APPEND BLANK
REPLACE queryno WITH mqueryno
REPLACE question WITH mquestion
REPLACE answer WITH manswer
```

```
        CLEAR
        CLEAR GETS
ENDDO
SET TALK ON
CLEAR
CLOSE DATA
RETURN
```

Program-Based Subject Searching

Character string searching was mentioned earlier. In the interest of making things easy for a number of library staff members doing quick searches, we will search using a routine that prompts for search term and displays on the screen all matches. Truncation is supported, for example, "S" and "Slay" will both bring up "Slayton," but only "S" will retrieve "Shepard" as well.

This routine is similar to those described elsewhere in this book. A generalized search module could be developed to serve a number of different programs.

```
** ARCHSRCH.PRG
** Prompts for search term, searches ARCHSUBJ.DBF, pulls
** information from linked file ARCHIVE.DBF
SET TALK OFF
CLOSE DATA
SELE 2
USE archive INDEX query
SELE 1
USE archsubj INDEX subjterm
SET RELATION TO queryno INTO archive

DO WHILE .T.

    CLEAR
    msubject=SPACE(40)
    @ 10,5 SAY "Subject term to be searched?  "
     ^^^^ GET msubject
    @ 22,20 SAY "Hit <RETURN> alone to end searching"
    READ
    IF LEN(TRIM(msubject))=0
        CLEAR
        EXIT
    ENDIF
    msubject=UPPER(TRIM(msubject))
    FIND &msubject
```

```
    IF .NOT. FOUND()
        CLEAR
        @ 10,10 SAY "Sorry, this subject isn't in the
     ^^^^ subject"
        @ 11,15 SAY "index."
        @ 22,1
        WAIT
        LOOP
    ENDIF

    CLEAR
    DO WHILE UPPER(TRIM(term))=msubject
        ? "    subject: "+UPPER(term)
        ? "Question: "+archive->question
        ? "Answer: "+archive->answer
        ?
        ?
        ? SPACE(20)+"Press any key to continue..."
        SET CONSOLE OFF
        WAIT
        SET CONSOLE ON
        ?
        SKIP
    ENDDO
    ?
    ? REPLICATE("*",60)
    ? "         There are no more entries indexed on "
     ^^^^ +msubject
    ?
    ?
    WAIT
ENDDO
CLOSE DATA
RETURN
```

Here's what we get when we run it:

```
. DO archsrch
```

//

```
Subject term to be searched?    [                      ]



                  Hit <RETURN> alone to end searching
```

//

The next screen lists matches:

```
/////////////////////////////////////////////////////
    subject: DATABASE MANAGEMENT
Question: What are the leading file management and
    ^^^^ database management software products?

Answer: PFS-File, dBase III.


                        Hit any key to continue...
/////////////////////////////////////////////////////
```

If we search on "S" alone (I don't know why we would except to demonstrate truncated term searching), here's what we would get:

```
/////////////////////////////////////////////////////
    subject: SCOTTISH DRESS
Question: What is the origin of the phrase "The Whole
    ^^^^ Nine Yards"?
Answer: Nine yards is the amount of cloth required for
    ^^^^ traditional men's Scottish attire

                        Hit any key to continue...
/////////////////////////////////////////////////////




/////////////////////////////////////////////////////
    subject: SHEPARD, ALAN
Question: What were the names of the Mercury astronauts

Answer: Alan Shepard, Gus Grissom, John Glenn, Walter
    ^^^^ Shirra, Scott Carpenter, Gordon Cooper, Deke
    ^^^^ Slayton

                        Hit any key to continue...
/////////////////////////////////////////////////////
```

//
      subject: SHIRRA, WALTER
Question: What were the names of the Mercury astronauts

Answer: Alan Shepard, Gus Grissom, John Glenn, Walter
     ^^^^ Shirra, Scott Carpenter, Gordon Cooper, Deke
     ^^^^ Slayton

                           Hit any key to continue...
//

//
      subject: SLAYTON, DEKE
Question: What were the names of the Mercury astronauts

Answer: Alan Shepard, Gus Grissom, John Glenn, Walter
     ^^^^ Shirra, Scott Carpenter, Gordon Cooper, Deke
     ^^^^ Slayton

                           Hit any key to continue...
//

//
      subject: SOFTWARE PUBLISHING, INC.
Question: What are the leading file management and
     ^^^^ database management software products?

Answer: PFS-File, dBase III.

                           Hit any key to continue...
//

//
      subject: SPHYGMOMANOMETER
Question: What's the official name of a blood pressure gauge?

Answer: A sphygmomanometer
                           Hit any key to continue...

           There are no more entries indexed on S
//

    To get an idea of what is in the archive, take a quick peek at
the ARCHSUBJ.DBF file. All it takes is a short command from the
dot-prompt.

```
. USE archsubj INDEX subjterm
. LIST term
Record#  term
     22  Alaska
     34  Architects
     38  Ashton-Tate, Inc.
      9  Avon, Inc.
     25  Bachman, Richard
     24  Bangor, Maine
      3  Blood pressure
***INTERRUPTED
```

ACQUISITIONS

dBase III+ is well suited to a wide range of acquisitions applications, both simple and independent, and complex and integrated.

An automated on-order file could answer, with just a few keystrokes, such questions as:

1. Is a specific title on order, and if so with what vendor and since when?
2. What titles have been on order more than ninety days?
3. How much money is encumbered as of today?
4. How many titles are on order from a particular vendor and how much money is involved?
5. What titles are on order from McGraw-Hill and Prentice-Hall in alphabetical order by author?
6. How much money is encumbered on behalf of a particular requesting individual or department?

What with the substantial overlap in information, why not automate the consideration file as well, capturing data for the on-order file at the beginning of the acquisition process? Such a consideration file ought to help answer questions like:

1. What high-priority titles have been in the file for more than seven days without being ordered?
2. How many titles has Joe Smith requested and what are they?
3. What top priority titles are published by Macmillan (or whatever vendor may have a special, limited-time discount offer)?
4. What is the sum of the retail prices of the books waiting to be ordered?

Once materials arrive, there is often a need to produce lists of them for library users. A given new books list may include every item received during a certain time period, only those in particular subject areas, only those requested by specified individuals, or only those which match a particular profile of subject interests. Once again, there is a great deal of overlap between the information required for on-order tracking and that needed for various new books lists.

The simplest approach is to use one data file, ACQ.DBF, to store information about titles in all three categories: under consideration, on-order, and newly arrived. Additional files can be related to ACQ.DBF to provide purchase order and vendor name-address information.

As long as all the information pertaining to books to be ordered is in one data file, it makes sense to look into generating purchase orders and handling encumbrance and fund tracking using *dBase III+* as well.

Acquisitions is one of the library applications to which *dBase III+* is particularly well suited. While simpler, less expensive file managers or a high-powered spreadsheet (*SuperCalc 3* or *Lotus 1-2-3*) could be pressed into service, the wide variety of reporting and inquiry requirements and the need to link purchase order and vendor files to the acquisitions file require the "bells and whistles" of a product like *dBase III+*.

Products and Queries

We want lists containing a wide variety of bibliographic and order information, arranged at various times by author, title, publisher, requesting individual, priority, request date, or order date. We may wish to qualify inclusion in a list by author, publisher, requesting individual, priority, request or order date, year of publication, price, cost, purchase order number, and perhaps other fields as well. A name-address list of vendors will be needed, as will a summary of purchase order information.

We also want to produce purchase orders. The arrangement of information will likely be dictated by existing forms and policies that vary widely from library to library.

We will want to rapidly locate and qualify records by the same elements by which we need to arrange printed listings of the database.

Data Structure

First, let's look at the structure of ACQ.DBF, the main file of bibliographic information for our acquisitions system:

```
Structure for database: C:acq.dbf
Number of data records:      12
Date of last update   : 08/15/86
Field  Field Name  Type        Width    Dec
    1  TITLENO     Character        6
    2  TITLE       Character      100
    3  AUTHFIRST   Character       15
    4  AUTHLAST    Character       20
```

5	PUBLISHER	Character	40	
6	EDITION	Character	10	
7	VOLUMES	Numeric	2	
8	DATE	Character	10	
9	ISBN	Character	15	
10	LCCN	Character	10	
11	QUANTITY	Numeric	2	
12	QTYRCVD	Numeric	2	
13	PRICE	Numeric	6	2
14	PONO	Character	6	
15	ONORDER	Logical	1	
16	CONSIDER	Logical	1	
17	NEWBOOKS	Logical	1	
18	RQDATE	Date	8	
19	REQUESTOR	Character	20	
20	PRIORITY	Character	1	
21	ORDERDATE	Date	8	
22	RECEIVDATE	Date	8	
23	COST	Numeric	6	2
24	FUNDA	Logical	1	
25	FUNDB	Logical	1	
26	FUNDC	Logical	1	
27	FUNDD	Logical	1	
28	ORDERNOW	Logical	1	
29	RECEIVED	Logical	1	
** Total **			305	

TITLENO is a unique sequential number assigned to each title as it is entered into the database. PRIORITY is a numeric indicator (stored in a character field for ease of concatenation with other fields to produce suitable indexes) of how urgent it is that a library acquire a particular title. CONSIDER is a logical field indicating that a title is under consideration. After it is ordered, CONSIDER is changed to .F. and ONORDER is set to .T. . When the book arrives, ONORDER goes to .F. and NEWBOOKS is given a value of .T. . These three logical fields serve as economical filters when we want to look at only records in one or the other of the three categories.

The fields ORDERDATE and PONO are used only after an item has been ordered. PONO is the purchase order number. It is the link between ACQ.DBF and ACQPONO.DBF and ACQVENDR.DBF. When the title is received, the fields QTYRCVD (quantity received), COST (as opposed to list PRICE), and RECEIVDATE are filled in.

In the approach described here, the FUNDA, FUNDB, etc. fields aren't used. They've been placed here to suggest one way to handle the problem some libraries have of keeping track of titles ordered by fund account. You could use the fields as filters to come up with rough encumbrances (based on list price and, perhaps, a standard estimated discount) by fund. The command line might look like this, assuming a twenty percent average discount off list price:

. SUM quantity * price * .8 FOR funda

The purchase order file, ACQPONO.DBF, keeps track of orders as opposed to individual titles:

```
Structure for database: C:acqpono.dbf
Number of data records:      5
Date of last update   : 08/15/86
Field  Field Name  Type       Width    Dec
   1   PONO        Character      6
   2   VENDORNO    Character      6
   3   ORGENCUMBR  Numeric        8      2
   4   CURENCUMBR  Numeric        8      2
   5   DATE        Date           8
** Total **                      37
```

VENDORNO is an identifier that links this file to ACQVENDR.DBF, the vendor name-address file. ORGENCUMBR is the original amount encumbered, at list price, for the order. CURENCUMBR is the current encumbrance, reflecting the list price of titles still undelivered less the list price of those that have been received.

Finally comes ACQVENDR.DBF. It isn't very different from the mailing list structure described elsewhere in this book:

```
Structure for database: C:acqvendr.dbf
Number of data records:      3
Date of last update   : 08/15/86
Field  Field Name  Type       Width    Dec
   1   VENDORNO    Character      6
   2   VENDOR      Character     40
   3   ADR2        Character     35
   4   ADR3        Character     35
   5   CITY        Character     20
   6   STATE       Character      2
   7   ZIP         Character      5
   8   PHONE       Character     30
   9   REP         Character     30
** Total **                     204
```

VENDOR is vendor name. REP is the name of the sale representative or other contact with which the library regularly deals.

Interactive Use

Before launching into a demonstration of the full-blown program-file approach to acquisitions, let's make a few inquiries from the dot-prompt. To view information about items on order, we might type:

```
. USE acq INDEX acqauth
. LIST TRIM(authlast)+", "+TRIM(authlast)+".  "+
    ^^^^ TRIM(title)+;". "+DTOC(orderdate)+
    ^^^^ ", "+c->vendor FOR onorder OFF

trim(authlast)+", "+trim(authlast)+".  "+
    ^^^^ trim(title)+". "+   dtoc(orderdate)+
    ^^^^ ", "+c->vendor

Feynman, Feynman.  "Surely You're Joking, Mr. Feynman!":
    ^^^^ Adventures of a Curious Character. 05/17/86,
    ^^^^ Eastern Book Company
Knecht, Knecht.  Microsoft BASIC. 05/25/86, Eastern
    ^^^^ Book Company
Smith, Smith.  Russians. 05/31/86, Eastern Book
    ^^^^ Company
Walter, Walter.  Secret Guide to Computers: Volume 1,
    ^^^^ Secret Skills. 05/05/86, Eastern Book Company
```

To find out when Richard Feynman's book was ordered:

```
. USE acq INDEX acqauth
. FIND Feynman
. DISPLAY TRIM(title)+", "+DTOC(orderdate)
Record#  Title                                orderdate
    7 "Surely You're Joking, Mr. Feynman!": Adventures
^^^^ of a Curious Character, 05/17/86
```

So what is the dollar value at list price of the titles under consideration for purchase, and on order in our little demonstration file?

```
. SUM quantity * price FOR consider
    3 records summed
    quantity*price
```

```
            42.85

. SUM quantity*price FOR onorder
    4 records summed
  quantity*price
          126.70
```

If you intend to spend a good deal of time with this interactive approach, it is helpful to store the operating set-up for each major category of operation. For example, if you frequently search through the consideration file, using a FILTER to make ACQ.DBF look like it contains only consideration records may be helpful:

```
. USE acq INDEX acqauth, acqtitle, acqpub, acqrq,
^^^^ acqrqdat, acqprior
. SET FILTER TO consider
. CREATE VIEW acqcons FROM ENVIRONMENT
```

From now on, you may set up the operating environment with one command line:

```
. SET VIEW TO acqcons
. DISPLAY STATUS
```

```
Currently Selected Database:
Select area:  1, Database in Use: C:ACQ.DBF    Alias: ACQ
  Master index file:  C:ACQAUTH.NDX  Key: authlast
    Index file:  C:ACQTITLE.NDX  Key: substr(title,1,20)
    Index file:  C:ACQPUB.NDX  Key: substr(publisher,
    ^^^^ 1,15)+substr(title,1,15)
    Index file:  C:ACQRQ.NDX  Key: requestor+substr
    ^^^^ (title,1,15)
    Index file:  C:ACQRQDAT.NDX  Key: dtoc(rqdate)+
    ^^^^ substr(title,1,15)
    Index file:  C:ACQPRIOR.NDX  Key: priority+substr
    ^^^^ (title,1,15)
Filter: CONSIDER
```

Notice the index keys used above. To conserve disk space, only the first fifteen or twenty characters of most fields are indexed, rather than the entire field. Note also the indexes that consist of two fields concatenated. This has the effect of putting consideration records in order by the first element and, where the first elements are identical, in order by the second element. The utility of this is more clearly evident in the programs that follow.

Viewing Files

Speaking of programs, the compact nature of the SET VIEW command has been exploited in the files used to fully automate this approach to acquisitions. What is gained by brevity is, perhaps, partially lost in ease of understanding. Looking at a given program file, it isn't possible to determine what files are open in which work area. For reference purposes, as well as for their possible utility in interactive use, here are the other view files employed in the program system:

```
. SET VIEW TO acqorder
. DISPLAY STATUS

Currently Selected Database:
Select area:  1, Database in Use: C:ACQ.DBF  Alias: ACQ
    Master index file:  C:ACQTITLE.NDX  Key:
    ^^^^ substr(title,1,20)
            Index file:  C:ACQPONUM.NDX  Key: pono
            Index file:  C:ACQODATE.NDX  Key:
    ^^^^ dtoc(orderdate)+substr(title,1,15)
Filter: consider

Select area:  2, Database in Use: C:ACQPONO.DBF
    ^^^^ Alias: ACQPONO
    Master index file:  C:ACQPNO.NDX  Key: pono
Press any key to continue...

Select area:  3, Database in Use: C:ACQVENDR.DBF
    ^^^^ Alias: ACQVENDR
    Master index file:  C:ACQVNAME.NDX  Key:
    ^^^^ substr(vendor,1,15)
            Index file:  C:ACQVNO.NDX  Key: vendorno

. SET VIEW TO acqrcv
. DISPLAY STATUS

Currently Selected Database:
Select area:  1, Database in Use: C:ACQ.DBF  Alias: ACQ
    Master index file:  C:ACQTITLE.NDX  Key:
    ^^^^ substr(title,1,20)
            Index file:  C:ACQRCDAT.NDX  Key:
    ^^^^ receivdate
Filter: onorder
    Related into: ACQPONO
    Relation: pono
```

```
Select area:  2, Database in Use: C:ACQPONO.DBF
     ^^^^ Alias: ACQPONO
    Master index file:  C:ACQPNO.NDX  Key: pono
    Related into: ACQVENDR
    Relation: vendorno

Select area:  3, Database in Use: C:ACQVENDR.DBF
     ^^^^ Alias: ACQVENDR
    Master index file:  C:ACQVNO.NDX  Key: vendorno

 . SET VIEW TO acqnewbk
 . DISPLAY STATUS

Currently Selected Database:
Select area:  1, Database in Use: C:ACQ.DBF  Alias: ACQ
    Master index file:  C:ACQAUTH.NDX  Key: authlast
          Index file:  C:ACQTITLE.NDX  Key:
     ^^^^ substr(title,1,20)
          Index file:  C:ACQRQ.NDX  Key: requestor+
     ^^^^ substr(title,1,15)
Filter: newbooks
```

Acquisitions System

ACQMENU.PRG is the access point to the acquisitions system. You must type DO ACQMENU in order to get things underway. The applications generator that is included with *dBase III+* was used to produce most of the menus that follow, as well as the routines to maintain the acquisitions and vendor databases. Modifications were done on the code generated to make it work more smoothly with the programs written from scratch.

The maintenance programs allow the user to directly manipulate the database with the APPEND, EDIT, and BROWSE commands. While quicker and simpler to set up, this approach carries the added risk that a user may inadvertently damage data and not realize it. If only one or a very few people will use the system (more likely in a typical acquisitions operation than in circulation, for example), and conscientious back-ups of all data files are made daily, then there shouldn't be too many problems with this scheme.

The first screen to appear when DO ACQMENU is entered offers a number of choices:

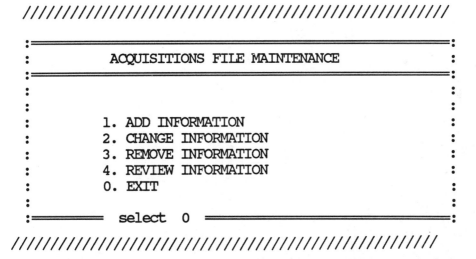

```
/////////////////////////////////////////////////////////
:=========================================================:
:               ACQUISITIONS  SYSTEM  MAIN  MENU          :
:=========================================================:
:                                                         :
:                                                         :
:                                                         :
:            1. Maintain Acquisitions File                :
:            2. Maintain Vendor File                      :
:            3. Place an Order                            :
:            4. Receive an Order                          :
:            5. Generate Reports                          :
:                                                         :
:            0. EXIT                                       :
:                                                         :
:======= select  0 =======================================:
/////////////////////////////////////////////////////////
```

If you hit RETURN without entering a number first, the default
choice of 0 exits the program. Choice 1 brings up a secondary menu,
courtesy of *dBase*'s APPSGEN.PRG applications generator:

```
/////////////////////////////////////////////////////////
:=========================================================:
:               ACQUISITIONS FILE MAINTENANCE             :
:=========================================================:
:                                                         :
:                                                         :
:                                                         :
:            1. ADD INFORMATION                           :
:            2. CHANGE INFORMATION                        :
:            3. REMOVE INFORMATION                        :
:            4. REVIEW INFORMATION                        :
:            0. EXIT                                       :
:                                                         :
:=======  select  0 ======================================:
/////////////////////////////////////////////////////////
```

Choice 1 put us in APPEND mode. A filled-out entry looks like
this:

```
/////////////////////////////////////////////////////////
           Entering Data Into Consideration File

TITLE      [Fifteen Minute Investor                       ]
AUTHFIRST [Chet        ]    AUTHLAST   [Currier           ]
EDITION    [            ]    PUBLISHER  [Watts            ]
DATE       [1986        ]   ISBN [0-531-15502-1   ]
     ^^^^ LCCN [85-31752   ]
QUANTITY  [ 2] Volumes [ 0]Price [ 14.95]
REQUESTOR [Oakes, Sherman ] Request Date [06/08/86]
     ^^^^ Priority [1]
ORDER IMMEDIATELY ! ! ! [F]
```

```
/////////////////////////////////////////////////////////
```

The format above was determined by a format file (ACQADD.FMT) specified when APPSGEN.PRG produced the program to maintain ACQ.DBF. If no format file had been specified, as none was for the second menu choice, editing, the display would have looked like this instead:

```
/////////////////////////////////////////////////////////
Record No.      12
TITLENO        [101121]
TITLE          [Fifteen Minute Investor
                                                      ]
AUTHFIRST      [Chet           ]
AUTHLAST       [Currier            ]
PUBLISHER      [Watts                                  ]
EDITION        [           ]
VOLUMES        [ 0]
DATE           [1986       ]
ISBN           [0-531-15502-1   ]
LCCN           [85-31752   ]
QUANTITY       [ 2]
QTYRCVD        [ 0]
PRICE          [ 14.95]
PONO           [200015]
ONORDER        [F]
CONSIDER       [T]
NEWBOOKS       [F]
RQDATE         [06/08/86]
REQUESTOR      [Oakes, Sherman      ]
PRIORITY       [1]
/////////////////////////////////////////////////////////
```

It is expected that if a record is to be deleted entirely, you will locate the record with choice 2 or choice 4 and mark it for deletion with ^U. Choice 3 packs the data file, permanently removing any records that have been marked for deletion in prior operations. The code presented here offers no safety net. If you have accidentally or temporarily marked a record for deletion, it will nevertheless evaporate. To provide utmost security, a routine could be added to choice 3 that would list records about to be deleted and ask for confirmation that the action should really take place.

Choice 4 activates the BROWSE command, a full-screen columnar view of data that should make spreadsheet aficionados feel at home. Here's the display it gives us for our small data file:

```
///////////////////////////////////////////////////////
AUTHFIRST------- AUTHLAST------------ PUBLISHER--------
Chet            Currier             Watts
Adam            Osborne             Avon
Ken             Knecht              Dilithium Press
Hedrick         Smith               Ballantine
Russ            Walter              The Author
Arthur T.       Hadley              Random House
Richard P.      Feynman             Norton


BROWSE    :<C:>:ACQ           :Rec: 12/12          :
:
                 View and edit fields.

///////////////////////////////////////////////////////
```

To see more, we can scroll to the right with ^B, and to the left with ^Z. If you have included the line SET MENU ON somewhere prior to making this choice, a menu listing these and other full-screen commands will appear on the screen. The down side is that the menu will subtract from the number of lines of the data file that can be seen.

Maintenance of the vendor file ACQVENDR.DBF works in exactly the same way.

Ordering

In maintaining the ACQ.DBF file, you may enter a "T" in the TOORDER field. When ordering is chosen from the main menu (choice 3), the system presents a list of titles under consideration that have been so marked and asks for confirmation:

//
Tentative List Of Titles To Be Ordered

Advanced Programmer's Guide: Castro, Luis. Ashton-Tate,
1985,   1 copies, $ 28.95 each.

Birnbaum's USA for Business Travelers: Birnbaum, ed.,
Stephen. Houghton Mifflin, 1985,   1 copies, $ 7.95
each.

Fifteen Minute Investor: Currier, Chet. Watts, 1986, 2
copies, $ 14.95 each.

Titles: 3   Copies: 4 Amount (at retail): $ 66.80

Okay to order?
(Y)es, (N)o, or <RETURN> alone to exit)

Press any key to continue...
//

Next we decide which vendor to use. Nonexistent vendor
numbers are rejected:

//
SELECT VENDOR - THE FOLLOWING ARE OUR REGULAR SOURCES

Record#   vendor   vendorno
     1   Eastern Book Company   555551
     2   Hospital Publishing   555552
     3   Seaway Books   555553

Vendor Number? (<RETURN> alone to exit order
     ^^^^ process) 55555533

There is no vendor with this number in the
   vendor file. Please recheck the listing
   that follows.

Press any key to continue...
//

```
//////////////////////////////////////////////////////////
SELECT VENDOR - THE FOLLOWING ARE OUR REGULAR SOURCES

Record#  vendor                          vendorno
      1  Eastern Book Company            555551
      2  Hospital Publishing             555552
      3  Seaway Books                    555553

Vendor Number? (<RETURN> alone to exit order
    ^^^^ process) 555553
//////////////////////////////////////////////////////////
```

A unique purchase order number is automatically generated, based on the last used purchase order number. The HEADING clause of REPORT FORM is used in an interesting way to place the multiline vendor address at the top of the purchase order.

```
Page No.  1      Purchase Order #200015 for...
                        Seaway Books
                         Suite 300
                    10332 Route 11 North
                     Latham, NY 12122
08/16/86

             ORDERED BY:  Anytown Public Library
                          5 Main Street
                      Anytown, PA 33221

Title            Author         Pub     Qty  List   Total

                                        Each at List


Advanced         Castro, Luis   Ashton- 1 28.95    28.95
Programmer's                    Tate
Guide
Birnbaum's USA   Birnbaum, ed., Houghton 1  7.95    7.95
for Business     Stephen        Mifflin
Travelers
Fifteen Minute   Currier, Chet  Watts   2 14.95    29.90
Investor
```

*** Total ***

4   66.80

Press any key to continue...

Receiving Materials

The receiving routine makes use of BROWSE. A list of all titles on order is presented, and .T. is entered to mark those that are to be checked in. Adjustments in the encumbrance figures of PONO.DBF are made, along with those necessary to convert the ACQ.DBF record from that of an on-order title to a new books title. Notice that the WIDTH option has been used with BROWSE to display fields at less than their assigned width. The cursor keys may be used to scroll within each field to find its end.

Lists of newly arrived materials, by the way, may be generated from the custom report menu described below.

Here's the first screen of the check-in sequence:

//
Receiving Ordered Materials

Hit any key to view titles listed as on-order

Change the RECEIVED field to .T. and enter cost for
        ^^^^ each item that has arrived
//

Changes are made to the QTYRCVD, RECEIVED, and COST fields before exiting BROWSE:

//

TITLE----------	AUTHLAST-	QUANTITY	QTYRCVD	RECEIVED	COST
Microsoft BASIC	Knecht	3	3	T	12.35
Russians	Smith	1	0	F	0.00
Secret Guide to	Walter	5	0	F	0.00
Surely You're J	Feynman	2	1	F	0.00

BROWSE   :<C:>:ACQ   :Rec: 10/12   :   :
                View and edit fields.

//

Further confirmation is requested:

```
//////////////////////////////////////////////////
Tentative List Of Titles To Be Checked In

Microsoft BASIC, Knecht, Ken. Dilithium Press, 1982,
          ^^^^ 3 copies, $ 12.35 each.

Titles:   1   Copies:   3    Amount (at cost): $ 37.05

Okay to Checkin?
(Y)es, (N)o, or <RETURN> alone to exit)
//////////////////////////////////////////////////
```

Reports

The permutations of reports that may be required are large in number. Rather than define a submenu item for all but a couple of reports, a Chinese restaurant approach is used: one from column A, one from column B, etc. This is a powerful technique that could be applied in a number of other applications described in this book. Serials reporting springs most immediately to mind.

The main reports menu offers a gateway into the custom reports module, and purchase order summaries by publisher and purchase order number. Depending on your needs, it might be useful to offer additional specialized report options at this level:

```
//////////////////////////////////////////////////

:===================================================:
:                                                   :
:              ACQUISITIONS REPORTS                 :
:                                                   :
:      1.  On-Order Summary By Purchase Order       :
:                                                   :
:      2.  On-Order Summary By Publisher            :
:                                                   :
:      3.  Custom Reports                           :
:                                                   :
:      0.  Return to Main Menu                      :
:                                                   :
:===================================================:


            SELECT ONE:
//////////////////////////////////////////////////
```

Here's the purchase order summary:

```
Page No.      1
08/16/86
              On-Order Summary By Purchase Order Number

Author        Title           Vendor   Order  Qty List Est.
                                       Date             Cost


** Purchase Order # 200001
Walter,       Secret Guide to Eastern  05/05/86 5  8.00 40.00
Russ          Computers:      Book
              Volume 1,       Company
              Secret Skils
** Subtotal **
                                              5       40.00


** Purchase Order # 200010
Feynman,      Surely You're   Hospital 05/17/86 2 16.95 33.90
Richard P.    Joking, Mr.     Publishing
              Feynman!:
              Adventures
              of a Curious
              Character
** Subtotal **
                                              2       33.90


** Purchase Order # 200012
Knecht,       Microsoft BASIC Eastern  05/25/86 3 15.95 47.85
Ken                           Book
                              Company
** Subtotal **
                                              3       47.85

** Purchase Order # 200014
Smith,        Russians        Seaway   05/31/86 1  4.95  4.95
Hedrick

** Subtotal **
                                              1        4.95
*** Total ***
                                             11      126.70
```

The summary by publisher uses the same report form but with a different index--one by publisher. Here's the custom report menu:

//
CUSTOM   REPORTS

Type of Report	Qualifiers	
1. Consideration File	13. Author	25. .AND.
2. On-Order File	14. Publisher	26. .OR.
3. New Books File	15. Order Date	27. .NOT.
4. All	16. Request Date	28. (
	17. Receive Date	29.)
Sort Order	18. Priority	
5. Title	19. Requestor	99. Do it
6. Author	20. Price	
7. Publisher	21. Cost	-1. EXIT
8. Order Date		
9. Request Date	Connections	-9. Redo
10. Receive Date	22. =	qualification
11. Priority	23. <	
12. Requestor	24. >	88. Data Entry

Type: Consideration   Order: Title

Qualifications:

//

A default value is displayed for "Type" of report (e.g., which REPORT FORM to use and which, if any, FOR clause to employ) and "Order" (e.g., index file). Options 1-4 change the report form and filter condition. Options 5-12 determine what index will be used. Additional qualifying (FOR) clauses can be constructed using choices 13-29. You must be familiar with *dBase* syntax to get such clauses right. A help screen or improved checking for syntactic validity would be a useful enhancement to the current set-up.

Choice 88 opens a window into which values for the qualification statement may be entered directly from the keyboard. If the qualification statement is botched, -9 wipes it out but leaves all other selections as before. Choice 99 runs the report.

Program Listings

```
* Program..: ACQMENU.PRG
*   Main menu routine.  Choices here call up programs.
```

```
SET TALK OFF
SET BELL OFF
SET ESCAPE OFF
DO WHILE .T.

    * ---Display menu options, centered on the screen.
    *     draw menu border and print heading
    CLEAR
    @ 2, 0 TO 15,79 DOUBLE
    @ 3,12 SAY [A C Q U I S I T I O N S   S Y S T E M
^^^^ M A I N   M E N U]
    @ 4,1 TO 4,78 DOUBLE
    * ---display detail lines
    @  7,26 SAY [1. Maintain Acquisitions File]
    @  8,26 SAY [2. Maintain Vendor File]
    @  9,26 SAY [3. Place an Order]
    @ 10,26 SAY [4. Receive an Order]
    @ 11,26 SAY [5. Generate Reports]
    @ 13, 26 SAY '0. EXIT'
    STORE 0 TO selectnum
    @ 15,33 SAY " select      "
    @ 15,42 GET selectnum PICTURE "9" RANGE 0,5
    READ

    DO CASE
        CASE selectnum = 0
            SET BELL ON
            SET TALK ON
            SET ESCAPE ON
            CLEAR ALL
            RETURN
        CASE selectnum = 1
        *  DO Maintain Acquisitions File

            DO acqmaint

        CASE selectnum = 2
        *  DO Maintain Vendor File

            DO acqvmain

        CASE selectnum = 3
        *  DO Place an Order

            DO acqorder

        CASE selectnum = 4
```

```
    *   DO Receive an Order

        DO acqrcv

    CASE selectnum = 5
    *   DO Generate Reports

        DO acqrpts

ENDCASE

ENDDO T
RETURN
* EOF: ACQMENU.PRG



* Program..: ACQMAINT.PRG
*   Program enables user to update ACQ.DBF

USE acq INDEX acqtitle,acqtitno,acqauth,acqpub,
    ^^^^ acqrq,acqrqdat

DO WHILE .T.

    * ---Display menu options, centered on the screen.
    *     draw menu border and print heading
    CLEAR
    @ 2, 0 TO 14,79 DOUBLE
    @ 3,12 SAY [A C Q U I S I T I O N S   F I L E
     ^^^^ M A I N T E N A N C E]
    @ 4,1 TO 4,78 DOUBLE
    * ---display detail lines
    @  7,30 SAY [1. ADD INFORMATION]
    @  8,30 SAY [2. CHANGE INFORMATION]
    @  9,30 SAY [3. REMOVE INFORMATION]
    @ 10,30 SAY [4. REVIEW INFORMATION]
    @ 12, 30 SAY '0. EXIT'
    STORE 0 TO selectnum
    @ 14,33 SAY " select      "
    @ 14,42 GET selectnum PICTURE "9" RANGE 0,4
    READ

    DO CASE
        CASE selectnum = 0
            RETURN

        CASE selectnum = 1
```

```
   *   DO ADD INFORMATION

       SET ORDER to 2
       GO BOTT
       mtitleno=STR(VAL(titleno)+1,6)
       SET FORMAT TO acqadd
       APPEND
       GO TOP
       DO WHILE LEN(TRIM(titleno))=0
          REPLACE titleno WITH mtitleno
          mtitleno=STR(VAL(mtitleno)+1,6)
          REPLACE consider WITH .T.
       ENDDO
       SET FORMAT TO
       SET ORDER TO 1
       STORE ' ' TO wait_subst
       @ 23,0 SAY 'Press any key to continue...'
^^^^ GET wait_subst
       READ
 CASE selectnum = 2
   *   DO CHANGE INFORMATION
       EDIT

       STORE ' ' TO wait_subst
       @ 23,0 SAY 'Press any key to continue...'
^^^^ GET wait_subst
       READ
 CASE selectnum = 3
   *   DO REMOVE INFORMATION
       SET TALK ON
       CLEAR
       @ 2,0 SAY ' '
       ? 'PACKING DATABASE TO REMOVE RECORDS MARKED
^^^^ FOR DELETION'
       PACK

       SET TALK OFF
       STORE ' ' TO wait_subst
       @ 23,0 SAY 'Press any key to continue...'
^^^^ GET wait_subst
       READ
 CASE selectnum = 4
   *   DO REVIEW INFORMATION

       BROWSE

       STORE ' ' TO wait_subst
```

```
               @ 23,0 SAY 'Press any key to continue...
          ^^^^ ' GET wait_subst
               READ
         ENDCASE
ENDDO T
RETURN
* EOF: ACQMAINT.PRG



* Program..: ACQVMAIN.PRG
*     Program enables user to update vendor file.
SET TALK OFF
SET BELL OFF
SET STATUS ON
SET ESCAPE OFF
USE ACQVENDR INDEX ACQVNO

DO WHILE .T.

   * ---Display menu options, centered on the screen.
   *     draw menu border and print heading
   CLEAR
   @ 2, 0 TO 14,79 DOUBLE
   @ 3,18 SAY [V E N D O R   F I L E
    ^^^^ M A I N T E N A N C E]
   @ 4,1 TO 4,78 DOUBLE
   * ---display detail lines
   @  7,30 SAY [1. ADD INFORMATION]
   @  8,30 SAY [2. CHANGE INFORMATION]
   @  9,30 SAY [3. REMOVE INFORMATION]
   @ 10,30 SAY [4. REVIEW INFORMATION]
   @ 12, 30 SAY '0. EXIT'
   STORE 0 TO selectnum
   @ 14,33 SAY " select       "
   @ 14,42 GET selectnum PICTURE "9" RANGE 0,4
   READ

   DO CASE
      CASE selectnum = 0
         CLEAR ALL
         RETURN

      CASE selectnum = 1
      *   DO ADD INFORMATION

         APPEND

         STORE ' ' TO wait_subst
```

```
        @ 23,0 SAY 'Press any key to continue...'
^^^^ GET wait_subst
        READ
  CASE selectnum = 2
   *   DO CHANGE INFORMATION

        EDIT

        STORE ' ' TO wait_subst
        @ 23,0 SAY 'Press any key to continue...'
^^^^ GET wait_subst
        READ
  CASE selectnum = 3
   *   DO REMOVE INFORMATION

        SET TALK ON
        CLEAR
        @ 2,0 SAY ' '
        ? 'PACKING DATABASE TO REMOVE RECORDS MARKED
^^^^ FOR DELETION'
        PACK

        SET TALK OFF
        STORE ' ' TO wait_subst
        @ 23,0 SAY 'Press any key to continue...'
^^^^ GET wait_subst
        READ
  CASE selectnum = 4
   *   DO REVIEW INFORMATION

        BROWSE

        STORE ' ' TO wait_subst
        @ 23,0 SAY 'Press any key to continue...'
^^^^ GET wait_subst
        READ
ENDCASE

ENDDO T
RETURN
* EOF: ACQVMAIN.PRG

** ACQORDER.PRG
**   Orders titles in ACQ.DBF marked for consideration
**   Optionally generates simple purchase orders

*** Set view to order view
```

```
SET VIEW TO acqorder
SELECT 2
GO BOTTOM
mpono=STR(VAL(pono)+1,6)
SELECT 1

CLEAR
@ 10,25 SAY "Order Production System"
@ 22,1 SAY "Hit any key to view titles under
     ^^^^ consideration"
SET CONSOLE OFF
WAIT
SET CONSOLE ON

** Browse through ACQ, changing ORDERNOW for items to
     ^^^^ be ordered

DO WHILE .T.

     STORE .F. TO done
     DO WHILE .NOT. done
        GO TOP
        BROWSE FIELDS title,authlast,publisher,date,
     ^^^^ quantity,ordernow WIDTH 15

*** Preview those marked for ordering.  Redesignate
     ^^^^ if necessary.

        ? "Tentative List Of Titles To Be Ordered"
        ?
        GO TOP
        DO WHILE .NOT. EOF()
           IF ordernow
              ? TRIM(title)+": "+TRIM(authlast)+", "+
     ^^^^ TRIM(authfirst)+ ". "+TRIM(publisher)+", "+
     ^^^^ TRIM(date)+", "+STR(quantity,3) +" copies, $"
     ^^^^ +STR(price,6,2)+" each."
                 ?
           ENDIF
           SKIP
        ENDDO eof
        SUM quantity*price, quantity TO msum,mcopies
     ^^^^ FOR ordernow
        COUNT TO mtitlecnt FOR ordernow
        ? "Titles: "+STR(mtitlecnt,3)+"    Copies: "+
     ^^^^ STR(mcopies,3)+ "
Amount (at retail): $"+STR(msum,6,2)
        answer=" "
```

```
      ?
      ? "Okay to order?"
      ACCEPT "(Y)es, (N)o, or <RETURN> alone to
^^^^ exit)  " TO answer
      IF LEN(TRIM(answer))=0
          REPLACE ALL ordernow WITH .F.
^^^^ FOR ordernow
          CLOSE DATA
          RETURN
      ENDIF
      IF UPPER(answer)="Y"
          STORE .T. TO done
      ENDIF
ENDDO done
```

*** Produce printed purchase order?

```
CLEAR
answer=" "
@ 10,10 SAY "Produce Printed Purchase Order?  "
 ^^^^ GET answer
READ
IF UPPER(answer)="Y"
    mtoprint="TO PRINT"
ELSE
    mtoprint=""
ENDIF
```

*** Select a vendor

```
STORE .F. to done
DO WHILE .NOT. done
    CLEAR
    ?  "SELECT A VENDOR -- THE FOLLOWING ARE OUR
  ^^^^ REGULAR SOURCES"
    ?
    SELE 3
    GO TOP
    LIST vendor, vendorno
    ?
    mvendorno=SPACE(6)
    ACCEPT "Vendor Number? (<RETURN> alone to exit
^^^^ order process) " TO mvendorno
    IF LEN(TRIM(mvendorno))=0
        SELE 1
        REPLACE ALL ordernow WITH .F. FOR ordernow
        CLOSE DATA
```

```
        RETURN
     ENDIF
     SET ORDER TO 2
     FIND &mvendorno
     IF FOUND()
        STORE .T. TO done
     ELSE
        ?
        ? "There is no vendor with this number in the"
        ? "  vendor file.  Please recheck the listing"
        ? "   that follows."
        ?
        WAIT
     ENDIF
     SET ORDER TO 1
     SELE 1
  ENDDO done


*** Do purchase order, change consider to onorder,
*    add order date

*    *** Prepare purchase order heading
     mheading= "Purchase Order #"+"&mpono"+" for..."+
      ^^^^ ";"+TRIM(acqvendr->vendor)+";"+
      ^^^^ TRIM(acqvendr->adr2)+";"+TRIM(acqvendr->adr3)
      ^^^^ +";"+TRIM(acqvendr->city)+", "+acqvendr->
      ^^^^ state+" "+TRIM(acqvendr->zip)
     REPORT FORM acqorder &mtoprint HEADING mheading
      ^^^^ FOR ordernow

     WAIT
     CLEAR
     @ 10,10 SAY "Hit <RETURN> to update files,
      ^^^^ confirm order"
     @ 12,15 SAY "To (R)edo, type R"
     answer=" "
     @ 14,20 GET answer
     READ
     IF LEN(TRIM(answer))=0
        REPLACE ALL consider WITH .F., onorder WITH
      ^^^^ .T., ordernow WITH .F., pono WITH mpono,
      ^^^^ orderdate with date() FOR ordernow
        SELECT 2
        APPEND BLANK
        REPLACE pono WITH mpono, vendorno WITH
      ^^^^ mvendorno, orgencumbr WITH msum, date
      ^^^^ WITH date()
```

```
        CLOSE DATA
        RETURN
    ENDIF
ENDDO T


** ACQRCV.PRG
**      Processes materials as they are received

SET VIEW TO acqrcv
CLEAR
@ 10,25 SAY "Receiving Ordered Materials"
@ 15,1 SAY "Hit any key to view titles listed as
      ^^^^ on-order"
@ 17,1 SAY "Change the RECEIVED field to .T. and enter
      ^^^^ cost for each item that has arrived"
SET CONSOLE OFF
WAIT
SET CONSOLE ON


** Browse through ACQ, changing RECEIVED for items
** that have arrived

DO WHILE .T.

    STORE .F. TO done
    DO WHILE .NOT. done
        GO TOP
        BROWSE FIELDS title,authlast,quantity,qtyrcvd,
    ^^^^ received,cost,publisher,date WIDTH 15

*** Preview those marked for ordering.
*** Redesignate if necessary.

        ? "Tentative List Of Titles To Be Checked In"
        ?
        GO TOP
        DO WHILE .NOT. EOF()
            IF received
                ? TRIM(title)+", "+TRIM(authlast)+", "+
    ^^^^ TRIM(authfirst)+". "+TRIM(publisher)+", "+
    ^^^^ TRIM(date)+", "+STR(qtyrcvd,3) +" copies, $"
    ^^^^ +STR(cost,6,2)+" each."
                ?
            ENDIF
            SKIP
        ENDDO eof
        SUM qtyrcvd*cost,qtyrcvd TO msum,mcopies
```

```
^^^^ FOR received
     COUNT TO mtitlecnt FOR received
     ? "Titles: "+STR(mtitlecnt,3)+"   Copies: "
^^^^ +STR(mcopies,3)+ "     Amount (at cost): $"+STR(msum,6,2)
     answer=" "
     ?
     ? "Okay to Checkin?"
     ACCEPT "(Y)es, (N)o, or <RETURN> alone to
^^^^ exit)  " TO answer
     IF LEN(TRIM(answer))=0
        REPLACE ALL received WITH .F., cost WITH 0,
^^^^ qtyrcvd WITH 0 FOR received
        CLOSE DATA
        RETURN
     ENDIF
     IF UPPER(answer)="Y"
        STORE .T. TO done
     ENDIF
  ENDDO done

  CLEAR
  GO TOP
  DO WHILE .NOT. EOF()
     IF received
        IF quantity=qtyrcvd
           REPLACE onorder WITH .F.
        ENDIF
        SELECT 2
        REPLACE curencumbr WITH orgencumbr-
^^^^ (curencumbr+A->qtyrcvd*A->price)
        SELECT 1
        REPLACE newbooks WITH .T., received WITH
^^^^ .F.,receivdate WITH date()
     ENDIF
     SKIP
  ENDDO not eof
  CLOSE DATA
  RETURN
ENDDO T


** ACQRPTS.PRG
** Main menu of report generator - acquisitions system
** Calls ACQRPT2.PRG for custom reports

DO WHILE .T.
   selectnum=" "
   CLEAR
```

```
    @  3, 25  SAY "ACQUISITIONS REPORTS"
    @  5, 17  SAY "1.  On-Order Summary By Purchase
     ^^^^ Order"
    @  7, 17  SAY "2.  On-Order Summary By Publisher"
    @  9, 17  SAY "3.  Custom Reports"
    @ 11, 17  SAY "0.  Return to Main Menu"
    @ 18, 16  SAY "SELECT ONE:  " GET selectnum
    @  2,  7  TO 13, 60    DOUBLE
    READ
    DO CASE
        CASE selectnum="0"
            RETURN
        CASE selectnum="1"
            SELE 3
            USE acqvendr INDEX acqvno
            SELE 2
            USE acqpono INDEX acqpno
            SET RELATION TO vendorno INTO acqvendr
            SELE 1
            USE acq INDEX acqponum
            SET RELATION TO pono INTO acqpono
            SET FILTER TO onorder
            REPORT FORM acqpo
            CLOSE DATA
            WAIT
        CASE selectnum="2"
            SELE 3
            USE acqvendr INDEX acqvno
            SELE 2
            USE acqpono INDEX acqpno
            SET RELATION TO vendorno INTO acqvendr
            SELE 1
            USE acq INDEX acqpub
            SET RELATION TO pono INTO acqpono
            SET FILTER TO onorder
            REPORT FORM acqpopub
            CLOSE DATA
            WAIT
        CASE selectnum="3"
            DO acqrpt2
    ENDCASE
ENDDO T

** ACQRPT2.PRG
**   Generates custom reports for acquisitions system
typedef="consider"
typetag="Consideration"
```

```
rptdef="aconsidr"
sortdef="acqtitle"
sorttag="Title"
qualdef=""
DO WHILE .T.
CLEAR
@  1, 27  SAY "CUSTOM REPORTS"
@  3,  2  SAY "Type of Report
     ^^^^ Qualifiers"
@  4,  7  SAY "1.  Consideration File
     ^^^^ 13. Author          25. .AND."
@  5,  7  SAY "2.  On-Order File
     ^^^^ 14. Publisher        26. .OR."
@  6,  7  SAY "3.  New Books File
     ^^^^ 15. Order Date       27. .NOT."
@  7,  7  SAY "4.  All
     ^^^^ 16. Request Date     28.  ("
@  8, 39  SAY "17. Receive Date      29.  )"
@  9,  2  SAY "Sort Order
     ^^^^ 18. Priority"
@ 10,  7  SAY "5.  Titl
     ^^^^ 19. Requestor         99. Do it"
@ 11,  7  SAY "6.  Author
     ^^^^ 20. Price"
@ 12,  7  SAY "7.  Publisher
     ^^^^ 21. Cost             -1. EXIT"
@ 13,  7  SAY "8.  Order Date"
@ 14,  7  SAY "9.  Request Date
     ^^^^ Connections             -9. Redo"
@ 15,  7  SAY "10. Receive Date
     ^^^^ 22. =          qualification"
@ 16,  7  SAY "11. Priority
     ^^^^ 23. <"
@ 17,  7  SAY "12. Requestor
     ^^^^ 24. >    88. Data Entry"
@ 18,  1  TO 18, 79     DOUBLE

DO WHILE .T.
@ 20,1
@ 20,1 SAY "Type: "+typetag
@ 20,40 SAY "Order: "+sorttag
@ 22,17
@ 22,1 SAY "Qualifications: "+qualdef
choice=0
@ 19,60 GET choice PICTURE "999"
READ
DO CASE
```

```
        CASE choice=99
CLEAR
        answer=" "
        @ 10,10 SAY "SEND TO PRINTER? (Y/N)" GET answer
        READ
        CLEAR
        IF UPPER(answer)="Y"
            printdef=" TO PRINT "
        ELSE
            printdef=""
        ENDIF
        SELE 3
USE acqvendr INDEX acqvno
SELE 2
USE acqpono INDEX acqpno
        SET RELATION TO pono INTO acqvendr
SELE 1
  USE acq
SET RELATION TO pono INTO acqpono
SET INDEX TO &sortdef
REPORT FORM &rptdef &printdef FOR &typedef
     ^^^^ &qualdef
CLOSE DATA
WAIT
    CASE choice=-1
 RETURN
    CASE choice=-9
qualdef=""
    CASE choice=88
temp=SPACE(30)
@ 23,20 SAY "Keyboard entry: " GET temp
READ
qualdef=qualdef+" "+TRIM(temp)+" "
        @ 23,1
    CASE choice >0 .AND. choice<5
        DO CASE
            CASE choice=1
typetag="Consideration"
                typedef="consider"
                rptdef="aconsidr"
            CASE choice=2
typetag="On Order"
                typedef="onorder"
                rptdef="aonorder"
            CASE choice=3
typetag="New Books"
                typedef="newbooks"
```

```
                        rptdef="anewbook"
                CASE choice=4
typetag="All"
                    typedef="len(trim(title))>1"
                    rptdef="ageneral"
            ENDCASE
    CASE choice>4 .AND. choice<13
          DO CASE
                CASE choice=5
sorttag="Title"
                    sortdef="acqtitle"
                CASE choice=6
sorttag="Author"
                    sortdef="acqauth"
                CASE choice=7
sorttag="Publisher"
                    sortdef="acqpub"
                CASE choice=8
sorttag="Order Date"
                    sortdef="acqodate"
                CASE choice=9
sorttag="Request Date"
                    sortdef="acqrqdate"
                CASE choice=10
sorttag="Receive Date"
                    sortdef="acqrcdat"
                CASE choice=11
sorttag="Priority"
                    sortdef="acqprior"
                CASE choice=12
sorttag="Requestor"
                    sortdef="acqrq"
ENDCASE
    CASE choice> 12 .AND. choice<22
DO CASE
                CASE choice=13
 qualdef=qualdef+"author"
    CASE choice=14
                    qualdef=qualdef+"publisher"
                CASE choice=15
                    qualdef=qualdef+"orderdate"
                CASE choice=16
                    qualdef=qualdef+"rqdate"
    CASE choice=17
qualdef=qualdef+"receivdate"
    CASE choice=18
qualdef=qualdef+"priority"
```

```
    CASE choice=19
qualdef=qualdef+"requestor"
    CASE choice=20
qualdef=qualdef+"price"
    CASE choice=21
qualdef=qualdef+"cost"
    ENDCASE
    CASE choice >21 .AND. choice<30
DO CASE
    CASE choice=22
conn="="
qualdef=qualdef+conn
    CASE choice=23
                conn="<"
qualdef=qualdef+conn
            CASE choice=24
            conn=">"
qualdef=qualdef+conn
    CASE choice=25
                conn=" .AND. "
qualdef=qualdef+conn
    CASE choice=26
        conn=" .OR. "
qualdef=qualdef+conn
    CASE choice=27
        conn=" .NOT. "
qualdef=qualdef+conn
    CASE choice=28
        conn=" ("
qualdef=qualdef+conn
    CASE choice=29
conn=") "
qualdef=qualdef+conn
ENDCASE
ENDCASE
IF choice=99
EXIT
ENDIF
ENDDO inner T
ENDDO outer T
RETURN
```

SERIALS CONTROL

Serials control is a difficult job to effectively automate using *dBase III+*. A large library may have thousands of bibliographic records representing the serials it receives. Organizing, maintaining, and producing reports from that file raise the same problems they would in other library bibliographic files. Checking in issues as they arrive, on the other hand, is a transaction-oriented job in which speed and simplicity come to the fore. Some of the issues that arise in circulation discussions also apply here. Then there are the claiming and routing functions, the likes of which are not found elsewhere among the applications treated in this book.

Check-in and maintenance functions will be spotlighted here, with brief outlines to suggest how you might attack claiming and routing. The system of programs that follows was designed with the needs of a particular library in mind. As a result, the data structure contains a number of cryptic fields, the meaning of which is not likely to be of interest to those outside that one library.

Structure

Here's the idiosyncratic data structure for the bibliographic file. Notice the "check boxes" to indicate processing treatment, frequency, and other useful information. I feel it is easier to move the cursor to a check box and type T or Y than to remember a list of code numbers or abbreviations for entry into a single catch-all field.

```
Structure for database: C:bib.dbf
Number of data records:       3
Date of last update    : 07/09/86
Field   Field Name   Type       Width    Dec
    1    TITLENO      Character      5
    2    TITLE        Character     60
    3    HOLDINGS     Character     60
    4    CURRVOLUME   Character     60
    5    FORMER1      Character     60
    6    FORMER2      Character     60
    7    ISSN         Character     15
    8    VENDORCODE   Character     15
    9    LOCATION     Character     15
   10    VENDOR       Character     10
   11    QUANTITY     Numeric        2
   12    FIRSTISSUE   Date           8
   13    LASTISSUE    Date           8
```

14	COST	Numeric	6	2
15	PONO	Character	10	
16	INVOICENO	Character	10	
17	CLAIMLAG	Numeric	3	
18	PENDGCLAIM	Numeric	3	
19	MULS	Logical	1	
20	OCLC	Logical	1	
21	GIFT	Logical	1	
22	NEWS	Logical	1	
23	MICROFORM	Logical	1	
24	DEAD	Logical	1	
25	ROUTE	Logical	1	
26	BIND	Logical	1	
27	MARKCARDS	Logical	1	
28	ANNUAL	Logical	1	
29	QUARTERLY	Logical	1	
30	BIMONTHLY	Logical	1	
31	MONTHLY	Logical	1	
32	BIWEEKLY	Logical	1	
33	WEEKLY	Logical	1	
34	DAILY	Logical	1	
35	IRREGULAR	Logical	1	
36	COMMENTS	Character	60	

** Total **   488

An entry is made in a second file, CHECKIN.DBF, for every issue received. TITLENO is the common field upon which a relation between CHECKIN.DBF and BIB.DBF is built. Here again we see the pattern of the many-to-one relationship--many individual serial issues, all associated with a particular bibliographic record.

```
Structure for database: C:checkin.dbf
Number of data records:      19
Date of last update   : 08/26/86
Field  Field Name  Type      Width   Dec
    1   TITLENO     Character     5
    2   ISSUEDATE   Date          8
    3   RECEIVEDAT  Date          8
    4   QUANTITY    Numeric       2
** Total **                      24
```

Method

The approach taken here makes use of a number of short programs combined into an omnibus procedure file. Each of the programs begins with a PROCEDURE (procedure name) line and must end with the command RETURN, to avoid instructions from a subsequent, unrelated procedure being executed.

This approach is appropriate here because (1) a single long program would be extremely cumbersome to write and modify--it certainly wouldn't fit in the *dBase* editor; (2) a number of the routines need to be executed from several places in other program routines, and over and over in ways that would make for extremely obscure logical relationships between the parts of a monolithic program file; and (3) if the required multiple programs were left as individual files on disk, execution would slow down each time one had to be loaded into internal memory--procedure files reside in memory to the extent there is room for them there.

Things did not necessarily start out this way. Individual program files to do a specific job--for example, predict the next expected issue--are written and debugged independently. Only after they function properly on their own are they combined in a large procedure file using the file import capabilities of a word processing or editing program.

DSERIALS.PRG is designed to ask the user what function is to be performed, and run the appropriate procedure file within DSER.PRG. Here's the main menu:

```
//////////////////////////////////////////////////////
            MAIN MENU

        1.  CHECK IN SERIALS

        2.  ADD NEW SERIALS TO FILE

        3.  EDIT EXISTING RECORDS

        4.  CLAIMING

        5.  PRINT LISTS

        6.  EDIT CHECK-IN FILE

        0.  EXIT PROGRAM

    YOUR CHOICE?    [ ]

//////////////////////////////////////////////////////
```

Serials Check-in

The check-in process follows this pattern:

1. Ask the user for the title of the periodical to be checked in. Accept right-truncated titles. Accept a null entry (RETURN alone) as indicating that you want to exit the check-in routine.
2. Check the bibliographic file, reporting back if the title can't be found. If it is found, display information about the title on the screen.
3. Ask the user to confirm that the right BIB.DBF record has been found, or to indicate whether the display should be paged forwards or backwards in search of the correct record. There is an option to abandon the search and return to the first screen, at which point another title may be specified or the check-in function exited with a RETURN.
4. Display the most recent issues of the title that have been received, and, based on the frequency shown in the bibliographic record, predict the date of the next issue to be received.
5. Give the user the opportunity to manually override the prediction and fill in other than the default values for issue date and check-in date and quantity.

Likely enhancements would be the addition of logic to predict volume and number as well as issue date, and a facility for scrolling backwards and forwards again within the list of issues received.

After entering DO DSERIALS, the first question is:

//

```
                    TITLE?   [PC                        ]


           |------------------------------------------------|
           |        To return to main menu, hit <RETURN>    |
           |------------------------------------------------|
```

//

The next screen asks for confirmation that the correct bibliographic record has been located. Note that the display has been horizontally compressed from the normal eighty-character-wide format of a display screen, in order to fit on this page.

```
////////////////////////////////////////////////////

PC Week                                    00001
HOLDINGS  Jan '85+
CURRENT VOL  3
FORMER TITLE 1
FORMER TITLE 2
FIRST ISSUE 01/04/85 LAST ISSUE  /  /  LOCATION Browsing
VENDOR  Ebsco  VCODE  33333  COST  46.00  QUANTITY  1
ISSN  0740-1604      PO#  1231    INV#  56-7844
CLAIMING DELAY  14   # CLAIMS PENDING   0 MARKCARDS  F
MULS T  OCLC F  GIFT F  NEWS T  MICRO F  DEAD F BIND  F
ANNUAL  F    QUARTERLY   F        BIMONTHLY  F
MONTHLY  F   BIWEEKLY  F    WEEKLY T    DAILY  F
COMMENTS
```

```
|-------------------------------------------------------------|
|    <RETURN> - Confirm, (F)orward, (B)ackward, (A)bandon     |
|-------------------------------------------------------------|
```

```
        Your choice
```

```
////////////////////////////////////////////////////
```

Once the title has been confirmed, the recent check-in history is displayed and a prediction is made, based on the frequency information contained in each bibliographic record, as to which issue ought to be in hand.

//

```
PC Week                                             00001
HOLDINGS  Jan '85+
CURRENT VOL  3
FORMER TITLE 1
FORMER TITLE 2
FIRST ISSUE 01/04/85 LAST ISSUE   /  /   LOCATION Browsing
VENDOR  Ebsco   VCODE  33333  COST  46.00   QUANTITY   1
ISSN  0740-1604      PO#  1231     INV#  56-7844
CLAIMING DELAY   14   # CLAIMS PENDING   0  MARKCARDS  F
MULS T  OCLC F  GIFT F  NEWS T  MICRO F  DEAD F BIND  F
ANNUAL  F     QUARTERLY  F        BIMONTHLY  F
MONTHLY  F   BIWEEKLY  F   WEEKLY  T   DAILY  F
COMMENTS
```

PREDICTED NEXT ISSUE:

07/27/86   08/26/86   1

```
-------------------------------------------------------------
|   <RETURN> - Confirm, (M)anual Entry, (A)bandon        |
-------------------------------------------------------------
```

Your choice

//

Hitting RETURN checks in the predicted issue. In most cases, check-in will involve entering the first few characters of the title, enough to uniquely distinguish a particular title, and then striking the RETURN key three times. The ability to go forward and backward in the bibliographic file compensates for those instances when the first few characters of the title are insufficiently unique to bring up the title desired.

If an issue is received out of sequence, whether due to subscription snags or as a result of claiming efforts, the (M) option from the display above allows the user to fill in the correct information. It offers an opportunity to change the issue date of "00/00/00" to an actual date and modify the check-in date and quantity.

///

```
  ------------------------------------------------
  :      Issue Date, Receipt Date, Quantity      :
  :          07/20/86  08/26/86   1              :
  :          07/13/86  08/26/86   1              :
  :          07/06/86  07/22/86   1              :
  ------------------------------------------------
```

ISSUE DATE: 00/00/00 RECEIPT DATE: 08/27/86 QUANTITY: 1

///

It then comes back with the question of whether to confirm, abandon, or go back into manual entry again:

///

```
  ------------------------------------------------
  :      Issue Date, Receipt Date, Quantity      :
  :          07/20/86  08/26/86   1              :
  :          07/13/86  08/26/86   1              :
  :          07/06/86  07/22/86   1              :
  ------------------------------------------------
```

ISSUE TO BE CHECKED IN

06/30/86   08/27/86   1

```
  ------------------------------------------------
  |   <RETURN> - Confirm, (M)anual Entry, (A)bandon   |
  ------------------------------------------------
```

Your choice

///

Serials that are issued irregularly, or at an interval not listed among the frequencies in the bibliographic record (annual, quarterly, bimonthly, monthly, biweekly, weekly, and daily) must be dealt with in the same fashion.

One of the most difficult parts of putting this program together was constructing the date prediction segment, the PREDICT procedure. Originally devised with *dBase III*, there may be some possibility of redoing it in more compact form using the facilities of *dBase III+*.

File Maintenance

Data entry (option 2 on the main menu) is done into the format defined in the procedure BIBDISP. While the representation below is horizontally compressed to fit the page, even the full-size data entry form makes use of the horizontal scrolling function (e.g., PICTURE "@s25" to define a twenty-five-character window into a longer field):

```
//////////////////////////////////////////////////
Title [                        ]  Title # 00004
Current Volume [           ]Holdings [              ]
Former Title 1 [           ]Former Title 2 [         ]
ISSN [         ]Vendor Code [      ] Location [       ]
Vendor [     ]Quantity [ 0]First Issue [ /  /  ]
            ^^^^ Last Issue [ /  /  ]
COST [   0.00]P.O. # [         ]Invoice # [          ]
Claiming Delay [   0]# of Claims Pending [        0]
MULS [F]OCLC [F]Gift [F]Mark Cards [F]Bind [F]Route [F]
          ^^^^ Dead Title [F]
Newspaper [F]Microform [F]
Annual [F]Quarterly [F]Bimonthly [F]Monthly [F]
          ^^^^ Biweekly [F]Weekly [F]Daily [F]
Irregular [F]
Comments [                                     ]

        Hit <ESC> to return to main menu
//////////////////////////////////////////////////
```

A typical data record is displayed for editing (option 3) in the same format. Notice, however, that no format file is used and that database fields are not directly manipulated. Instead, changes are made in memory variables and only copied over into fields after the editing process has ended.

Editing the contents of the CHECKIN.DBF file uses the same approach, embodied in procedure CHKEDIT. The name of the title is requested (this time calling up only an abbreviated display controlled by procedure SHORTREC), then confirmation of the title is asked for based on an abbreviated display of some of its fields. Subsequently, a list of all check-ins is displayed and the user is asked to indicate which record # needs to be changed:

///
PC Week   00001

Record#	issuedate	receivedate	quantity
21	07/27/86	08/26/86	1
20	07/20/86	08/26/86	1
19	07/13/86	08/26/86	1
17	07/06/86	07/22/86	1
13	06/29/86	07/09/86	1
5	06/22/86	07/09/86	1
4	06/15/86	07/09/86	1
3	06/08/86	07/09/86	1
2	06/01/86	07/08/86	1
1	05/01/86	07/08/86	1

Enter record # to be changed, <RETURN> to exit 21
Issue date (mm/dd/yy) 08/03/86
Receive date (mm/dd/yy) 08/26/86
Quantity 1

//

After prompting for changes, the routine writes them to the corresponding disk record in CHECKIN.DBF.

Claiming

Claiming hasn't yet been added to this system of programs. When it is, a "batch" approach will be taken. At user-determined intervals:

1. Each record in BIB.DBF will be compared to CHECKIN.DBF. If the most recent issue in the check-in file is longer ago than the CLAIMLAG specified in the bibliographic record, and the missing issue(s) isn't already in CLAIMS.DBF, then the user will be asked whether a claim should be produced.
2. If the answer is no, nothing happens. If yes, the program compares the last recorded issue received with the frequency of

issue and displays a list of those issues that should have been received since, right up to the current date.

3.   The user is asked to confirm claims individually for each missing issue, including those since the CLAIMLAG cut-off. Whenever claims are confirmed, a .T. value is inserted in the CLAIMS field of BIB.DBF. All issues confirmed for claiming are entered into CLAIMS.DBF. This is its structure:

```
Structure for database: C:claims.dbf
Number of data records:       0
Date of last update   : 01/01/80
Field  Field Name  Type        Width    Dec
    1   TITLENO     Character     5
    2   ISSUEDATE   Date          8
    3   CLAIMDATE   Date          8
    4   QUANTITY    Numeric       2
** Total **                      24
```

4.   A change will have to be made to check-in routines to automatically check whether the CLAIMS field in BIB.DBF is .T. If it is, then "CLAIMS" will be displayed next to the predicted next issue date. Every check-in for that title will automatically be compared to the CLAIMS.DBF file and matching issue dates will cause the CLAIMS.DBF record to be deleted.

Routing

A routing system would be a separate routine activated by a value of .T. in the ROUTE field of BIB.DBF. This would cause the program to look to the ROUTING.DBF file for the information to print a routing slip.

A simple way to set up a routing file would involve a record for each title with enough additional fields to hold the names of all conceivable individuals likely to want a given title. Each time that title arrives, the program would instruct the user to get the printer ready, then issue the command:

```
. LIST NEXT 1 person1+";"+person2+";"+person3+";"+
        ^^^^ person4+ TO PRINT
```

The limitation here is principally in the fixed number of people who can easily be put on a particular routing list. A more flexible alternative is the creation of a file with a record for each individual and serial title combination. We might have something like this:

```
Structure for database: C:routing.dbf
Number of data records:        0
Date of last update    : 01/01/80
Field  Field Name  Type        Width     Dec
    1  TITLENO     Character       5
    2  PERSON      Date           20
    3  PRIORITY    Date            1
** Total **                       27
```

An index on TITLENO+PRIORITY+PERSON would result in a listing of unlimited length, the order of which could be changed by changing the value (1 to 9) for PRIORITY. Where egalitarianism is of utmost concern, you could devise a means of comparing a character or two from the current date with part of the person's name to come up with a more or less random order each time a list is produced.

The Listings

Here's the listing of the two program files that make the serials system work. Note that DSERIALS.PRG is mainly a menu program. All the actual work is done by small procedure files stored within DSER.PRG. Keeping the procedures short and somewhat generalized allows you to use them over and over, as well as to better maintain them.

```
*** DSERIALS.PRG ****
**
* MAIN MENU OF A SERIALS CHECK-IN SYSTEM
SET SCOREBOARD OFF
SET TALK OFF
SET BELL OFF
SET SAFETY OFF
CLOSE DATABASES

SET PROCEDURE TO DSER.PRG

* DISPLAY MAIN MENU OF PROGRAM OPTIONS

DO WHILE .T.
    CLEAR
    @ 2,20 SAY "MAIN MENU"
    @ 4,20 SAY "1.  CHECK IN SERIALS"
    @ 6,20 SAY "2.  ADD NEW SERIALS TO FILE"
    @ 8,20 SAY "3.  EDIT EXISTING RECORDS"
    @ 10,20 SAY "4.  CLAIMING"
```

```
       @ 12,20 SAY "5.    PRINT LISTS"
       @ 14,20 SAY "6.    EDIT CHECK-IN FILE"
       @ 16,20 SAY "0.    EXIT PROGRAM"
       choice=" "
       @ 18,2 SAY "YOUR choice?  " GET choice PICTURE "9"
       READ
       DO CASE
            CASE choice="1"
                DO check
            CASE choice="2"
                DO bibadd
            CASE choice="3"
                DO bibedit
            CASE choice="4"
            CASE choice="5"
            CASE choice="6"
                DO chkedit
            CASE choice="0"
                CLEAR ALL
                RELEASE ALL
                SET SAFETY ON
                SET TALK ON
                SET BELL ON
                CLOSE DATABASES
                SET SCOREBOARD ON
            SET PROCEDURE TO
                EXIT
            ENDCASE
     ENDDO
*   SET PROCEDURE TO


** DSER.PRG
*  Files holds procedures called from DSERIALS.PRG

PROCEDURE check
* CHECK IN MODULE OF SERIALS MANAGEMENT SYSTEM
* RELATE check-IN FILE TO BIBLIOGRAPHIC FILE
PUBLIC pdate
SELECT 2
USE bib INDEX bibtitle
SELECT 1
USE checkin INDEX CHECKNO
SELECT 2

DO WHILE .T.
     DO GETTITLE
```

```
    CLEAR
    IF .NOT. EOF()
        confirm=0
        DO WHILE confirm=0
            DO brecord
            DO PAGER
        ENDDO  &&confirm
        SELECT 1
        SET INDEX TO checkno
        MBTITLENO=bib->TITLENO
        FIND &MBTITLENO
        IF FOUND()
            DO newdates
            DO PREDICT
            DO predprnt
        ELSE
            PDATE=Date()
            DO predprnt
        ENDIF  && FOUND()
        SELECT 2
    ELSE
        @ 10,10 SAY 'Title not found'
        @ 12,10 SAY 'Hit <RETURN> TO continue'
        SET CONSOLE OFF
        WAIT
        SET CONSOLE ON
    ENDIF     *****NOT EOF()

ENDDO   Main LOOP
CLOSE DATABASES
RETURN


PROCEDURE GETTITLE
**   Routine TO ask for title, FIND it in bib.DBF
    CLEAR
    MTITLE=SPACE(20)
    @ 15,15 SAY "TITLE? " GET MTITLE
    @ 21,5 TO 23,52
    @ 22,10 SAY "To RETURN TO main menu, hit <RETURN>"
    READ
    IF LEN(TRIM(mtitle))=0
        CLOSE DATABASES
        RETURN TO MASTER
    ENDIF
MTITLE=upper(TRIM(MTITLE))
FIND &mtitle
RETURN
```

```
PROCEDURE BRECORD
CLEAR
@ 1,2 SAY title
@ 1,63 SAY titleno
@ 2,1 SAY "HOLDINGS"
@ 2,11 SAY holdings
@ 3,1 SAY "CURRENT VOL"
@ 3,14 SAY currvolume
@ 4,1 SAY "FORMER TITLE 1"
@ 4,17 SAY former1
@ 5,1 SAY "FORMER TITLE 2"
@ 5,17 SAY former2
@ 6,1 SAY "FIRST ISSUE"
@ 6,14 SAY FIRSTISSUE
@ 6,25 SAY "LAST ISSUE"
@ 6,37 SAY LASTISSUE
@ 6,47 SAY "LOCATION"
@ 6,57 SAY LOCATION
@ 7,1 SAY "VENDOR"
@ 7,9 SAY VENDOR
@ 7,19 SAY "VCODE"
@ 7,26 SAY VENDORCODE
@ 7,41 SAY "COST"
@ 7,47 SAY COST
@ 7,57 SAY "QUANTITY"
@ 7,67 SAY QUANTITY
@ 8,1 SAY "ISSN"
@ 8,7 SAY ISSN
@ 8,21 SAY "PO#"
@ 8,26 SAY PONO
@ 8,36 SAY "INV#"
@ 8,42 SAY INVOICENO
@ 9,1 SAY "CLAIMING DELAY"
@ 9,17 SAY CLAIMLAG
@ 9,26 SAY "# CLAIMS PENDING"
@ 9,44 SAY PENDGCLAIM
@ 9,56 SAY "MARKCARDS"
@ 9,67 SAY MARKCARDS
@ 10,1 SAY "MULS"
@ 10,7 SAY MULS
@ 10,12 SAY "OCLC"
@ 10,18 SAY OCLC
@ 10,23 SAY "GIFT"
@ 10,29 SAY GIFT
@ 10,34 SAY "NEWS"
@ 10,40 SAY NEWS
@ 10,45 SAY "MICRO"
```

```
@ 10,52 SAY MICROform
@ 10,58 SAY "DEAD"
@ 10,64 SAY DEAD
@ 10,69 SAY "BIND"
@ 10,75 SAY BIND
@ 11,1 SAY "ANNUAL"
@ 11,9 SAY ANNUAL
@ 11,16 SAY "QUARTERLY"
@ 11,27 SAY QUARTERLY
@ 11,37 SAY "BIMONTHLY"
@ 11,48 SAY BIMONTHLY
@ 12,1 SAY "MONTHLY"
@ 12,10 SAY MONTHLY
@ 12,18 SAY "BIWEEKLY"
@ 12,28 SAY BIWEEKLY
@ 12,37 SAY "WEEKLY"
@ 12,45 SAY WEEKLY
@ 12,52 SAY "DAILY"
@ 12,59 SAY DAILY
@ 13,1 SAY "COMMENTS"
@ 13,11 SAY COMMENTS
RETURN


PROCEDURE pager.prg
**  Routine TO offer forward/backward paging of display
PUBLIC currtitle
@ 20,5 TO 22,67
@ 21,10 SAY '<RETURN> - Confirm, (F)orward, (B)ackward,
      ^^^^ (A)bandon'
choice=" "
@ 23,10 SAY 'Your choice ' get choice PICTURE '!'
READ
DO CASE
   CASE LEN(TRIM(choice))=0
      currtitle=title
      confirm=1
   CASE upper(choice)='F'
      IF .NOT. EOF()
        SKIP
      ELSE
        SKIP-1
      ENDIF
   CASE upper(choice)='B'
     IF .NOT. bof()
        SKIP -1
     ELSE
        SKIP
```

```
      ENDIF
   CASE upper(choice)='A'
     CLOSE data
     RETURN TO MASTER
ENDCASE
@ 20,5 CLEAR
RETURN

PROCEDURE GETDATES

IF .NOT. EOF()
    mrecent1=DTOC(issuedate)+"  "+DTOC(receivedate)+
        ^^^^ "  "+STR(quantity,2)
    IF .NOT. EOF()
     SKIP
     IF titleno=mbtitleno
        mrecent2=DTOC(issuedate)+"  "+
     ^^^^ DTOC(receivedate)+" "+STR(quantity,2)
     ELSE
        mrecent2=space(20)
        mrecent3=space(20)
     ENDIF
    ELSE
     mrecent2=space(20)
     mrecent3=space(20)
    ENDIF
    IF .NOT. EOF()
     SKIP
     IF titleno=mbtitleno
        mrecent3=DTOC(issuedate)+"  "+DTOC(receivedate)
          ^^^^ +" "+STR(quantity,2)
     ELSE
        mrecent3=space(20)
     ENDIF
    ELSE
     MRECENT3=SPACE(20)
    ENDIF
    @ 14,15 TO 19,59 double
    @ 15,20 SAY "Issue Date, Receipt Date, Quantity"
    @ 16,25 SAY mrecent1
    @ 17,25 SAY mrecent2
    @ 18,25 SAY mrecent3
ENDIF
RETURN

PROCEDURE PREDICT &&Predicts next expected issue
FIND &MBTITLENO
```

```
LASTDATE=ISSUEDATE
  DO CASE
     CASE B->DAILY
          PDATE=LASTDATE+1
     CASE B->WEEKLY
          PDATE=LASTDATE+7
     CASE B->BIWEEKLY
          PDATE=LASTDATE+14
     CASE B->MONTHLY
          IF MONTH(LASTDATE)+1<13
             MMONTH=STR(MONTH(LASTDATE)+1,2)
             MDAY="/01/"
             MYEAR=SUBSTR(STR(YEAR(LASTDATE),4),3,2)
             PDATE=CTOD(MMONTH+MDAY+MYEAR)
          ELSE
             MMONTH="01"
             MDAY="/01/"
             MYEAR=SUBSTR(STR(YEAR(LASTDATE)+1,4),3,2)
             PDATE=CTOD(MMONTH+MDAY+MYEAR)
          ENDIF
     CASE B->BIMONTHLY
          IF MONTH(LASTDATE)+1<13
             MMONTH=STR(MONTH(LASTDATE)+2,2)
             MDAY="/01/"
             MYEAR=SUBSTR(STR(YEAR(LASTDATE),4),3,2)
             PDATE=CTOD(MMONTH+MDAY+MYEAR)
          ELSE
             LASTDATE=LASTDATE+366
             IF MONTH(LASTDATE)+2=13
                 MMONTH="01"
                 MDAY="/01/"
                 MYEAR=SUBSTR(STR(YEAR(LASTDATE)+1,4),
    ^^^^ 3,2)
                 PDATE=CTOD(MMONTH+MDAY+MYEAR)
             ELSE
                 MMONTH="02"
                 MDAY="/01/"
                 MYEAR=SUBSTR(STR(YEAR(LASTDATE)+1,4),
    ^^^^ 3,2)
                 PDATE=CTOD(MMONTH+MDAY+MYEAR)
             ENDIF
          ENDIF
     CASE B->QUARTERLY
          IF MONTH(LASTDATE)+3<13
             MMONTH=STR(MONTH(LASTDATE)+3,2)
             MDAY="/01/"
             MYEAR=SUBSTR(STR(YEAR(LASTDATE),4),3,2)
```

```
                    PDATE=CTOD(MMONTH+MDAY+MYEAR)
            ELSE
                LASTDATE=LASTDATE+366
                IF MONTH(LASTDATE)+3=13
                    MMONTH="01"
                    MDAY="/01/"
                    MYEAR=SUBSTR(STR(YEAR(LASTDATE)+1,4),
    ^^^^ 3,2)
                    PDATE=CTOD(MMONTH+MDAY+MYEAR)
                ELSE
                    IF MONTH(LASTDATE)+3=14
                        MMONTH="02"
                        MDAY="/01/"
                        MYEAR=SUBSTR(STR(YEAR(LASTDATE)+1,
    ^^^^ 4),3,2)
                        PDATE=CTOD(MMONTH+MDAY+MYEAR)
                    ELSE
                        MMONTH="03"
                        MDAY="/01/"
                        MYEAR=SUBSTR(STR(YEAR(LASTDATE)+1,
    ^^^^ 4),3,2)
                        PDATE=CTOD(MMONTH+MDAY+MYEAR)
                    ENDIF
                ENDIF
            ENDIF
    CASE B->ANNUAL
        IF INT(YEAR(LASTNAME)/4)=YEAR(LASTNAME)/4
            PDATE=LASTDATE+366
        ELSE
            PDATE=LASTDATE+365
        ENDIF
    OTHERWISE
        PDATE=DATE()
ENDCASE
RETURN

PROCEDURE predprnt
**PRINTS PAST AND PREDICTED ISSUE DATES
PREDHEADING= "PREDICTED NEXT ISSUE: "
PRCVDATE=DATE()
PQUANTITY=B->QUANTITY
flag2=1
DO WHILE FLAG2<>0
    @ 20,20 SAY PREDHEADING
    @ 21,25 SAY DTOC(PDATE)+"  "+DTOC(PRCVDATE)+"   "+
    ^^^^ STR(PQUANTITY,2)
    @ 22,5 TO 24,60
```

```
      @ 23,10 SAY '<RETURN> - Confirm, (M)anual Entry,
       ^^^^ (A)bandon'
      choice=" "
      @ 23,62 SAY 'Your choice ' get choice FUNCTION '!'
      READ
      DO CASE
        CASE LEN(TRIM(choice))=0
            APPEND BLANK
            REPLACE TITLENO WITH MBTITLENO
            REPLACE ISSUEDATE WITH PDATE
            REPLACE RECEIVEDAT WITH PRCVDATE
            REPLACE QUANTITY WITH PQUANTITY
            flag2=0
            FLAG1=0
        CASE upper(choice)='M'
            MISSUEDATE='00/00/00'
            MRCVDATE=DTOC(DATE())
            MQUANTITY=B->QUANTITY
            @ 20,1 CLEAR
            @ 20,2 SAY 'ISSUE DATE: ' GET MISSUEDATE
       ^^^^ FUNCTION 'D'
            @ 20,26 SAY 'RECEIPT DATE: ' GET MRCVDATE
       ^^^^ FUNCTION 'D'
            @ 20,52 SAY 'QUANTITY: ' GET MQUANTITY
       ^^^^ PICTURE '99'
            READ
            PDATE=CTOD(MISSUEDATE)
            PRCVDATE=CTOD(MRCVDATE)
            PQUANTITY=MQUANTITY
            PREDHEADING="ISSUE TO BE CHECKED IN"
            @ 20,1 CLEAR
        CASE upper(choice)='A'
            FLAG1=0
            CLOSE DATABASES
            RETURN TO MASTER
      ENDCASE
   ENDDO
   RETURN


PROCEDURE BIBADD &&Routine TO add, edit bib.dbf records
USE bib INDEX bibno, bibtitle

DO WHILE .T.

   IF reccount()>0
      GO BOTTOM
      number=ltrim(STR(VAL(titleno)+1,5))
```

```
        lennum=LEN(number)
        zeros=5-lennum
        number=replicate("0",zeros)+number
   ELSE
        number="00001"
   ENDIF

     CLEAR
     DO BIBINIT
     DO bibdisp
     append blank
     DO bibyes
     answer=" "
     @ 22,1 SAY "Hit <RETURN> TO add more, N TO stop "
      ^^^^ get answer
     READ
     IF LEN(TRIM(answer))<>0
      CLEAR
      CLOSE DATABASES
      RETURN
     ENDIF
ENDDO
RETURN


PROCEDURE BIBINIT
**Initialize variables preparatory TO appending
PUBLIC MTITLENO,MTITLE,MHOLDINGS,MCURRVOLUME,MFORMER1,
          ^^^^ MFORMER2,MISSN
PUBLIC MVENDORCODE,MLOCATION,MVENDOR,MQUANTITY,
      ^^^^ MFIRSTISSUE,MLASTISSUE,MCOST,MPONO
PUBLIC MINVOICENO,MCLAIMLAG,MPENDGCLAIM,MMULS,MOCLC,
      ^^^^ MGIFT,MNEWS,MMICROFORM,MDEAD
PUBLIC MROUTE,MBIND,MMARKCARDS,MANNUAL,MQUARTERLY,
      ^^^^ MBIMONTHLY,MMONTHLY
PUBLIC MBIWEEKLY,MWEEKLY,MDAILY,MIRREGULAR,MCOMMENTS
MTITLENO       =number
MTITLE         =SPACE(60)
MHOLDINGS      =SPACE(60)
MCURRVOLUME    =SPACE(60)
MFORMER1       =SPACE(60)
MFORMER2       =SPACE(60)
MISSN          =SPACE(15)
MVENDORCODE    =SPACE(15)
MLOCATION      =SPACE(15)
MVENDOR        =SPACE(10)
```

```
MQUANTITY      =00
MFIRSTISSUE    =CTOD(" / / ")
MLASTISSUE     =CTOD(" / / ")
MCOST          =000.00
MPONO          =SPACE(10)
MINVOICENO     =SPACE(10)
MCLAIMLAG      =000
MPENDGCLAIM    =000
MMULS          =.F.
MOCLC          =.F.
MGIFT          =.F.
MNEWS          =.F.
MMICROFORM     =.F.
MDEAD          =.F.
MROUTE         =.F.
MBIND          =.F.
MMARKCARDS     =.F.
MANNUAL        =.F.
MQUARTERLY     =.F.
MBIMONTHLY     =.F.
MMONTHLY       =.F.
MBIWEEKLY      =.F.
MWEEKLY        =.F.
MDAILY         =.F.
MIRREGULAR     =.F.
MCOMMENTS      =SPACE(60)
RETURN


PROCEDURE BIBDISP
**  Routine TO DO display for add, edit bib.dbf records
CLEAR
DO WHILE .T.
SET escape OFF
@  0,  0  SAY "Title"
@  0,  6  GET  MTITLE  picture "@S30"
@  0, 41  SAY "Title #"
@  0, 49  SAY  MTITLENO
@  2,  0  SAY "Current Volume"
@  2, 15  GET  MCURRVOLUME  picture "@s25"
@  2, 42  SAY "Holdings"
@  2, 51  GET  MHOLDINGS  picture "@s25"
@  4,  0  SAY "Former Title 1"
@  4, 15  GET  MFORMER1  picture "@s23"
@  4, 40  SAY "Former Title 2"
@  4, 55  GET  MFORMER2  picture "@s23"
@  6,  0  SAY "ISSN"
@  6,  5  GET  MISSN  PICTURE "XXXXXXXXXXXXXXX"
```

```
@  6, 22  SAY "Vendor Code"
@  6, 34  GET  MVENDORCODE   PICTURE "XXXXXXXXXXXXXXXX"
@  6, 52  SAY "Location"
@  6, 61  GET  MLOCATION
@  8,  0  SAY "Vendor"
@  8,  7  GET  MVENDOR
@  8, 19  SAY "Quantity"
@  8, 28  GET  MQUANTITY picture "99"
@  8, 32  SAY "First Issue"
@  8, 44  GET  MFIRSTISSUE picture "@D"
@  8, 54  SAY "Last Issue"
@  8, 65  GET  MLASTISSUE picture "@D"
@ 10,  0  SAY "COST"
@ 10,  5  GET  MCOST picture "999.99"
@ 10, 13  SAY "P.O. #"
@ 10, 20  GET  MPONO
@ 10, 32  SAY "Invoice #"
@ 10, 42  GET  MINVOICENO
@ 12,  0  SAY "Claiming Delay"
@ 12, 15  GET  MCLAIMLAG PICTURE "999"
@ 12, 20  SAY "# of Claims Pending"
@ 12, 40  GET  MPENDGCLAIM
@ 14,  0  SAY "MULS"
@ 14,  5  GET  MMULS PICTURE "L"
@ 14,  8  SAY "OCLC"
@ 14, 13  GET  MOCLC PICTURE "L"
@ 14, 16  SAY "Gift"
@ 14, 21  GET  MGIFT PICTURE "L"
@ 14, 24  SAY "Mark Cards"
@ 14, 35  GET  MMARKCARDS PICTURE "L"
@ 14, 38  SAY "Bind"
@ 14, 43  GET  MBIND PICTURE "L"
@ 14, 46  SAY "Route"
@ 14, 52  GET  MROUTE PICTURE "L"
@ 14, 55  SAY "Dead Title"
@ 14, 66  GET  MDEAD PICTURE "L"
@ 15,  0  SAY "Newspaper"
@ 15, 10  GET  MNEWS PICTURE "L"
@ 15, 13  SAY "Microform"
@ 15, 23  GET  MMICROFORM PICTURE "L"
@ 17,  0  SAY "Annual"
@ 17,  7  GET  MANNUAL PICTURE "L"
@ 17, 10  SAY "Quarterly"
@ 17, 20  GET  MQUARTERLY PICTURE "L"
@ 17, 23  SAY "Bimonthly"
@ 17, 33  GET  MBIMONTHLY PICTURE "L"
@ 17, 36  SAY "Monthly"
```

```
@ 17, 44  GET   MMONTHLY PICTURE "L"
@ 17, 47  SAY  "Biweekly"
@ 17, 56  GET   MBIWEEKLY PICTURE "L"
@ 17, 59  SAY  "Weekly"
@ 17, 66  GET   MWEEKLY PICTURE "L"
@ 17, 69  SAY  "Daily"
@ 17, 75  GET   MDAILY PICTURE "L"
@ 18,  0  SAY  "Irregular"
@ 18, 10  GET   MIRREGULAR PICTURE "L"
@ 20,  0  SAY  "Comments"
@ 20,  9  GET   MCOMMENTS
@ 22,10 SAY "Hit <ESC> TO RETURN TO main menu"
READ
SET escape ON
IF readkey()=12 .or. readkey()=268
    CLOSE database
    RETURN TO MASTER
ENDIF
@ 22,10 CLEAR

answer=" "
@ 22,10 SAY "Hit <RETURN> TO confirm, M TO modify,
         ^^^^ A TO Abandon " get answer
READ
DO CASE
    CASE LEN(TRIM(answer))=0
     CLEAR
     RETURN
    CASE upper(answer)="A"
     RELEASE ALL
     RETURN TO MASTER
    ENDCASE
@ 22,10
ENDDO
RETURN


PROCEDURE BIBYES
**Routine TO put memory values in fields
CLEAR
@ 15,5 SAY "Adding new information about "+
          ^^^^ TRIM(mtitle)+" TO database"
REPLACE title WITH mtitle
REPLACE titleno WITH mtitleno
REPLACE currvolume WITH mcurrvolume
REPLACE holdings WITH mholdings
REPLACE former1 WITH mformer1
REPLACE former2 WITH mformer2
```

```
REPLACE issn WITH missn
REPLACE vendorcode WITH mvendorcode
REPLACE location WITH mlocation
REPLACE vendor WITH mvendor
REPLACE quantity WITH mquantity
REPLACE firstissue WITH mfirstissue
REPLACE lastissue WITH mlastissue
REPLACE cost WITH mcost
REPLACE pono WITH mpono
REPLACE invoiceno WITH minvoiceno
REPLACE claimlag WITH mclaimlag
REPLACE pendgclaim WITH mpendgclaim
REPLACE muls WITH mmuls
REPLACE oclc WITH moclc
REPLACE gift WITH mgift
REPLACE markcards WITH mmarkcards
REPLACE bind WITH mbind
REPLACE route WITH mroute
REPLACE dead WITH mdead
REPLACE news WITH mnews
REPLACE microform WITH mmicroform
REPLACE annual WITH mannual
REPLACE quarterly WITH mquarterly
REPLACE bimonthly WITH mbimonthly
REPLACE monthly WITH mmonthly
REPLACE biweekly WITH mbiweekly
REPLACE weekly WITH mweekly
REPLACE daily WITH mdaily
REPLACE irregular WITH mirregular
REPLACE comments WITH mcomments
CLEAR
RETURN


PROCEDURE BIBEDIT &&Routine TO edit bib.dbf records
USE bib INDEX bibtitle

DO WHILE .T.
DO gettitle
CLEAR
IF .NOT. FOUND()
    response=" "
    @ 12,10 SAY "Sorry, no title found.  Please hit
        ^^^^ <RETURN> TO continue" get response
    READ
    LOOP
ENDIF
confirm=0
```

```
DO WHILE confirm=0
    DO brecord
    DO pager
ENDDO
    DO bibsetup
    DO bibdisp
    DO bibyes
    answer=" "
    @ 22,1 SAY "Finish editing <RETURN>,  (M)ore "
            ^^^^ GET answer
    READ
    IF LEN(TRIM(answer))=0
     CLEAR
     CLOSE DATABASES
     RETURN
    ENDIF
ELSE
    CLOSE DATABASES
    RETURN
ENDIF
ENDDO
CLOSE DATABASES
RETURN


PROCEDURE BIBSETUP
**Initialize variables before editing.
PUBLIC MTITLENO,MTITLE,MHOLDINGS,MCURRVOLUME,MFORMER1,
      ^^^^ MFORMER2,MISSN
PUBLIC MVENDORCODE,MLOCATION,MVENDOR,MQUANTITY,
       ^^^^ MFIRSTISSUE,MLASTISSUE,MCOST,MPONO
PUBLIC MINVOICENO,MCLAIMLAG,MPENDGCLAIM,MMULS,MOCLC,
       ^^^^ MGIFT,MNEWS,MMICROFORM,MDEAD
PUBLIC MROUTE,MBIND,MMARKCARDS,MANNUAL,MQUARTERLY,
       ^^^^ MBIMONTHLY,MMONTHLY
PUBLIC MBIWEEKLY,MWEEKLY,MDAILY,MIRREGULAR,MCOMMENTS
MTITLENO      =TITLENO
MTITLE        =TITLE
MHOLDINGS     =HOLDINGS
MCURRVOLUME   =CURRVOLUME
MFORMER1      =FORMER1
MFORMER2      =FORMER2
MISSN         =ISSN
MVENDORCODE   =VENDORCODE
MLOCATION     =LOCATION
MVENDOR       =VENDOR
```

```
MQUANTITY       =QUANTITY
MFIRSTISSUE     =FIRSTISSUE
MLASTISSUE      =LASTISSUE
MCOST           =COST
MPONO           =PONO
MINVOICENO      =INVOICENO
MCLAIMLAG       =CLAIMLAG
MPENDGCLAIM     =PENDGCLAIM
MMULS           =MULS
MOCLC           =OCLC
MGIFT           =GIFT
MNEWS           =NEWS
MMICROFORM      =MICROFORM
MDEAD           =DEAD
MROUTE          =ROUTE
MBIND           =BIND
MMARKCARDS      =MARKCARDS
MANNUAL         =ANNUAL
MQUARTERLY      =QUARTERLY
MBIMONTHLY      =BIMONTHLY
MMONTHLY        =MONTHLY
MBIWEEKLY       =BIWEEKLY
MWEEKLY         =WEEKLY
MDAILY          =DAILY
MIRREGULAR      =IRREGULAR
MCOMMENTS       =COMMENTS
RETURN


PROCEDURE CHKEDIT
** Edit checkin record module
SELECT 2
USE bib INDEX bibtitle
SELECT 1
USE checkin INDEX checkno
SELECT 2

DO WHILE .T.
    DO gettitle
    CLEAR
    confirm=0
    DO WHILE confirm=0
        DO shortrec
        DO pager
    ENDDO
    CLEAR
    IF .NOT. EOF()
    DO WHILE .T.
```

```
    SELECT 1
    mbtitleno=B->titleno
    FIND &mbtitleno
    IF FOUND()
        ? currtitle, mbtitleno
        ?
        DISPLAY issuedate, receivedate, quantity
^^^^ WHILE titleno=mbtitleno .AND. .NOT. EOF()
        ?
        ?
        missue="  /  /  "
        mreceive="  /  /  "
        mquantity=" "
        modrecno="     "
        ACCEPT "Enter record # TO be changed,
^^^^ <RETURN> TO EXIT " TO modrecno
        IF LEN(TRIM(modrecno))=0
            RETURN
        ENDIF
        modrecno=int(VAL(modrecno))
        GOTO modrecno
        IF titleno<>mbtitleno
            ?
            ? "This is an unacceptable record number"
            WAIT
            CLEAR
            LOOP
        ENDIF
        ACCEPT "Issue date (mm/dd/yy) " TO missue
        IF LEN(TRIM(missue))=0
            missue=DTOC(issuedate)
        ENDIF
        ACCEPT "Receive date (mm/dd/yy) " TO
^^^^ mreceive
        IF LEN(TRIM(mreceive))=0
            mreceive=DTOC(receivedate)
        ENDIF
        ACCEPT "Quantity " TO mquantity
        IF LEN(TRIM(mquantity))=0
            mquantity=STR(quantity,3)
        ENDIF
        ?
        ? "This:                ",issuedate,
    ^^^^ receivedate,quantity
        ? "Will be replaced by: ",CTOD(missue),
    ^^^^ CTOD(mreceive) , int(VAL(mquantity))
        ?
```

```
                    answer=" "
                    ACCEPT "<RETURN> - Replace, (A)bandon,
              ^^^^ (R)edo " TO answer
                    DO CASE
                    CASE upper(answer)="A"
                        CLOSE DATABASES
                        RETURN TO MASTER
                    CASE LEN(TRIM(answer))=0
                        REPLACE issuedate WITH CTOD(missue)
                        REPLACE receivedate WITH CTOD(mreceive)
                        REPLACE quantity WITH VAL(mquantity)
                        CLEAR
                    ENDCASE
              ELSE
                    @ 10,10 SAY "No issues of this title
              ^^^^ have been checked in"
                    @ 12,10 SAY "Hit <RETURN> TO continue"
                    SET CONSOLE OFF
                    WAIT
                    SET CONSOLE ON
              ENDIF
         ELSE
              @ 10,10 SAY "Title not found"
              @ 12,10 SAY "Hit <RETURN> TO continue"
              SET CONSOLE OFF
              WAIT
              SET CONSOLE ON
         ENDDO EOF()
         ENDIF
SELECT 2
ENDDO
RETURN


PROCEDURE SHORTREC   &&A short record display
CLEAR
SET COLOR TO I
@ 1,2 SAY title
SET COLOR TO W
@ 1,63 SAY titleno
@ 2,1 SAY "HOLDINGS"
@ 2,11 SAY holdings
@ 3,1 SAY "CURRENT VOL"
@ 3,13 SAY CURRVOLUME
@ 4,1 SAY "ANNUAL"
@ 4,9 SAY ANNUAL
@ 4,16 SAY "QUARTERLY"
@ 4,27 SAY QUARTERLY
```

```
@ 4,37 SAY "BIMONTHLY"
@ 4,48 SAY BIMONTHLY
@ 5,1 SAY "MONTHLY"
@ 5,10 SAY MONTHLY
@ 5,18 SAY "BIWEEKLY"
@ 5,28 SAY BIWEEKLY
@ 5,37 SAY "WEEKLY"
@ 5,45 SAY WEEKLY
@ 5,52 SAY "DAILY"
@ 5,59 SAY DAILY
@ 6,1 SAY "QUANTITY"
@ 6,11 SAY QUANTITY
RETURN
```

THE LIBRARY CATALOG

High-capacity, fast, and inexpensive hard disks have made microcomputer-based library catalogs a realistic possibility for small and even not-so-small libraries. The question of whether to use a small computer, and if so whether to use *dBase III+* to handle the job, is not answered simply, however.

The primary limitations of microcomputer technology in support of a public access catalog are the immaturity of multiuser network hardware and library applications software. Almost any situation in which the user community will do its own searching demands that more than one workstation be available. The ideal solution would be a large-capacity hard disk with network connections to a variable number of low-cost terminals or micros. But sophisticated network software is needed to coordinate the demands placed by various users. Relatively few adequate online catalog software packages integrate smoothly with micro-oriented network environments, as of this writing.

Then there is the cost. In some networks, the cost per network connection plus the cost of the terminal/workstation can exceed the cost of a respectable stand-alone computer. Network hardware will decrease in cost with increased competition, more universal adherence to one or two standards, and the incorporation of network functions into custom chips. Yet, the cost of single-user systems, against which network costs have to be measured, will also continue to decrease.

An alternative to networks is the use of multiple, stand-alone PCs, each with its own copy of the library database. If the database isn't too large and if daily batch updates to the database via floppy disk are adequate, this may be the more cost-effective approach.

Another set of issues emerges with respect to bibliographic standards. Many libraries will eventually want to add information about their holdings to some larger database encompassing records from a number of libraries. It is highly unlikely that any other library will have built a *dBase* database exactly the same as any other. Different field names, field lengths, and data types will be fairly difficult to resolve in order to create a useful combined file. Invariably, records coming from one source will be richer and more informative than those from other sources. The best way to create a shared database is to start from a standard format and, ideally, a common and rich resource file of bibliographic information.

The MARC II format is the *lingua franca* of bibliographic information transfer. It is highly likely that any extensive *dBase III+* file of bibliographic information will eventually have to be converted to the MARC II format. To make that process as easy as possible, include the Library of Congress Card Number (LCCN) and the International Standard Book Number (ISBN) in every record. Running these in batch mode against a MARC resource file will easily handle a large percentage of the conversion job.

But for now, let's assume that the library is small, that only one or a few search stations are required, that catalog access with *dBase III+* is badly needed right now, that a library staff person will be available to provide assistance in searching when necessary, and that there is someone ready, willing, and able to enter data in the first place.

Many-to-One Approach

The data structure of a *dBase III+* catalog must allow for the unitary nature of some of the data elements and the many-to-one relationships characteristic of other data elements. Generally, a book has one title, one publisher, one publication date, one physical description, etc. It may, however, have multiple authors, editors, subjects, series, etc. associated with it. The library may also have multiple copies of a title, each with a slightly different call number and maybe a different location. If information on cost and source is maintained for internal use, that, too, will differ among multiple copies.

There is no satisfactory way of dealing with the many-to-one relationships using a single data file. An arbitrary number of subject fields (SUBJ1, SUBJ2, SUBJ3) restricts access to records that should have more subject entries and wastes space in records where fewer would be sufficient. Indexing by subject for quick online access or to produce a single printed list of references by subject won't work because INDEX can't merge multiple subject fields into one. Stuffing all subject references into one large field allows access by subject only through use of the slow (when it's faced with wading through thousands of records) string-searching function ($) of *dBase III+*.

But *dBase III+* is a *relational* database. There is no reason to restrict ourselves to a single data file when multiple data files can be used to easily and conveniently handle unitary, access point, and copy-specific information.

Data Structure

The files below form the basis of one way to handle many-to-one relationships. The unitary information about each item is stored in CBIB.DBF. Only a few sample elements are shown here. ISBN, LCCN, and a number of additional bibliographic elements would be required in a full-scale system.

Subject terms, authors, editors, added title entries, and series references are held in CACCESS.DBF. While it is generally a unitary element of bibliographic description, title is also placed in this file to make it easier to search by title proper, subtitles, and alternative titles all in one step. The field TERMTYPE indicates during processing whether that particular access point is a subject term, author name, or whatever. In some circumstances, you will want retrieval based on a particular type of access point, while at other times a global search of all access points may be preferable.

You could just as easily have created several access files, one for each type of access point. This would have made a global search (e.g., books by *and* about Mark Twain) more time consuming, however.

Copy-specific information is contained in the CCOPY.DBF file. Only copy number, call number, and location are recorded here. A full working version of this system would include such things as price, vendor source, date received, etc.

```
Structure for database: C:cbib.dbf
Number of data records:        10
Date of last update   : 08/22/86
Field  Field Name  Type      Width    Dec
    1  BIBNO       Character     5
    2  TITLE       Character    50
    3  EDITION     Character    10
    4  PUBLISHER   Character    25
    5  DATE        Character    10
** Total **                    101
```

```
Structure for database: C:caccess.dbf
Number of data records:        45
Date of last update   : 08/22/86
Field  Field Name  Type      Width    Dec
    1  BIBNO       Character     5
    2  TERM        Character    50
    3  AUTHOR      Character     1
    4  SUBJECT     Character     1
```

```
      5  SERIES        Character    1
      6  TITLE         Character    1
      7  ADDEDTITLE    Character    1
** Total **                        61
```

```
Structure for database: C:ccopy.dbf
Number of data records:      16
Date of last update    : 08/22/86
Field  Field Name  Type      Width    Dec
      1  BIBNO       Character     5
      2  COPYNO      Character     2
      3  CALLNO      Character    15
      4  LOCATION    Character    15
** Total **                       38
```

Method

Searching the catalog involves these steps:

1. Prompt for search term.
2. Prompt for type of search (global, subject, author, title, series).
3. Find (FIND) search term.
4. Tell user if search is unsuccessful; restart process.
5. Display one at a time those records that meet search criteria, allowing user to page backwards and forwards and to print the screen display if desired.

Adding new information to the catalog database involves three files. In outline form, the process is:

1. Open the three files along with their index files.
2. Prompt for unitary information to be stored in CBIB.DBF.
3. Prompt for copy-specific information, giving the user opportunity to enter a realistically high number of sets of information into CCOPY.DBF.
4. Prompt for a similarly high number of entries to the CACCESS.DBF file (screen-handling complications are the only reason to limit the number of entries to an arbitrary figure).

The command files shown below manage the tasks of searching and adding to the catalog database. Searching is dependent on this working environment:

```
Currently Selected Database:
Select area:  1, Database in Use: C:caccess.dbf
       ^^^^ Alias: CACCESS
```

```
    Master index file:  C:caccterm.ndx  Key: upper(term)
    Index file:  C:caccno.ndx  Key: bibno+addedtitle+
       ^^^^series+subject+title+author+substr(term,1,10)
      Related into: CBIB
      Relation: bibno

  Select area:  2, Database in Use: C:cbib.dbf
        ^^^^ Alias: CBIB
      Master index file:  C:cbibno.ndx  Key: bibno
      Related into: CCOPY
      Relation: bibno

  Select area:  3, Database in Use: C:ccopy.dbf
        ^^^^ Alias: CCOPY
    Master index file:  C:ccopyno.ndx  Key: bibno+copyno
```

Access to the main programs in the catalog system is controlled by CATMENU.PRG:

```
** CATMENU.PRG
*    Calls CATINPUT.PRG and CATFIND.PRG
SET TALK OFF
SET BELL OFF
SET ESCAPE OFF

DO WHILE .T.

    * ---Display menu options, centered on the screen.
    *    draw menu border and print heading
    CLEAR
    @ 2, 0 TO 12,79 DOUBLE
    @ 3,12 SAY [D E M O N S T R A T I O N   C A T A L O G
     ^^^^ S Y S T E M]
    @ 4,1 TO 4,78 DOUBLE
    * ---display detail lines
    @  7,26 SAY [1. Search the Catalog]
    @  8,26 SAY [2. Add records to the Catalog]
    @ 10, 26 SAY '0. EXIT'
    STORE 0 TO selectnum
    @ 12,33 SAY " select      "
    @ 12,42 GET selectnum PICTURE "9" RANGE 0,2
    READ

    DO CASE
       CASE selectnum = 0
          SET BELL ON
```

```
        SET TALK ON
        CLEAR ALL
        RETURN

     CASE selectnum = 1
     *   DO Search the Catalog
        DO catfind
     CASE selectnum = 2
     *   DO Add records to the Catalog
        DO catinput

ENDCASE

ENDDO T
RETURN
* EOF: CATMENU.PRG
```

Entering Information into the Catalog

The database is built using CATINPUT.PRG:

```
** CATINPUT.PRG   Handles input to CBIB.DBF, CCOPY.DBF
***     and CACCESS.DBF
CLEAR
SET TALK OFF
CLOSE DATA
SELECT 3
USE caccess INDEX caccno, caccterm
SELECT 2
USE ccopy INDEX ccopyno
SELECT 1
USE cbib INDEX cbibno

DO WHILE .T.

*** Initialize memory variables for unitary information
     mbibno=SPACE(5)
     mtitle=SPACE(60)
     medition=SPACE(10)
     mpublisher=SPACE(25)
     mdate=SPACE(10)

*** Initialize memory variables for access file input
     counter=1
          DO WHILE counter<7  && 6 is current, arbitrary
     ^^^^ limit on access fields
```

```
            mterm="mterm"+STR(counter,1)
            &mterm=SPACE(40)
            mtype="mtype"+STR(counter,1)
            &mtype=SPACE(2)
            counter=counter+1
       ENDDO

*** Initialize memory variables for copy file input
     cctr=1
     DO WHILE cctr<7
        mcopyno="mcopyno"+STR(cctr,1)
        &mcopyno=SPACE(2)
        mcallno="mcallno"+STR(cctr,1)
        &mcallno=SPACE(15)
        mlocation="mlocation"+STR(cctr,1)
        &mlocation=SPACE(10)
        cctr=cctr+1
      ENDDO

*** Prompt for input of unitary information
     @  3,  5  SAY "Title Number " GET mbibno
     @  5,  5  SAY "Edition " GET medition
     @  5, 25  SAY "Publisher " GET mpublisher
     @  5, 62  SAY "Date " GET mdate
     @ 23, 5 SAY "<ESC> to abandon"
     READ
     IF READKEY()=12 .OR. READKEY()=268 .OR.
      ^^^^ LEN(TRIM(mbibno))=0
         EXIT
     ENDIF

*** Prompt for input of copy file information
     cctr=0
     @ 7,12 say "Copy #"
     @ 7,19 say "Call Number"
     @ 7,47 say "Location"
     startpos=ROW()
     DO WHILE .t.
        cctr=IIF(cctr<1,1,cctr+1)
        mcopyno="mcopyno"+STR(cctr,1)
        mcallno="mcallno"+STR(cctr,1)
        mlocation="mlocation"+STR(cctr,1)
        IF TYPE(mterm)="U"
            &mterm=SPACE(40)
        ENDIF

        @  startpos+cctr, 12  GET &mcopyno
```

```
            @  startpos+cctr, 19  GET &mcallno
            @  startpos+cctr, 47  GET &mlocation
            READ
            @ startpos+cctr, 12 SAY &mcopyno
            @ startpos+cctr, 19 SAY &mcallno
            @ startpos+cctr, 47 SAY &mlocation
            IF READKEY()=12 .or. READKEY()=268
                 SET TALK ON
                 CLOSE DATA
                 RETURN
            ENDIF
            IF READKEY() = 4 .OR. READKEY() = 260
                 cctr = cctr - 2
            ELSE
                 IF LEN(TRIM(&mcopyno))=0 .OR. cctr=6
                     EXIT
                 ENDIF
            ENDIF
      ENDDO

   *** Prompt for input of access file information
      counter=0
      @ 15,25 say "Term(s) and Term Type (AU, TI, SU, SE)"
      startpos=ROW()
      @ 22,0 SAY REPLICATE("*",79)
      @ 23,40 SAY "<RETURN> alone to save, move on"

DO WHILE .t.
          counter=IIF(counter<1,1,counter+1)
          mterm="mterm"+STR(counter,1)
          mtype="mtype"+STR(counter,1)
          IF TYPE(mterm)="U"
              &mterm=SPACE(40)
          ENDIF

          @  startpos+counter, 12  GET &mterm
          @  startpos+counter, 65  GET &mtype
          READ
          @ startpos+counter, 12 SAY &mterm
          @ startpos+counter, 65 SAY &mtype
          IF READKEY()=12 .or. READKEY()=268
              SET TALK ON
              CLOSE DATA
              RETURN
          ENDIF
*      **** re-edit fields with PgUp
          IF READKEY() = 4 .OR. READKEY() = 260
```

```
                counter = counter - 2
        ELSE
            IF LEN(TRIM(&mterm))=0 .OR. counter=6
                EXIT
            ENDIF
        ENDIF
    ENDDO
    CLEAR
    @ 10,10 SAY "The information just entered is now
     ^^^^ being"
    @ 12,10 SAY "added to the database.  Please wait..."

*** Replace values into fields in CACCESS.DBF

    SELECT 3
    counter=counter-1
     DO WHILE counter>0
        APPEND BLANK
        mterm="mterm"+STR(counter,1)
        mtype="mtype"+STR(counter,1)
        REPLACE bibno with mbibno
        REPLACE term WITH &mterm
        DO CASE
            CASE UPPER(&mtype)="AU"
                REPLACE author WITH "T"
            CASE UPPER(&mtype)="SU"
                REPLACE subject WITH "T"
            CASE UPPER(&mtype)="SE"
                REPLACE series WITH "T"
            CASE UPPER(&mtype)="TI"
                REPLACE title WITH "T"
        ENDCASE
        counter=counter-1
    ENDDO

*** Information being added to CCOPY.DBF
    SELECT 2
    cctr=cctr-1
    DO WHILE cctr>0
        APPEND BLANK
        mcopyno="mcopyno"+STR(cctr,1)
        mcallno="mcallno"+STR(cctr,1)
        mlocation="mlocation"+STR(cctr,1)
        REPLACE bibno WITH mbibno
        REPLACE copyno WITH &mcopyno
        REPLACE callno WITH &mcallno
        REPLACE location WITH &mlocation
```

```
        cctr=cctr-1
     ENDDO
*** Information being added to CBIB.DBF
     SELECT 1
     APPEND BLANK
     REPLACE bibno WITH mbibno
     REPLACE title WITH mtitle
     REPLACE edition WITH medition
     REPLACE publisher WITH mpublisher
     REPLACE date WITH mdate

     CLEAR
     CLEAR GETS
ENDDO
SET TALK ON
CLEAR
CLOSE DATA
RETURN
```

The screen display for data entry is nothing fancy. A more attractive screen display could easily be incorporated into the program file above, once it is decided what additional data elements need to be solicited from the user. As it stands, the user sees the following, having almost completed entering information to describe the item in hand:

///

```
Title Number  50011

Edition  2nd   Publisher  McGraw-Hill        Date  1985

     Copy # Call Number                 Location
        01      630




          Term(s) and Term Type (AU, TI, SU, SE)
    Applied Agronomy                              TI
    Peterson, John                                AU
    Fenderson, Frank                              AU
    Agronomy                                      SU
    Source books in agriculture                   SE


    ****************************************************
    <ESC> to abandon        <RETURN> alone to save, move on
```

///

Notice how all subjects stay on the screen as they are entered. PgUp moves backward one term until the first term is reached. PgDn moves the user back down the list again.

Searching the Catalog

Searches are run with CATFIND.PRG:

```
** CATFIND.PRG
*Searches catalog files: CBIB.DBF,CACCESS.DBF,CCOPY.DBF

*      set up working environment
SET TALK OFF
SELE 3
USE ccopy INDEX ccopyno
SELE 2
USE cbib INDEX cbibno
SET relation TO bibno INTO ccopy
SELE 1
USE caccess INDEX caccterm, caccno
SET relation TO bibno INTO cbib

DO WHILE .T.

*      *** Ask for search term, type of search
       CLEAR
       mterm=SPACE(20)
       @ 7,20 SAY "Term TO be searched?  " GET mterm
       @ 10,27 SAY "Type of Search"
       @ 12,25 SAY "1.  Global Search  "
       @ 13,25 SAY "2.  Subject Search"
       @ 14,25 SAY "3.  Author Search"
       @ 15,25 SAY "4.  Title Search"
       @ 16,25 SAY "5.  Series Search"
       @ 17,25 SAY "6.  Author & Subject"
       @ 18,25 SAY "7.  Title & Subject"
       manswer=1
       @ 20,30 SAY "Type of search? " GET manswer RANGE 1,7
       @ 22,10 SAY "<RETURN> alone TO finish searching"
       READ

*      *** Exit program if no term or search type specified
       IF len(TRIM(mterm))=0 .OR. manswer=0
           exit
       ENDIF

*** Construct qualifying clause for non-global searches
```

```
       answer=STR(manswer,1)
   DO CASE
    CASE answer="1"
      qualifier=""
    CASE answer="2"
      qualifier=" .AND. subject='T'"
    CASE answer="3"
      qualifier=" .AND. author='T'"
    CASE answer="4"
      qualifier=" .AND. (title='T' .OR. addedtitle='T')"
    CASE answer="5"
      qualifier=" .AND. series='T'"
    CASE answer="6"
      qualifier=" .AND. (author='T' .OR. subject='T')"
    CASE answer="7"
      qualifier=" .AND. (title='T' .OR. subject='T')"
   ENDCASE

*    *** Find desired term, report and go to beginning
*        if term isn't in CACCESS.DBF
    mterm=upper(TRIM(mterm))
    FIND &mterm
    IF .NOT. FOUND()
        CLEAR
        @ 10,10 SAY "This term isn't listed"
        @ 22,1 SAY " "
        WAIT
        LOOP
    ENDIF

*    *** Initialize some variables used in program
    mrecno=RECNO()        && Current record number
    firstrecno=RECNO()  && First record number found
    mbibno=bibno && Current bibliographic record
    foundstr="" && Records already displayed once
    printit=.F. && Output to screen or printer?
    CLEAR

*    *** Process records as long as each includes
*        a TERM that meets the search term requirements

    DO WHILE upper(term)=mterm

*    *** Count in printer or in screen terms?
            IF printit
                mrow=prow()
            ELSE
```

```
            mrow=2
        ENDIF

*   *** Don't display record a second time, even if
*       2 access points would normally cause the record
*       to display twice.  Apply qualifying clause.

        IF .NOT. bibno $foundstr &qualifier

*   *** Display unitary information from CBIB.DBF

            @ mrow,5 SAY "Publisher: "+cbib->
^^^^ publisher + " Pub. Date: "+cbib->date
            @ mrow+1,5 SAY "Holdings:"

*   *** Display possibly multiple copy-specific entries

            SELE 3
            copyctr=0
            DO WHILE bibno=mbibno
                @ mrow+1+copyctr,15 SAY "Call # "
^^^^ +ccopy->callno+" Copy # "+ ccopy->copyno+
^^^^ " Location: "+ccopy->location
                copyctr=copyctr+1
                SKIP
            ENDDO

*   *** Return to CACCESS.DBF, but arrange by bibno and
*       look for access terms with same bibno.  This
*       reconstructs a variable number of access
*       elements into a single screen display.

            SELE 1
            SET ORDER TO 2
            FIND &mbibno

            ctr=0
            mrow=mrow+copyctr
            DO WHILE bibno=mbibno

*     *** Set up for display of appropriate access
*         point types

                DO CASE
                    CASE author="T"
                        tag="Author:     "
                    CASE title="T"
                        tag="Title:      "
```

```
                              CASE subject="T"
                                   tag="Subject:      "
                              CASE series="T"
                                   tag="Series:       "
                              CASE addedtitle="T"
                                   tag="Added Title: "
                         ENDCASE
```

*   *** Display access points, in inverse video if
*   they match the search term

```
                    IF UPPER(term)=mterm
                        SET color TO I
                        @ mrow+4+ctr,5 SAY tag+TRIM(term)
                        SET color TO
                    ELSE
                        @ mrow+4+ctr,5 SAY tag+TRIM(term)
                    ENDIF
                    ctr=ctr+1
                    SKIP
                ENDDO
```

*   *** Add current bibno to list of records already
*   found, get ready for looking at next term in
*   the access file in order by term

```
                    foundstr=foundstr+mbibno+"/"
                    SET ORDER TO 1
                    GOTO mrecno
                    SKIP
                    mrecno=RECNO()
                    mbibno=bibno
```

*   *** If current record didn't qualify, move to next

```
                ELSE
                    SKIP
                    mrecno=RECNO()
                    mbibno=bibno
                    LOOP
                ENDIF
```

*   *** If printer on, turn it off

```
                IF printit
                    @ PROW()+1,0 SAY CHR(10)
                    SET DEVICE TO SCREEN
```

```
            printit=.F.
     ENDIF

     IF term<>mterm
            @ 21, 40 SAY "LAST MATCHING RECORD"
     ENDIF
```

*   *** Page backwards, print, or go forward

```
     answer=" "
     @ 22,10 SAY "PgUp TO go backward,(P)rint,
^^^^ <RETURN> TO go forward" GET answer
     READ
```

*   *** Page backward routine

```
     IF READKEY()=6
         SKIP -1
         IF RECNO()<>firstrecno
             SKIP -1
         ENDIF
         mrecno=RECNO()
         mbibno=bibno
         IF LEN(TRIM(foundstr))>12
             foundstr=LEFT(foundstr,LEN(TRIM
^^^^ (foundstr))-12)
         ELSE
             foundstr=""
         ENDIF
         DO WHILE bibno $foundstr
             SKIP -1
         ENDDO
         mrecno=RECNO()
         mbibno=bibno
     ENDIF
```

*   *** Print to paper routine

```
     IF UPPER(answer)="P"
         SKIP-1
         mbibno=bibno
         mrecno=RECNO()
         foundstr=SUBSTR(foundstr,1,LEN(TRIM
^^^^ (foundstr))-6)
         SET DEVICE TO PRINT
         printit=.T.
     ELSE
```

```
            CLEAR
        ENDIF
    ENDDO
ENDDO
CLOSE DATA
SET TALK ON
RETURN
```

Here's a search for anything in the database about Adam Osborne. Truncating the search term pulls in misspellings and, it turns out, a subject heading. Since the author and subject references are attached to the same item, it doesn't make much difference here, but in other circumstances, the global search with truncation would have added significantly to the material retrieved:

///

Term TO be searched?   Osborn

Type of Search

1.   Global Search
2.   Subject Search
3.   Author Search
4.   Title Search
5.   Series Search
6.   Author & Subject
7.   Title & Subject

Type of search?   1

<RETURN> alone to finish searching
///

Here's the record display that results:

//

Publisher: Avon   Pub. Date: 1984

Holdings: Call # 338.7/O667h   Copy # 01 Location: off
          Call # 338.7/O667h/c2 Copy # 02 Location:

Author: Dvorak, John
Author: Osborne, Adam
Title: Hypergrowth: the rise and fall of Osborne
     ^^^^ Computer
Subject: Computer industry -- United States
Subject: Microcomputers
Subject: Osborne Computer Corporation

                    LAST MATCHING RECORD

PgUp TO go backward,(P)rint, <RETURN> TO go forward

//

CATALOG CARD PRODUCTION

A major advantage of producing catalog cards with *dBase III+* is the incidental creation of a permanent, easy-to-manipulate database of bibliographic information about the materials processed.

Any card typing system should include fields for the Library of Congress Card Number (LCCN) and the International Standard Book Number (ISBN). These numbers are the key to upgrading of the database to MARC II format, should eventual automation activities require it. Producing a list of LCCNs, titles, and other search keys on disk or on paper is a snap using *dBase*, *if* the information exists in machine-readable form in the first place. However limited your current objectives, it is virtually guaranteed that conversion to a standardized format (i.e., MARC) and enrichment of the information contained in a standardized bibliographic record from a source database will one day be desired.

Card printing is a task that is simple in concept but complex, tricky, and demanding in execution. A finely tuned card-typing program takes a lot of work and far more code than there is room for here. What follows is a quick and dirty demonstration of how one feasible approach could be implemented. It does not purport to follow any particular conventions as to form or content. It is meant to illustrate a pattern that can be modified and expanded as need dictates.

Our approach will consist of the following steps:

1. Input cataloging information into a bibliographic file (or use information that is already there through input from an acquisitions system or from some other source).
2. Place an indicator that a record is to be used for generation of cards in a field set aside for that purpose (MAKECARDS in this example). BROWSE or EDIT mode will be most convenient for this.
3. Invoke a *dBase III+* program file when cards are to be previewed and/or printed.
4. Answer the program prompt as to whether cards are to be printed; set up printer if necessary.
5. If cards are to be printed, print all designated records; otherwise display one card set at a time and wait for user to prompt for the next card set.
6. Break out of program with ESC, if desired.
7. Reset card-printing parameters by using RESTORE FROM (parameter file name) PARAMS.MEM, doing DISPLAY MEMORY,

changing values as necessary, and finally saving to (parameter file name).

The data elements can be input in a number of ways. Using *dBase* interactively,

- USE cdbib
- APPEND

will allow for entry of the requisite information. In some circumstances, the ten-character limit on the length of field names will be inadequate to convey sufficient information to the occasional user about what is to be entered in each field. A screen format file could be created (CREATE SCREEN) that would include easily understood, explanatory prompts. SET FORMAT TO (format file name) would then precede the USE and APPEND commands.

Data Structure

To make the card production process clearer, we assume here that bibliographic information is stored in a single data file. The discussion regarding a *dBase* online catalog and the discussions elsewhere about searching a bibliographic database make it pretty clear that a single file won't cut the mustard as far as interactive access is concerned. Either the information stored in the data structure that follows will have to be transferred into a multiple, linked file system, or the card production program itself will have to be expanded to place information in multiple files. For now, however, let's assume that card typing, not online access, is the issue. Here is the data structure we will use:

```
Structure for database: C:cdbib.dbf
Number of data records:        12
Date of last update    : 08/17/86
Field  Field Name  Type       Width    Dec
    1   MAKECARDS   Character      1
    2   CALLNO      Character     25
    3   AUTHFIRST   Character     15
    4   AUTHLAST    Character     20
    5   AUTHSTATE   Character    100
    6   TITLE       Character    100
    7   PUBLISHER   Character     40
    8   EDITION     Character      5
    9   DATE        Character     10
   10   PAGES       Character     10
   11   NOTES       Character    100
```

12	SUBJECT1	Character	50
13	SUBJECT2	Character	50
14	SUBJECT3	Character	50
15	ADDEDAUTH1	Character	50
16	ADDEDAUTH2	Character	50
17	ALTTITLE	Character	100
18	SERIES	Character	50
19	ISBN	Character	10
20	LCCN	Character	8
** Total **			845

Parameters Stored in a Memory File

The key to making any kind of text-formatting program flexible is to make as much of it as possible "parameter driven." In this instance, parameters are values used in various parts of the program that can be changed simply and easily. Changes are simple because, internally, the values are stored in just one place and thus only one change is needed.

dBase III+ allows you to store values that will be used over and over in a memory file with the .MEM file extension (not to be confused with MEMO fields, which are an entirely different concept). The file CDPARAMS.MEM holds values for such parameters as the line on which to start the main entry (MEPOS), the call number indention (CALLNOINDENT), the first indention (INDENT1), etc.

A fully articulated card production program would have a separate parameter-setting module with informative explanations of the choices and range-checking routines to ensure that inappropriate values (main entry starting on card line 15) are not selected. For our purposes, using RESTORE FROM on the .MEM file, making a change (e.g., MEPOS=5), and using SAVE TO on the .MEM file is the only recourse.

These are the parameters set up for this run-through:

```
. RESTORE FROM cdparams
. DISP MEMO
HEADINGPOS    pub   N          2  (          2.00000000)
MEPOS         pub   N          4  (          4.00000000)
TRACEPOS      pub   N         15  (         15.00000000)
LEFTOFFSET    pub   N          2  (          2.00000000)
CALLINDENT    pub   N          2  (          2.00000000)
INDENT1       pub   N          9  (          9.00000000)
```

INDENT2	pub	N			12	(	12.00000000)
MAXLENGTH	pub	N			40	(	40.00000000)
TITLEPUNC	pub	C	". "				
AUTHORPUNC	pub	C	". "				
PUBPUNC	pub	C	", "				
DATEPUNC	pub	C	". "				
EDPUNC	pub	C	". "				
PAGEPUNC	pub	C	"p. "				
NOTEPOS	pub	N			10	(	10.00000000)

```
   15 variables defined,      106 bytes used
  241 variables available,   2966 bytes available
```

The Method

The logic behind the program below consists of these steps:

1. Ask whether cards are to be printed or just displayed on the screen. Find the first of the entries in CDBIB.DBF with a "T" in the MAKECARDS field. Process each such record in turn, as described below.
2. Determine whether main entry is to be under author or title by checking whether there is anything in AUTHLAST.
3. Concatenate the elements of the card into several major sections, each of which is likely to require further processing for multiple line presentation. These sections are: main entry, body, pagination, notes, ISBN, LCCN, and tracing. The assumption is made that none of these major sections will exceed the *dBase III+* limit of 255 characters on the length of a single variable.
4. Process each of these major character strings into lines of appropriate length, as specified by parameter file. Assign each line to a LINEn memory variable, where the "n" stands for a row position between 1 and 18.
5. Insert call number line segments into their appropriate LINEn memory variables.
6. Print cards by reprinting the LINEn lines, inserting a heading line if appropriate.

Here is the program, consisting of CDPRINT.PRG and the modules EXPROD and EXPRNTER contained in the procedure file CARDS.PRG, followed by the results of a sample run:

```
** CDPRINT.PRG
**   Print catalog cards from file CDBIB.DBF
SET TALK OFF
SET PROCEDURE TO cards
```

```
CLEAR

*** Retrieve card printing parameters from .MEM file
RESTORE FROM cdparams
maxlength=maxlength+indent1+leftoffset
indent1=indent1+leftoffset
indent2=indent2+leftoffset

*** Prompt for whether to send cards to printer
yesprint=" "
@ 10,10 SAY "Do you wish to produce cards on the
      ^^^^ printer? "
@ 12,40 GET yesprint
READ
IF UPPER(yesprint)="Y"
   @ 16,20 SAY "SET UP PRINTER NOW"
   @ 21, 1 SAY ""
   WAIT
   SET PRINT ON
ENDIF
CLEAR

*** Locate the first record to be printed
USE cdbib INDEX cdmake
FIND T

*** Begin processing all marked records
DO WHILE makecards="T"
   CLEAR
   @ 10,10 SAY "Please wait while card image is
    ^^^^ being formed"

*      *** initialize line memory variables
   num=1
   DO WHILE num<19
      mnum=IIF(num<10,STR(num,1),STR(num,2))
      memvar="line"+"&mnum"
      &memvar=""
      num=num+1
   ENDDO
   num=1

   mbody=""
   mentry=SPACE(indent1)
   mbody=SPACE(indent2)
* Decide if author or title main entry, concatenate me
   IF LEN(TRIM(authlast))>0
```

```
        mentry=mentry+TRIM(authlast)+", "+
  ^^^^ TRIM(authfirst)+authorpunc
        mbody=mbody+TRIM(title)+titlepunc
ELSE
        mentry=mentry+TRIM(title)+titlepunc
ENDIF
? "Main entry processed"

*       *** Concatenate to form body of card
IF LEN(TRIM(edition))>0
        mbody=mbody+TRIM(edition)+edpunc
ENDIF
IF LEN(TRIM(publisher))>0
        mbody=mbody+TRIM(publisher)+pubpunc
ENDIF
IF LEN(TRIM(date))>0
        mbody=mbody+TRIM(date)+datepunc
ENDIF
? "Body of card processed"

*       *** Form collation, notes sections
mpages=SPACE(indent2)+TRIM(pages)
mnotes=SPACE(indent2)+TRIM(notes)
? "Pagination and notes processed"

*       *** Form tracing
mtrace=SPACE(indent1)
IF LEN(TRIM(subject1))>0
        mtrace=mtrace+"1. "+TRIM(subject1)+". "
ENDIF
IF LEN(TRIM(subject2))>0
        mtrace=mtrace+"2. "+TRIM(subject2)+". "
ENDIF
IF LEN(TRIM(subject3))>0
        mtrace=mtrace+"3. "+TRIM(subject3)+". "
ENDIF
IF LEN(TRIM(authlast))>0
      mtrace=mtrace+"I. Title.  "
ENDIF
IF LEN(TRIM(addedauth1))>0
      mtrace=mtrace+"II. "+TRIM(addedauth1)+". "
ENDIF
IF LEN(TRIM(addedauth2))>0
      mtrace=mtrace+"III. "+TRIM(addedauth2)+". "
ENDIF
IF LEN(TRIM(series))>0
      mtrace=mtrace+"Series: "+TRIM(series)+"."
ENDIF
```

```
    ? "Tracing processed"

*** Process main entry line(s), testing for line length
    rowpos=mepos
    IF LEN(mentry)>maxlength
        step=0
        DO WHILE .T.
          IF SUBSTR(mentry,maxlength-step,1) $(" ,-.;:")
              EXIT
          ELSE
              step=step+1
          ENDIF
        ENDDO
        mrow=IIF(rowpos<10,STR(rowpos,1),STR(rowpos,2))
        memvar=("line"+"&mrow")
        &memvar=SUBSTR(mentry,1,maxlength-step)
        rowpos=rowpos+1
        mrow=IIF(rowpos<10,STR(rowpos,1),STR(rowpos,2))
        memvar=("line"+"&mrow")
        &memvar=SPACE(indent2)+SUBSTR(mentry,maxlength
     ^^^^ -step+1)
    ELSE
        mrow=IIF(rowpos<10,STR(rowpos,1),STR(rowpos,2))
        memvar=("line"+"&mrow")
        &memvar=TRIM(mentry)
    ENDIF
    rowpos=rowpos+1
    ? "Main entry lines done"

*     Print body, testing for line length
    section=mbody
    DO exprnter
    ? "Body lines done"

*       *** Print pagination
    IF LEN(mpages)>0
        mrow=IIF(rowpos<10,STR(rowpos,1),STR(rowpos,2))
        memvar=("line"+"&mrow")
        &memvar=TRIM(mpages)+pagepunc
        rowpos=rowpos+1
    ENDIF

*       *** Process notes
    rowpos=notepos
    IF LEN(mnotes)>0
        section=mnotes
        DO exprnter
```

```
      ENDIF
      ? "Pagination and notes lines done"

*         *** Process ISBN, LCCN
      IF LEN(TRIM(LCCN))>0
          mrow=IIF(rowpos<10,STR(rowpos,1),STR(rowpos,2))
          memvar=("line"+"&mrow")
          &memvar=SPACE(indent2)+"LCCN:   "+lccn
          rowpos=rowpos+1
      ENDIF
      IF LEN(TRIM(ISBN))>0
          mrow=IIF(rowpos<10,STR(rowpos,1),STR(rowpos,2))
          memvar=("line"+"&mrow")
          &memvar=SPACE(indent2)+"ISBN:   "+isbn
          rowpos=rowpos+1
      ENDIF
      ? "ISBN and LCCN lines done"

*         *** Process tracing
      rowpos=tracepos
      IF LEN(mtrace)>0
          section=mtrace
          DO exprnter
      ENDIF
      ? "Tracing done"
*         *** Insert call numbers if they exist.
      IF LEN(TRIM(callno))>0
          n=0
          mcallno=TRIM(callno)
       `  IF "/" $mcallno
              DO WHILE "/" $mcallno
                  segment=SUBSTR(mcallno,1,AT("/",
    ^^^^ mcallno)-1)
                  memvar="line"+STR(mepos+n,1)
                  blanks=SPACE(leftoffset+callindent)
                  &memvar=blanks+segment+space(indent1
    ^^^^ -1-LEN(blanks+segment))+SUBSTR
    ^^^^ (&memvar,indent1)
                  mcallno=LTRIM(SUBSTR(mcallno,AT("/",
    ^^^^ mcallno)+1))
                  n=n+1
              ENDDO
          ENDIF
          IF LEN(TRIM(mcallno))>0
              memvar="line"+STR(mepos+n,1)
              blanks=SPACE(leftoffset+callindent)
              &memvar=blanks+mcallno+space(indent1-1-LEN
```

```
     ^^^^ (blanks+mcallno))+SUBSTR(&memvar,indent1)
        ENDIF
     ENDIF
     ? "Call number lines done"

*      *** Print cards
     DO exprod
     IF LEN(TRIM(authlast))>0
        memvar="line"+STR(headingpos,1)
        &memvar=SPACE(indent1)+TRIM(title)
        DO exprod
     ENDIF
     IF LEN(TRIM(subject1))>0
        memvar="line"+STR(headingpos,1)
        &memvar=SPACE(indent1)+UPPER(TRIM(subject1))
        DO exprod
     ENDIF
     IF LEN(TRIM(subject2))>0
        memvar="line"+STR(headingpos,1)
        &memvar=SPACE(indent1)+UPPER(TRIM(subject2))
        DO exprod
     ENDIF
     IF LEN(TRIM(subject3))>0
        memvar="line"+STR(headingpos,1)
        &memvar=SPACE(indent1)+UPPER(TRIM(subject3))
        DO exprod
     ENDIF
     IF LEN(TRIM(series))>0
        memvar="line"+STR(headingpos,1)
        &memvar=SPACE(indent1)+TRIM(series)
        DO exprod
     ENDIF
     IF LEN(TRIM(addedauth1))>0
        memvar="line"+STR(headingpos,1)
        &memvar=SPACE(indent1)+TRIM(addedauth1)
        DO exprod
     ENDIF
     IF LEN(TRIM(addedauth2))>0
        memvar="line"+STR(headingpos,1)
        &memvar=SPACE(indent1)+TRIM(addedauth2)
        DO exprod
     ENDIF

     IF yesprint<>"Y"
        SET CONSOLE OFF
        WAIT
        SET CONSOLE ON
```

```
      ENDIF
      SKIP
ENDDO
SET PROCEDURE TO
SET PRINT OFF
SET TALK ON
RETURN   && end of cdprint.prg


** CARDS.PRG
**    Contains procedures EXPRNTER and EXPROD

PROCEDURE EXPRNTER

    DO WHILE LEN(section)>maxlength
        step=0
        DO WHILE .T.
         IF SUBSTR(section,maxlength-step,1) $(" ,-.;:")
             EXIT
         ELSE
             step=step+1
         ENDIF
        ENDDO
        mnum=IIF(rowpos<10,STR(rowpos,1),STR(rowpos,2))
        memvar="line"+"&mnum"
        &memvar=SUBSTR(section,1,maxlength-step)
        rowpos=rowpos+1
        section=SPACE(indent1)+LTRIM(SUBSTR(section,
    ^^^^ maxlength-step+1))
    ENDDO
    IF LEN(section)>0
        mnum=IIF(rowpos<10,STR(rowpos,1),STR(rowpos,2))
        memvar="line"+"&mnum"
        &memvar=section
        rowpos=rowpos+1
    ENDIF
    RETURN


PROCEDURE EXPROD

num=1
DO WHILE num<19
        mnum=IIF(num<10,STR(num,1),STR(num,2))
        memvar="line"+"&mnum"
        ? &memvar
        num=num+1
ENDDO
RETURN   && end CARDS.PRG procedure file
```

After putting a "T" in the MAKECARDS field of CDBIB.DBF, cards are produced from all marked records by performing DO CDPRINT.PRG. First, the following lines are displayed on the screen to let the user know something is happening during the twenty-five-second processing wait:

//

```
        Main entry processed
        Body of card processed
        Pagination and notes processed
        Tracing processed
        Main entry lines done
        Body lines done
        Pagination and notes lines done
        ISBN and LCCN lines done
        Tracing done
        Call number lines done
```

//

Then the cards start coming:

```
001     Castro, Luis.
.645        Advanced Programmer's Guide. Ashton-
C223a   Tate, 1985.
1985        567p.



            Covers dBase II and III, but not III+
            LCCN:   82023322
            ISBN:   01-9983882



        1. dBase II. 2. dBase III. 3. Computer
        programming. I. Title.   II. Hanson, Jay.
        III. Rettig, Tom. Series: Ashton-Tate
        Guides.

        Advanced Programmer's Guide

001     Castro, Luis.
.645        Advanced Programmer's Guide. Ashton-
C223a   Tate, 1985.
1985        567p.
```

Covers dBase II and III, but not III+
LCCN: 82023322
ISBN: 01-9983882

1. dBase II. 2. dBase III. 3. Computer
programming. I. Title. II. Hanson, Jay.
III. Rettig, Tom. Series: Ashton-Tate
Guides.

DBASE II

001   Castro, Luis.
.645   Advanced Programmer's Guide. Ashton-
C223a   Tate, 1985.
1985   567p.

Covers dBase II and III, but not III+
LCCN: 82023322
ISBN: 01-9983882

1. dBase II. 2. dBase III. 3. Computer
programming. I. Title. II. Hanson, Jay.
III. Rettig, Tom. Series: Ashton-Tate
Guides.

DBASE III

001   Castro, Luis.
.645   Advanced Programmer's Guide. Ashton-
C223a   Tate, 1985.
1985   567p.

Covers dBase II and III, but not III+
LCCN: 82023322
ISBN: 01-9983882

1. dBase II. 2. dBase III. 3. Computer
programming. I. Title. II. Hanson, Jay.
III. Rettig, Tom. Series: Ashton-Tate
Guides.

COMPUTER PROGRAMMING

```
001     Castro, Luis.
.645        Advanced Programmer's Guide. Ashton-
C223a   Tate, 1985.
1985        567p.
```

```
            Covers dBase II and III, but not III+
            LCCN:  82023322
            ISBN:  01-9983882
```

```
        1. dBase II. 2. dBase III. 3. Computer
        programming. I. Title.  II. Hanson, Jay.
        III. Rettig, Tom. Series: Ashton-Tate
        Guides.
```

Ashton-Tate Guides

```
001     Castro, Luis.
.645        Advanced Programmer's Guide. Ashton-
C223a   Tate, 1985.
1985        567p.
```

```
            Covers dBase II and III, but not III+
            LCCN:  82023322
            ISBN:  01-9983882
```

```
        1. dBase II. 2. dBase III. 3. Computer
        programming. I. Title.  II. Hanson, Jay.
        III. Rettig, Tom. Series: Ashton-Tate
        Guides.
```

Hanson, Jay

```
001     Castro, Luis.
.645        Advanced Programmer's Guide. Ashton-
C223a   Tate, 1985.
1985        567p.
```

```
            Covers dBase II and III, but not III+
            LCCN:  82023322
            ISBN:  01-9983882
```

```
          1. dBase II. 2. dBase III. 3. Computer
          programming. I. Title.  II. Hanson, Jay.
          III. Rettig, Tom. Series: Ashton-Tate
          Guides.

          Rettig, Tom

  001     Castro, Luis.
  .645        Advanced Programmer's Guide. Ashton-
  C223a   Tate, 1985.
  1985        567p.



          Covers dBase II and III, but not III+
          LCCN:  82023322
          ISBN:  01-9983882
          1. dBase II. 2. dBase III. 3. Computer
          programming. I. Title.  II. Hanson, Jay.
          III. Rettig, Tom. Series: Ashton-Tate
          Guides.
  Press any key to continue...
```

Extensions

The improvements, refinements, and niceties that could be added to this approach are legion. By building on the memory-variable-oriented approach, you could prompt for input directly from the keyboard and print one card set at a time. After entry and before printing, the information would be appended (APPEND) to the bibliographic file. This may or may not be more convenient than entering data into the file first.

You could develop and store several parameter files corresponding to conventions of card form used widely in libraries (e.g., AACR2, Akers', etc.). Some additional IF/THEN logic in the program could control whether or not fields display (level 1 vs. level 2 description).

A good deal of code tightening and greater use of macro substitution techniques (like the &MEMVAR approach) could probably reduce the size of the program. This would, hopefully, increase its speed. The principal shortcoming of the program as it stands is that it is slow. You can wait thirty seconds or more for character manipulations before a new card set starts to print. Running the program through a compiler like *Clipper* (Nantucket Software) or on a faster machine than the PC would probably improve performance substantially.

Producing printed cards in sort order would be a welcome enhancement. One way to do that would be to store each card image, along with any applicable heading, in a temporary data file with fields for each of the eighteen lines plus one for heading. Indexing the temporary file on heading and then printing each record in sequence would produce cards in sort order. A more sophisticated variation would involve two files, one for the "unit card" information and the other for heading and a pointer back to the corresponding unit card. This should be faster and more space efficient.

Speaking of multifile variants, the structure of CDBIB is pretty primitive. Only three subject headings and two author-added entry headings can be accommodated. There is no reason, other than the increased complexity of developing a successful command file, why the line-by-line card image that CDPRINT produces couldn't be derived from more than one file.

Those familiar with the computer language C, or with assembly language, may see ways to speed up the text manipulation many times just by offloading a few routines to an external program module. That is beyond the scope of this book, and beyond the present competence of its author, but die-hards will be interested.

REGISTRATION

A registration file is an integral part of just about any circulation system. Its use as part of such a larger system will be discussed at length in the sections of this book dealing with overdues management, reserves, and charging and discharging materials. Here we will focus on automating the library registration file independent of any other function.

So, absent a full-blown circulation system, what good is it to have instant access to the names of library patrons?

1. Accurate statistics on the number of registered borrowers, their addresses, and other demographic factors are available, assuming that the relevant information was collected at the time of registration.
2. Mailings to patrons whose cards are about to expire, who are interested in a particular type of library program or service, or who simply want to receive the library newsletter are easy, given *dBase III*'s label-generation capabilities.
3. Lists of patrons with reserves to be picked up, holds against their borrowing privileges, or expired cards can be generated daily for use at the circulation desk. Those lists can be by name, by patron's card number, or by any other element in the registration database.

Data Structure

The REGISTER.DBF data structure below might be adequate for a smaller public library. The MESSAGE field indicates whether there is additional information regarding the patron in the MESSAGES.DBF file. The message is stored in a separate data file because (1) this arrangement saves space, assuming that there will be no messages stored that relate to the majority of library borrowers; and (2) there will be multiple messages, not easily accommodated in a single file with just one message field, in the case of other patrons.

```
Structure for database: C:register.dbf
Number of data records:        5
Date of last update   : 07/27/86
Field  Field Name  Type        Width    Dec
    1  BORROWERNO  Character       5
    2  FIRSTNAME   Character      15
    3  LASTNAME    Character      20
    4  ADR2        Character      35
    5  ADR3        Character      35
    6  CITY        Character      15
```

7	STATE	Character	2
8	ZIP	Character	9
9	PHONE	Character	15
10	ISSUEDATE	Date	8
11	RESIDENCE	Character	15
12	MESSAGES	Logical	1
** Total **			176

Structure for database: C:messages.dbf
Number of data records: 3
Date of last update   : 07/22/86

Field	Field Name	Type	Width	Dec
1	BORROWERNO	Character	5	
2	MESSAGE	Character	150	
** Total **			156	

Inquiries

To locate information about a patron, type:

. SELECT 2
. USE messages INDEX msgborno
. SELE 1
. USE register INDEX reglast
. SET RELATION TO borrowerno INTO messages

DISPLAY STATUS would, at this point, provide the following description of the state of affairs:

Currently Selected Database:
Select area: 1, Database in Use: C:register.dbf
    ^^^^ Alias: REGISTER
    Master index file: C:reglast.ndx Key: lastname
    Related into: MESSAGES
    Relation: borrowerno

Select area: 2, Database in Use: C:messages.dbf
    ^^^^ Alias: MESSAGES
    Master index file: C:msgborno.ndx Key: borrowerno

After setting up the working environment for inquiries, find (FIND) the surname of the borrower of interest, look at the record with EDIT (F10 unless you have redefined the function keys), and check whether there are any messages in the MESSAGE file pertaining to that borrower. Checking for messages involves selecting (SELECT) work area 2, checking to see whether there are any messages at all for the given BORROWERNO, and determining whether there are multiple messages rather than just one. The program file CHECKER.PRG greatly simplifies the check:

```
** CHECKER.PRG
**   Given a BORROWERNO from REGISTER.DBF, checks
**   MESSAGES.DBF for any messages, notes, holds or
**   whatever.
SELECT 2
IF .NOT. EOF()   && If no messages, EOF() will be true
    regrecno=recno()
    ?
    ? TRIM(register->firstname)+" "+
     ^^^^ TRIM(register->lastname)
    ?
    LIST message WHILE borrowerno=register->borrowerno
     ^^^^ OFF
    GOTO regrecno
ELSE          && If there are no messages, do this
    ?
    ? "No messages regarding this borrower"
    ?
ENDIF
SELECT 1
RETURN
```

To find out whether there are messages or not, just type:

    . DO checker

Even that can be simplified by assigning the character string "DO checker;" to a function key. The semicolon, by the way, is interpreted by *dBase* as a carriage-return. While we're assigning a new value to a function key, we might as well save ourselves even more typing by setting up the environment for the FIND command.

Using a view file to open files and define their relationships is preferable. To create it, enter the five lines listed on page 206 (after subhead "Inquiries") followed by this instruction:

    . CREATE VIEW regis FROM ENVIRONMENT

The result will be a file called REGIS.VUE that can henceforth be invoked at the beginning of a session by entering

    . SET VIEW TO regis

The command file to set up the environment and reassign the value of a function key looks like this:

```
** REGSETUP.PRG
**    Set up environment for searches on REGISTER.DBF, linked to
**    MESSAGES.DBF.
SET VIEW TO regis
CLEAR
SET FUNCTION 8 TO "DO checker;"
```

To summarize, the steps involved in making simple inquiries of the registration database by borrower name are:

1.   Do regsetup once.
2.   Do FIND, do EDIT to inspect a record, and do F8 (DO checker) to check for messages, if desired.

Here's an example:

```
. DO regsetup
. FIND Franklin
. DO checker
      3

Sanford Franklin

message
Remind him of November ski program he's agreed to do.
   . FIND Summers
   . DO checker

No messages regarding this borrower
```

Statistics on Registered Borrowers

Generating statistics on the demographics of library usage may be one of the main reasons for automating a registration file. One simple way to count (COUNT) the number of borrowers from each of a small number of communities is illustrated here. The user enters the line that begins with the dot-prompt, and the system replies with a record count.

```
. COUNT FOR residence="Bookcity"
   452 records
. COUNT FOR residence="Endicott"
   2201 records
```

```
. COUNT FOR residence="Framingham"
   392 records
```

A library serving a large number of communities, or wishing to compile statistics based on some other field in the registration record, might want to take a more generalized approach. Such an approach would consist of the following steps:

1. Do INDEX ON (fieldname) to (name of index file) UNIQUE. The UNIQUE is important. It ensures that only the first record containing each value will be indexed.
2. Do COPY TO temp FIELD (fieldname). This creates a temporary file with just one occurrence of each possible value for (fieldname), for example, just one of each of the zip codes represented among registered borrowers, just one of each of the places of employment represented (assuming such things are tracked in the first place).
3. Type DO (command file) that uses the temporary file in one work area and REGISTER.DBF in another, and for each value of the chosen fieldname in TEMP.DBF selects the other work area and counts (COUNT FOR (fieldname) = TEMP-> (fieldname)) the number of occurrences. Each count is printed and/or displayed before advancing to the next value.

Mailing Labels

To produce labels, a plain, vanilla label form is defined as follows:

```
firstname,lastname
adr2
adr3
trim(city)+", "+state=" "+zip
(blank line)
(blank line)
```

The result of running it with a small trial database:

```
. LABEL FORM reglabel
Sanford Franklin
Director of Community Affairs
WWME TV
Frye, ME 04434

Edward Senter
22 West Ave.
Endicott, ME 04122
```

Fred Smith
52 Evensong Road
Bookcity, ME 04422

Frances Smith
Parsons Insurance
53 Center St.
Bookcity, ME 04422

Blakely Summers
Endicott Broadcasting
P.O. Box 55
Endicott, ME 04122

A full range of reports listing all or selected categories of registered borrowers, displaying all or selected fields, and arranged in order by any field element are accomplished in a straightforward manner. Creating appropriate report forms and indexes and qualifying those report forms by FOR clauses when they are run gives the user complete control of the situation. See the chapter on mailing list management for examples.

OVERDUES

Managing overdues is one of the most time-consuming and frustrating tasks in school and public libraries. Producing reminder notices, generating bills, tracking subsequent collection activities, and blocking further library use by patrons badly in arrears are all unrewarding and tedious clerical jobs that most library staff would happily transfer to any adequate computer-based system.

It is possible to set up an automated overdues approach, either as part of a larger integrated system or independently. In this section we will take the independent approach. We will assume, however, that because of its usefulness in doing overdues as well as the benefits cited in the section on registration files, there is a *dBase* patron registration file already in existence. If there is no such file available, a library staff member will have to enter name and address information each time a first notice is prepared. That data can be held in a temporary file for the duration of the overdues management cycle and deleted when materials are returned and accounts cleared.

We will want the following printed products:

1. Lists of overdue materials by title, author, call number, date due, and patron name, for phone reminders and other purposes
2. Overdue notices listing titles and due dates along with information about the patron who checked the materials out
3. Bills listing items unreturned and explaining the consequences of continued lack of response
4. Labels for mailing the notices (assuming window envelopes are not used)
5. Counts and amounts of bills, general statistics on overdues

In addition, it must be easy to answer the following questions through keyboard inquiry:

1. What does a particular patron have overdue and when is each item due?
2. Who has a particular item and when was it due?

Data Structure

We will be using two files: REGISTER.DBF, the data file containing information about registered library patrons, and a new data file called OVERDUE.DBF. MESSAGES.DBF, a file used in conjunction with REGISTER.DBF to record and retrieve a wide variety of information about patrons (see the section on registration), is not used in this approach to handling overdues. Here's the structure of our two data files:

```
Structure for database: C:OVERDUE.DBF
Number of data records:        7
Date of last update   : 07/27/86
Field  Field Name  Type       Width    Dec
    1  BORROWERNO  Character      5
    2  TITLE       Character     50
    3  AUTHFIRST   Character     15
    4  AUTHLAST    Character     20
    5  COPYNO      Character      2
    6  CALLNO      Character     15
    7  DATEDUE     Date           8
    8  FIRST       Date           8
    9  SECOND      Date           8
   10  BILL        Date           8
** Total **                    140
```

```
Structure for database: C:REGISTER.DBF
Number of data records:        5
Date of last update   : 07/27/86
Field  Field Name  Type       Width    Dec
    1  BORROWERNO  Character      5
    2  FIRSTNAME   Character     15
    3  LASTNAME    Character     20
    4  ADR2        Character     35
    5  ADR3        Character     35
    6  CITY        Character     15
    7  STATE       Character      2
    8  ZIP         Character      9
    9  PHONE       Character     15
   10  ISSUEDATE   Date           8
   11  RESIDENCE   Character     15
   12  MESSAGES    Logical        1
** Total **                    176
```

There are at least two reasonable ways to add information to OVERDUE.PRG. If notices are always prepared as the first step in reminding borrowers to return materials, then the notice routine could serve as the data entry vehicle as well. If a variety of approaches is used, none with 100 percent predictability, then it is better to separate data entry from the preparation of notices and other lists.

MAINTAIN.PRG, at the end of this section, was prepared using the *dBase* Applications Generator (APPSGEN.PRG). It provides a menu-based approach to adding, editing, deleting, and viewing the contents of OVERDUE.DBF. The program has been augmented by lines that cause it to update multiple indexes if a change is made by the user, that open REGISTER.DBF for report preparation, and that offer a few other enhancements.

Materials must be entered into OVERDUE.DBF using MAINTAIN.PRG. After they are confirmed by the user, the MTLSDUE field of the REGISTER database is changed to indicate that at least one item is overdue and held by that borrower. When overdue notices are prepared, the date fields FIRST, SECOND, and BILL are automatically filled in with the date on which the notice was prepared. If notices are sometimes given by phone or other means, the dates will have to be added from within MAINTAIN.PRG.

Simple Lists

Producing lists by date due, call number, title, and author is fairly straightforward. First, we relate OVERDUE.DBF to REGISTER.DBF using BORROWERNO as the field to link them together:

```
. SELECT 2
. USE register INDEX regborno
. SELECT 1
. USE overdue INDEX overdate
. SET RELATION TO borrowerno INTO register
```

An index by title, author, or call number rather than date could just as well have been invoked in doing USE OVERDUE.DBF. It will be more convenient for future use if we save this relationship as a view file:

```
. CREATE VIEW overdues FROM ENVIRONMENT
```

The general outline for doing inquiries interactively from the keyboard is:

1. Do SET VIEW TO overdues.
2. Do SET INDEX TO (index file name) (if an arrangement other than by date due is required).
3. Do FIND or SEEK (search key, e.g., date, title, author, call number).
4. Do LIST (fieldnames from OVERDUE.DBF and REGISTER.DBF) (A

FOR or WHILE clause could be appended); or do EDIT to see all
of the OVERDUE.DBF record.

As an example, let's seek titles with a specific due date (FIND
won't work with date fields):

```
. SET VIEW TO overdues
. SEEK ctod('08/08/86')
. LIST title WHILE datedue=CTOD('08/08/86')
Record#  title
      3  USA for Business Travelers
      4  Library Automation
```

Additional data can be displayed if desired:

```
. seek ctod('08/08/86')
. LIST title,datedue,TRIM(register->firstname)+" "+
   ^^^^ TRIM(register->lastname) OFF WHILE datedue=
   ^^^^ CTOD('08/08/86')
 title                        datedue  TRIM(register->
                             ^^^^ firstname)+" "+
                             ^^^^ TRIM(register->lastname)
USA for Business Travelers   08/08/86 Blakely Summers
Library Automation           08/08/86 Fred Smith
```

It may be more convenient to define a report form for screen
display rather than reissue complex interactive commands as to what
fields are to be displayed in what order. A simple report form,
OVERRPT.FRM, produces a list like the one below:

```
. SET INDEX TO overdate
. REPORT FORM overrpt
```

```
Page No.      1
07/27/86
                        Overdues

Date Due Title     Copy Call #   Borrower        Phone


07/23/86 Catseye     1  YA FIC   Sanford         777-2231
                                 Franklin        x245
07/31/86 Thinner     2  Fic      Fred Smith      555-6765
```

08/04/86	BASIC Handbook	1	001.64	Blakely Summers 666-4322
08/04/86	Thinner	1	Fic	Blakely Summers 666-4322
08/05/86	Space	1	Fic	Blakely Summers 666-4322
08/08/86	USA for Business Travelers	2	914.74	Blakely Summers 666-4322
08/08/86	Library Automation	1	025.3028	Fred Smith 555-6765

Setting the index to (SET INDEX TO) something else will change the order in which the overdues come up on the report.   A FOR clause will pull out only those records of particular interest.   For instance, to display or to print only items checked out to Blakely Summers, issue the following command:

```
. REPO FORM overrpt HEADING 'Blakely Summers' FOR
  ^^^^ register->lastname='Summers'
```

Page No.   1   Blakely Summers
07/27/86

                        Overdues

Date Due	Title	Copy	Call #	Borrower	Phone
08/05/86	Space	1	Fic	Blakely Summers	666-4322
08/04/86	BASIC Handbook	1	001.64	Blakely Summers	666-4322
08/08/86	USA for Business Travelers	2	914.74	Blakely Summers	666-4322
08/04/86	Thinner	1	Fic	Blakely Summers	666-4322

Overdue Lists by Borrower Name

The one essential capability that is lacking under the approach just described is that of producing lists of overdues in order by borrower name. (Borrower number would be a snap because it is present in the same file as the other elements that need to be listed.   Just create an index to the BORROWERNO field in OVERDUE.DBF, perhaps first doing MODIFY REPORT to include a column for the BORROWERNO field, and run the report.)

The preferable approach to alphabetizing by name requires the addition of a field to REGISTER.DBF and the creation of a new index to that database. The field called MTLSDUE is designed to trigger the retrieval of related information from OVERDUE.DBF for those borrowers who have at least one item that is overdue. The new index, REGBYLAS.NDX, concatenates the MTLSDUE field with the LASTNAME field, ensuring that all records retrieved will be in order by last name.

The purpose of this index is to make it possible to avoid all the borrowers listed in the registration file who do not currently have an overdue title charged against them. Only those records with a "T" or "t" in the MTLSDUE field will be processed, and in alphabetical order by last name. Notice that the MTLSDUE field is a character-type rather than a logical-type field. This was done because logical fields cannot be concatenated with character fields. Unfortunately, the current release of *dBase III+* has no logical-type to character-type conversion functions analogous to those for numeric to character conversion.

An alternative that may appeal to some is to add a field for last name to OVERDUE. However, this approach involves a penalty in additional storage for redundant information. Given the relatively small size of the data files generally involved in overdues, it is probably a toss-up.

In any case, the modified REGISTER.DBF looks like this:

```
Structure for database: C:register.dbf
Number of data records:        5
Date of last update    : 07/30/86
Field  Field Name  Type       Width    Dec
    1   BORROWERNO  Character      5
    2   FIRSTNAME   Character     15
    3   LASTNAME    Character     20
    4   ADR2        Character     35
    5   ADR3        Character     35
    6   CITY        Character     15
    7   STATE       Character      2
    8   ZIP         Character      9
    9   PHONE       Character     15
   10   ISSUEDATE   Date           8
   11   RESIDENCE   Character     15
   12   MESSAGES    Logical        1
   13   MTLSDUE     Character      1
** Total **                     177
```

The operating environment can be summarized as:

```
Currently Selected Database:
Select area:  1, Database in Use: C:register.dbf
    ^^^^ Alias: REGISTER
    Master index file:  C:regbylas.ndx  Key:
    ^^^^ upper(mtlsdue)+substr(lastname,1,10)
    Related into: OVERDUE
    Relation: borrowerno

Select area:  2, Database in Use: C:overdue.dbf
    ^^^^ Alias: OVERDUE
    Master index file:  C:ovborttl.ndx  Key:
    ^^^^ borrowerno+substr(title,1,10)
```

The following command file prints overdues lists by borrower.
Additional fields could be made to display by slight alteration of the
program file. SET PRINT ON issued before entering DO OVERLAST
would direct output to the printer, albeit with no provision for
skipping over page breaks. If your printer can be set up to
automatically skip over the perforation between sheets in continuous
feed paper, this is the time to use that feature. The only other
alternative is to build a loop into the program that will count the
number of lines printed, and after fifty-five or sixty do an EJECT
to get to the top of the next page.

```
** OVERLAST.PRG
*Prints list of overdues alphabetically by borrower name

** Open files and define relation between them
CLEAR
SELECT 2
USE overdue INDEX ovborttl  && By borrowerno and title
SELECT 1
USE register INDEX regbylas  && By mtlsdue and lastname
SET RELATION TO borrowerno INTO overdue
** Find the first record for a patron with books overdue
FIND T

** Process all records in registration file for which
** overdue books are indicated.

DO WHILE UPPER(mtlsdue)="T" .AND. .NOT. EOF()

    SELECT 2  && Switch to OVERDUE.DBF
    ? TRIM(register->firstname)+" "+TRIM(register->
      ^^^^ lastname);+ ", Phone: "+TRIM(register->phone)
```

```
     DO WHILE borrowerno=register->borrowerno
        ? "   "+TRIM(title)+", "+DTOC(datedue)+", "+
     ^^^^ trim(callno)
        SKIP  && Look at next record for overdue title
     ENDDO borrowerno check

     ?
     SELECT 1    && Back to REGISTER.DBF
     SKIP  && Look at next record for overdue borrower
ENDDO  eof
CLOSE DATABASES
WAIT
RETURN
```

The result of running OVERLAST.PRG is this:

```
. DO overlast
Sanford Franklin, Phone: 777-2231 x245
   Catseye, 07/23/86, YA FIC

Fred Smith, Phone: 555-6765
   Library Automation, 08/08/86, 025.3028
   Thinner, 07/31/86, Fic

Blakely Summers, Phone: 666-4322
   BASIC Handbook, 08/04/86, 001.64
   Space, 08/05/86, Fic
   Thinner, 08/04/86, Fic
   USA for Business Travelers, 08/08/86, 914.74
```

Notice that titles appear in alphabetical order under each borrower. This is due to OVBORTTL.NDX, an index that combines BORROWERNO and TITLE into a single key.

Overdue Inquiries by Borrower Name

A simple question as to what titles are overdue and the responsibility of a given borrower is handled differently. While the essential commands could be issued interactively at the dot prompt, they are more conveniently stored in a command file:

```
** BORRFIND.PRG
**  Given a borrower name, lists books overdue
SELECT 2
USE overdue INDEX ovrborno
SELECT 1
```

```
USE register INDEX reglast
SET RELATION TO borrowerno INTO overdue

DO WHILE .T.
    CLEAR
    mname=space(20)
    @ 10, 10 SAY "Borrower name?  " GET mname
    @ 20, 20 SAY "Type surname, followed by <RETURN>"
    @ 22, 20 SAY "  Enter <RETURN> alone to end
     ^^^^ searching"
    READ
    mname=TRIM(mname)
    IF LEN(mname)=0
        CLEAR
        EXIT
    ENDIF
    FIND &mname
    IF .NOT. FOUND()
        CLEAR
        @ 10,10 SAY "That surname is not in the
      ^^^^ registration file"
        @ 20,1 SAY " "
        WAIT
        LOOP
    ELSE
        DO WHILE lastname=mname
            IF UPPER(mtlsdue)="T"
                CLEAR
                ? TRIM(firstname)+" "+TRIM(lastname)
                SELECT 2
                DO WHILE borrowerno=REGISTER->borrowerno
                    ? datedue, title
                    SKIP
                ENDDO  borrowerno check
                SELECT 1
                @ 20,1 SAY " "
                WAIT
            ENDIF
            SKIP
        ENDDO  lastname check
    ENDIF
ENDDO
CLOSE DATABASES
RETURN
```

This is the result of performing DO BORRFIND.PRG and giving "Smith" in response to the full-screen prompt for a last name:

Fred Smith
08/08/86 Library Automation
07/31/86 Thinner

Press any key to continue...

The routine will match on the root or just the first letter of a name. If "S" is specified, for instance, the result is:

Fred Smith
08/08/86 Library Automation
07/31/86 Thinner

Press any key to continue...

Pressing a key as directed brings up a second borrower whose last name begins with "S" and who also has overdue materials:

Blakely Summers
08/05/86 Space
08/04/86 BASIC Handbook
08/08/86 USA for Business Travelers
08/04/86 Thinner

Notices and Bills

Notices and bills are produced by NOTICE.PRG. Here's the program, followed by a demonstration session:

```
** NOTICE.PRG
*Produces printed notices from OVERDUE.PRG/REGISTER.PRG
CLEAR
***  Set up working environment
SELECT 2
USE register INDEX regborno
SELECT 1
USE overdue INDEX ovrborno
SET RELATION TO borrowerno INTO register
***  Prompt for type of notices to be produced
CLEAR
@ 10,10 SAY "What are to be produced?"
answer=" "
@ 12,15 SAY "(F)irst notices,   (S)econd notices,
     ^^^^ (B)ills?  " GET answer
READ
answer=UPPER(answer)
```

```
***   Assign values to WHICH and CUTOFF
DO CASE
    CASE answer="F"
        which="FIRST"
        cutoff=date()-7
    CASE answer="S"
        which="SECOND"
        cutoff=date()-14
    CASE answer="B"
        which="BILL"
        cutoff=date()-21
ENDCASE
***   Display cutoff date, give user chance to change it
@ 15,10 SAY "What is cut-off date prior to which action
    ^^^^ is to be taken?"
@ 17,15 GET cutoff
@ 22,20 SAY "Hit <RETURN> to accept date indicated"
@ 23,25 SAY "New date followed by <RETURN> to change
    ^^^^ cutoff date"
READ
***   Main processing starts here
CLEAR
STORE .F. TO done
DO WHILE .NOT. EOF()
***       Check if date is before cut-off date
***         and notice/bill hasn't already been produced
    IF datedue < cutoff .AND. .NOT. YEAR(&which)>0
      startpt=RECNO()
      mborrower=borrowerno
      ?
      ? SPACE(20)+which+iif(which="BILL"," "," NOTICE")
      ?
***       Select heading for notice
        DO CASE
        CASE which="FIRST"
            ? "The following items charged out to "+
    ^^^^ TRIM(register->firstname)+" "+
    ^^^^ TRIM(register->lastname)
            ? "are overdue.  Please return them as
    ^^^^ soon as possible:"
        CASE which="SECOND"
            ? "Please return the following items,
    ^^^^ charged out to "+TRIM(register->firstname)+
    ^^^^ " "+TRIM(register->lastname)+","
            ? "within 7 days.  A bill for replacement
    ^^^^ cost will follow."
        CASE which="BILL"
```

```
                    ? "The following books, charged out to "+
        ^^^^ TRIM(register->firstname)+" "+trim(register->
        ^^^^ lastname)+" have not been returned."
                    ? "Please return IMMEDIATELY, or pay costs,
        ^^^^ listed below."
            ENDCASE
***         List each title that is overdue
            ?
            ?
            ?  "Title and author"+space(35)+"Due Date"
            ?
            DO WHILE borrowerno=mborrower .AND. .NOT. EOF()
                IF datedue<cutoff
                    ? title, datedue
                    ? "  "+TRIM(authlast)+", "+TRIM
        ^^^^ (authfirst)+ " -- "+ TRIM(callno)
                        IF done
                            REPLACE &which WITH DATE()
                        ENDIF
                ENDIF
                SKIP
            ENDDO
            ?
            ?
            ?
            ?
            ?
        ELSE
            SKIP
            LOOP
        ENDIF
***  Send notice to printer?
IF .NOT. done
    @ 24,5 SAY "(Y)es to confirm and print, (N)o to
     ^^^^ skip printing"
    answer=" "
    @ 24,65 GET answer
    READ
ENDIF

IF UPPER(answer)="Y" .AND. .NOT. done
    SET PRINT ON
    GOTO startpt
    STORE .T. TO done
    CLEAR
    LOOP
ELSE
    SET PRINT OFF
```

```
    STORE .F. TO done
    CLEAR
ENDDO eof

RETURN
```

First, the user is asked to indicate what kind of notices/bills are to be prepared. A default cut-off date is supplied, but the user can override it:

///
        What are to be produced?

        (F)irst notices,   (S)econd notices, (B)ills?   b

What is cut-off date prior to which action is to be taken?

        08/08/86

    Hit <RETURN> to accept date indicated
    New date followed by <RETURN> to change cutoff date

///

The user sees a preview of all the notices, or in this case bills that will be prepared. Only after they have been confirmed are they sent to the printer, and changes made in the relevant data files:

///

BILL

The following books, charged out to Blakely Summers have
not been returned. Please return IMMEDIATELY, or pay
costs, listed below.

Title and author   Due Date

Space   08/05/86
  Michener, James -- Fic
BASIC Handbook   08/04/86
  Lien, David -- 001.64
Thinner   08/04/86
  Bachman, Richard -- Fic
Winds of War   07/28/86
  Wouk, Herman -- FIC Wou

(Y)es to confirm and print, (N)o to skip printing

///

Here's the second bill that, according to the program file, ought
to be issued:

///

BILL

The following books, charged out to Fred Smith have not
been returned. Please return IMMEDIATELY, or pay costs,
listed below.

Title and author   Due Date

Thinner   07/31/86
  Bachman, Richard -- Fic

(Y)es to confirm and print, (N)o to skip printing

///

An Overdues Menu

To knit everything together, ODUES.PRG is provided:

```
* Program..: ODUES.PRG
SET TALK OFF
SET BELL OFF
SET CONFIRM ON

DO WHILE .T.

    * ---Display menu options, centered on the screen.
    *      draw menu border and print heading
    CLEAR
    @ 2, 0 TO 15,79 DOUBLE
    @ 3,20 SAY [O V E R D U E S  - -  M A I N   M E N U]
    @ 4,1 TO 4,78 DOUBLE
    * ---display detail lines
    @  7,27 SAY [1. File Maintenance]
    @  8,27 SAY [2. Query Overdues By Borrower]
    @  9,27 SAY [3. List Overdues By Borrower]
    @ 10,27 SAY [4. Produce Overdue Notices]
    @ 11,27 SAY [5. Statistics]
    @ 13, 27 SAY '0. EXIT'
    STORE 0 TO selectnum
    @ 15,33 SAY " select       "
    @ 15,42 GET selectnum PICTURE "9" RANGE 0,5
    READ

    DO CASE
       CASE selectnum = 0
           SET BELL ON
           SET TALK ON
           CLEAR ALL
           RETURN

       CASE selectnum = 1
       *  DO File Maintenance
           DO maintain

       CASE selectnum = 2
       *  DO Query Overdues By Borrower
           DO borrfind
```

```
        CASE selectnum = 3
        *  DO List Overdues By Borrower
           DO overlast

        CASE selectnum = 4
        *  DO Produce Overdue Notices
           DO notice

        CASE selectnum = 5
        *  DO Statistics
           DO ovrstats

   ENDCASE

   ENDDO T
   RETURN
   * EOF: ODUES.PRG
```

Here is the display it creates (in slightly compressed form):

```
/////////////////////////////////////////////////////////
:=======================================================:
:          O V E R D U E S  - -  M A I N   M E N U      :
:=======================================================:
:                                                       :
:                                                       :
:            1. File Maintenance                        :
:            2. Query Overdues By Borrower              :
:            3. List Overdues By Borrower               :
:            4. Produce Overdue Notices                 :
:            5. Statistics                              :
:                                                       :
:            0. EXIT                                    :
:                                                       :
:================== select 0 ===========================:
/////////////////////////////////////////////////////////
```

Data Entry

APPSGEN.PRG was used to create the skeleton of MAINTAIN.PRG below. To it were added choices for checking overdue materials back in and producing reports.

Selecting choice 1 in the main overdues menu puts the user in the MAINTAIN.PRG submenu:

```
* Program..: MAINTAIN.PRG
DO WHILE .T.

    * ---Display menu options, centered on the screen.
    *      draw menu border and print heading
    CLEAR
    @ 2, 0 TO 15,79 DOUBLE
    @ 3,24 SAY [F I L E   M A I N T E N A N C E]
    @ 4,1 TO 4,78 DOUBLE
    * ---display detail lines
    @  7,30 SAY [1. ADD INFORMATION]
    @  8,30 SAY [2. CHANGE INFORMATION]
    @  9,30 SAY [3. REMOVE INFORMATION]
    @ 10,30 SAY [4. REVIEW INFORMATION]
    @ 11,30 SAY [5. CHECK-IN OVERDUES]
    @ 12,30 SAY [6. PRINT REPORT]
    @ 14, 30 SAY '0. EXIT'
    STORE 0 TO selectnum
    @ 16,33 SAY " select       "
    @ 16,42 GET selectnum PICTURE "9" RANGE 0,5
    READ

    DO CASE
       CASE selectnum = 0
           SET BELL ON
           SET TALK ON
           CLEAR ALL
           RETURN

       CASE selectnum = 1
       *  DO ADD INFORMATION

           USE overdue
           SET SAFETY OFF
           COPY STRUCTURE TO temp
           USE temp
           APPEND
           SET CONFIRM ON
```

```
IF RECCOUNT()>0
    INDEX ON borrowerno TO tempborr UNIQUE
    SET SAFETY ON
    SELECT 2
    USE register INDEX regborno,regbylas
    SELECT 1
    SET RELATION TO borrowerno INTO register
    GO TOP
    CLEAR
    DO WHILE .NOT. EOF()
        IF borrowerno=register->borrowerno
            REPLACE register->mtlsdue WITH "T"
        ELSE
            ? borrowerno+" is not in
^^^^ registration file"
            DELETE
        ENDIF
        SKIP
    ENDDO
    WAIT
    USE overdue INDEX ovborttl,overdate,
^^^^ overauth,overcall,ovrborno,overttl
    SET DELETED ON
    APPEND FROM temp
    SET DELETED OFF
ENDIF
CLOSE DATA

CASE selectnum = 2
*  DO CHANGE INFORMATION

    USE overdue INDEX overttl, ovborttl, overdate,
^^^^ overauth,overcall, ovrborno
    EDIT

    SET CONFIRM OFF
    STORE ' ' TO wait_subst
    @ 23,0 SAY 'Press any key to continue...' GET
^^^^ wait_subst
    READ
    SET CONFIRM ON
    CLOSE DATA

CASE selectnum = 3
*  DO REMOVE INFORMATION

    USE overdue INDEX overttl, ovborttl, overdate,
```

```
^^^^ overauth,overcall, ovrborno
    SET TALK ON
    CLEAR
    @ 2,0 SAY ' '
    ? 'PACKING DATABASE TO REMOVE RECORDS MARKED
^^^^ FOR DELETION'
    PACK

    SET TALK OFF
    SET CONFIRM OFF
    STORE ' ' TO wait_subst
    @ 23,0 SAY 'Press any key to continue...'
^^^^ GET wait_subst
    READ
    SET CONFIRM ON
    CLOSE DATA

 CASE selectnum = 4
 *  DO REVIEW INFORMATION

    USE overdue INDEX overttl, ovborttl, overdate,
^^^^ overauth, overcall, ovrborno
    BROWSE

    SET CONFIRM OFF
    STORE ' ' TO wait_subst
    @ 23,0 SAY 'Press any key to continue...'
^^^^ GET wait_subst
    READ
    SET CONFIRM ON
    CLOSE DATA

 CASE selectnum = 5
 *  DO CHECK-IN OVERDUES
    DO returns

 CASE selectnum = 6
 *  DO PRINT REPORT

    USE overdue INDEX overttl
    SELECT 2
    USE register INDEX regborno
    SELECT 1
    SET RELATION TO borrowerno INTO register
    CLEAR
    answer=" "
    @ 10,10 SAY "Send to (P)rinter or (S)creen?   "
```

```
    ^^^^ GET answer
         READ
         IF UPPER(answer)="P"
             REPORT FORM overrpt TO PRINT
         ELSE
             REPORT FORM overrpt
         ENDIF
         SET CONFIRM OFF
         STORE ' ' TO wait_subst
         ?
         @ 23,0 SAY 'Press any key to continue...'
    ^^^^ GET wait_subst
         READ
         SET CONFIRM ON
ENDCASE

ENDDO T
RETURN
* EOF: MAINTAIN.PRG
```

Overdue Statistics

Here is the program to produce a statistical summary of overdue
activity, followed by its output working with a small demonstration
file:

```
** OVRSTATS.PRG
**   Statistical summary of overdues
SET SAFETY OFF
CLEAR
@ 10,10 SAY "Please wait while statistics are
     ^^^^ tabulated..."
USE OVERDUE
COUNT TO odtotal
COUNT FOR YEAR(bill)>YEAR(CTOD('00/00/00')) TO billtot
COUNT FOR YEAR(second)>YEAR(CTOD('00/00/00')) .AND.
   ^^^^ YEAR(bill)=YEAR(CTOD('00/00/00')) TO secondtot
COUNT FOR YEAR(first)> YEAR(CTOD('00/00/00')) .AND.
   ^^^^ YEAR(second)=YEAR(CTOD('00/00/00')) .AND.
   ^^^^ YEAR(bill)=YEAR(CTOD('00/00/00')) TO firsttot
SUM cost TO costtot FOR YEAR(bill)>YEAR
   ^^^^ (CTOD('00/00/00'))
INDEX ON borrowerno TO tempuniq UNIQUE
COUNT TO uniqtotal
CLEAR
?
```

```
? DTOC(DATE())+SPACE(20)+"Overdue Materials Summary"
?
? "Total Overdues:    "+STR(odtotal)
? "  Billed:            "+STR(billtot)+"     Cost: "+
  ^^^^ STR(costtot,,2)
? "  Second Notices: "+STR(secondtot)
? "  First Notices:  "+STR(firsttot)
? "  Number of Overdue Patrons:  "+STR(uniqtotal)
?
?
CLOSE DATABASES
WAIT
SET SAFETY ON
RETURN
```

///

08/29/86   Overdue Materials Summary

Total Overdues: 7
   Billed: 0   Cost: 0.00
   Second Notices: 1
   First Notices: 6
   Number of Overdue Patrons: 2

Press any key to continue...

///

RESERVES

Reserves--books currently unavailable that are to be provided to a patron when they do become available--are the subject of this discussion. While reserves are best handled in conjunction with a computer-based circulation system (see the section on circulation), they can also be significantly expedited on a stand-alone basis using *dBase III+*.

I am assuming the existence of a separate *dBase* file containing name and address information about patrons. REGISTER.DBF, as discussed in the section on registration of library users, is a suitable model. Absent such a file, modifications will have to be made to the approach presented here to enter patron data each time a reserve is added to the system.

A separate bibliographic file listing all materials held by the library would make reserves processing much easier. Its existence is also assumed.

We will want to produce:

1. List of books and the number of reserves for them
2. List of reserves more than a specific number of days old
3. List of reserves and patrons by title
4. List of reserves and patrons by patron

We must be able to handle such queries as:

1. Who is waiting for a particular title?
2. What books are on reserve for a particular patron?
3. How many patrons are ahead of a particular patron waiting for a specific book?

Data Structure

The structure of REGISTER.DBF is the same as in the previous section on overdues, except for the addition of the field RESERVED to indicate that at least one title has been put on reserve for the borrower:

```
Structure for database: C:register.dbf
Number of data records:       5
Date of last update   : 08/23/86
Field  Field Name  Type        Width    Dec
    1  BORROWERNO  Character       5
```

```
       2   FIRSTNAME   Character     15
       3   LASTNAME    Character     20
       4   ADR2        Character     35
       5   ADR3        Character     35
       6   CITY        Character     15
       7   STATE       Character      2
       8   ZIP         Character      9
       9   PHONE       Character     15
      10   ISSUEDATE   Date           8
      11   RESIDENCE   Character     15
      12   MESSAGES    Logical        1
      13   MTLSDUE     Character      1
      14   RESERVED    Character      1
** Total **                        178
```

BIB.DBF is a greatly simplified bibliographic file which saves a library staff member from having to manually enter a lot of information about the title being placed on reserve. It isn't essential to doing reserves with a computer, but it certainly makes things easier:

```
Structure for database: a:bib.dbf
Number of data records:       7
Date of last update   : 08/08/86
Field   Field Name  Type        Width    Dec
    1   BOOKNO      Character       5
    2   TITLE       Character      50
    3   AUTHFIRST   Character      15
    4   AUTHLAST    Character      20
    5   COPYNO      Character       2
    6   CALLNO      Character      15
    7   RESERVED    Character       1
** Total **                       109
```

RESERVES.DBF is a transaction record. All bibliographic and patron information is stored in other files:

```
Structure for database: C:reserves.dbf
Number of data records:       8
Date of last update   : 08/23/86
Field   Field Name   Type        Width    Dec
    1   BORROWERNO   Character       5
    2   BOOKNO       Character       5
    3   RSVDATE      Date            8
** Total **                        19
```

Adding Reserves

The program RSVADD.PRG handles adding reserves to the list maintained in *dBase III+*. It follows these steps:

1. Prompts for a borrower number, finds the borrower name to which it corresponds
2. Reports borrower name and asks for confirmation
3. Asks for the title to be put on reserve
4. Presents a list of all titles matching the title term entered and asks which is to be put on reserve
5. Shows both borrower and title information and gives user one last chance to back out of placing the reserve
6. Upon confirmation, enters new record in RESERVES.DBF, stores "T" to RESERVED in both BIB.DBF and REGISTER.DBF

Here's the listing:

```
** RSVADD.PRG
*Adds reserves information to RESERVES.DBF, BIB.DBF and
**       REGISTER.DBF
close data
SET BELL OFF
USE reserves INDEX rsvborrn, rsvbibno
SELECT 2
USE register INDEX regborno
SELECT 3
USE bib INDEX bibtitle

set talk off
DO WHILE .T.
   CLEAR
   mborrno=SPACE(5)
   @ 10,10 SAY "Borrower Number " GET mborrno PICTURE
    ^^^^ '99999'
   @ 17,10 SAY "To exit, hit <RETURN> alone"
   READ
   @ 17,10
   IF LEN(TRIM(mborrno))=0
       CLEAR
       EXIT
   ENDIF
   SELECT 2
   FIND &mborrno
   IF .NOT. FOUND()
       @ 15,10 SAY "There is no borrower with the
    ^^^^ number "+mborrno
```

```
    @ 16,15 SAY "registered at this library.
^^^^ Please check and "
    @ 17,15 SAY "re-enter."
    @ 22,1 SAY " "
    WAIT
    LOOP
ELSE
    @ 15,10 SAY "Book(s) will be reserved for "+
^^^^ TRIM(firstname)+" "+TRIM(lastname)
    answer=" "
    @ 22,10 SAY "(N)o to abort, <RETURN> to
^^^^ confirm" GET answer
    READ
    @ 22,10
    IF UPPER(answer)="N"
        LOOP
    ENDIF
ENDIF

SELECT 3
DO WHILE .T.
    mtitle=SPACE(50)
    @ 17,10 SAY "Title?  " GET mtitle
    @ 22,20 SAY "<RETURN> alone discontinues
^^^^ transaction"
    READ
    @ 22,20
    mtitle=TRIM(mtitle)
    IF LEN(mtitle)=0
        EXIT
    ENDIF
    FIND &mtitle
    IF .NOT. FOUND()
        @ 17,10
        @ 17,10 SAY "Title is not listed.
^^^^ Please re-enter."
        @ 22,1 SAY " "
        WAIT
        @ 16,0 CLEAR TO 23,79
        LOOP
    ENDIF
    CLEAR
    ctr=0
    ? "-------------- Titles That Match
^^^^ ----------------"
    ?
    ?
```

```
        DO WHILE TITLE=mtitle
            ctr=ctr+1
            ? STR(ctr,2)+"  "+TRIM(title)+
    ^^^^ IIF(copyno>"1",", Copy # "+copyno," ")
            SKIP
        ENDDO
        answer=" "
        ?
        ?
        ?
        ACCEPT "Which title? " TO answer
        SKIP -(ctr-VAL(answer)+1)
        CLEAR
        @ 15,10 SAY "A reserve will be placed on "
        @ 16,20 SAY title
        @ 18,10 SAY "For "+TRIM(register->firstname)+
    ^^^^ " "+TRIM(register->lastname)+", Card # "+
    ^^^^ register->borrowerno
        answer=" "
        @ 22,10 SAY "<RETURN> to confirm, (N)o to
    ^^^^ abort" GET answer
        READ
        @ 22,10
        IF UPPER(answer)="N"
            abandon="T"
            EXIT
        ELSE
            CLEAR
            abandon="F"
            EXIT
        ENDIF
    ENDDO
    IF abandon<>"T"
        SELECT 1
        REPLACE register->reserved WITH "T"
        REPLACE bib->reserved WITH "T"
        APPEND BLANK
        REPLACE borrowerno WITH register->borrowerno
        REPLACE bookno WITH bib->bookno
        REPLACE rsvdate WITH DATE()
    ENDIF
ENDDO
CLOSE DATA
RETURN
SET TALK ON
SET BELL ON
```

Querying the Database and Performing Deletions

Having the ability to delete entries in the reserves system in combination with a general query facility is convenient. RSVQRY.PRG searches the system by title or borrower, at the user's choice, and lists the reserves that correspond to it. Along the way, the user may choose whether to delete one of the transactions.

Note the use of relative addressing to display information using the @ ... SAY construction. A counter, called CTR here, is increased by one every time a line is sent to the screen. It is used to position each succeeding line when it is added to a base value, held in MROW. While at first the construction @ MROW+CTR,10 SAY (whatever) looks unwieldy, it is actually a great convenience and a source of substantial flexibility in screen design. Changing MROW in one spot will cause the entire screen to be shifted vertically. Using a variable rather than the number 10 for the column position would have left even greater leeway to change things later on.

Keep in mind that there is a maximum of twenty-four allowable values for the vertical coordinates of an @ ... SAY command. An error condition will bring everything to a halt if you attempt to increase MROW+CTR beyond that limit within a program file.

In this circumstance, we could have that problem if we attempted to search on a very short segment of a name or title. Specifying "S" rather than "Smith" might cause problems. Use of the ON ERROR construction and multiple display screens would be a tricky but feasible way of handling the problem.

Notice also how the same program segments are used to make inquiries both by borrower and by title. This is made possible by use of macros, variables preceded with a "&" that can represent the names (as opposed to the contents) of other variables.

Annotations within the listing that follows further explain what each section of the routine does:

```
** RSVQRY.PRG
*    Makes inquiries into reserves systems, allows for
*    deletions

SET TALK OFF

DO WHILE .T.
```

```
*    *** Ask for type of inquiry, name/title to search
     CLEAR
     answer=" "
     findterm=SPACE(30)
     @ 10,10 SAY "Inquiry by (T)itle or (B)orrower?
      ^^^^ ( (E)xit )" GET answer
     @ 13,10 SAY "To be located: " GET findterm
     READ

     IF UPPER(answer)="E"
         CLEAR
         CLOSE DATA
         EXIT
     ENDIF

     IF .NOT. UPPER(answer) $"TB"
         LOOP
     ENDIF

     IF LEN(TRIM(findterm))=0
         LOOP
     ENDIF

     findterm=TRIM(findterm)

*    *** Set up for a title query

     IF UPPER(answer)="T"
         SELE 3
         USE register INDEX regborno
         SELE 2
         USE reserves INDEX rsvbibno, rsvborrno
         SET RELATION TO borrowerno INTO register
         SELE 1
         USE bib INDEX bibttl
         SET RELATION TO bookno INTO reserves
         mfindtype="Title"
         mfindfld="title"
         orderfld="bookno"
         opporder="borrowerno"
         mretrieve="TRIM(register->firstname)+' '+
             TRIM(register->lastname)"
         moreflds="TRIM(callno)+'  Copy: '+copyno"
     ENDIF
*    *** Set up for borrower query

     IF UPPER(answer)="B"
         SELE 3
```

```
            USE bib INDEX bibno
            SELE 2
            USE reserves INDEX rsvborrno, rsvbibno
            SET RELATION TO bookno INTO bib
            SELE 1
            USE register INDEX reglast
            SET RELATION TO borrowerno INTO reserves
            mfindtype="Borrower"
            mfindfld="TRIM(lastname)+', '+TRIM(firstname)"
            orderfld="borrowerno"
            opporder="bookno"
            mretrieve="TRIM(c->title)"
            moreflds="borrowerno"
        ENDIF

        FIND &findterm
        IF .NOT. FOUND()
            CLOSE DATA
            LOOP
        ENDIF

*       *** Display multiple matches on title/name

        CLEAR
        ctr=1
        mrow=2
        DO WHILE &mfindfld=findterm
            IF reserved="T"
                @ mrow+ctr,10 SAY STR(ctr,2)+'  '+
^^^^ TRIM(&mfindfld)+' '+&moreflds
                ctr=ctr+1
            ENDIF
            SKIP
        ENDDO

        IF ctr=1
            CLEAR
            @ 10,20 SAY "This &mfindtype has no reserves"
            @ 22,1 SAY " "
            WAIT
            CLOSE DATA
            LOOP
          ENDIF

*       *** Select from among the matches

        mnum=" "
```

```
@ mrow+ctr+2,10 SAY "Which &mfindtype is to be
^^^^ processed? " GET mnum
mnum=VAL(mnum)
READ
SKIP -(ctr-mnum)
DO WHILE reserved<>"T"
    SKIP-1
ENDDO
CLEAR
```

```
*     *** Display reserves involving title/borrower,
*     *** select which one to process
```

```
mrow=2
ctr=1
@ mrow, 10 SAY TRIM(&mfindfld)+' '+&moreflds
SELE 2
? "bookno, a->bookno"+bookno+a->bookno
DO WHILE &orderfld=A->&orderfld
    @ mrow+ctr,10 SAY STR(ctr,2)+' '+
^^^^ DTOC(rsvdate)+'  '+&mretrieve
    ctr=ctr+1
    SKIP
ENDDO
answer=" "
mnum=" "
@ mrow+ctr+2,10 SAY "Which reserve is to be
^^^^ processed? " GET mnum
mnum=VAL(mnum)
@ mrow+ctr+4,10 SAY "(D)elete, (C)ontinue "
^^^^ GET answer
READ
SKIP -(ctr-mnum)
CLEAR
SELE 3
crecno=recno()
SELE 2
```

```
IF UPPER(answer)="C"
    CLOSE DATA
    LOOP
ENDIF
```

```
*     *** Processing of deletions starts here
```

```
IF UPPER(answer)="D"
    DELETE
    morder1=&orderfld
```

```
        morder2=&opporder

* Check whether there are any other reserves for this
* title/borrower.  If not, mark record to be packed out
* of existence, change reserved flag.

        SET DELETED ON
        FIND &morder1
        topack=.F.
        IF .NOT. FOUND()
            SELE 1
            REPLACE A->reserved with "F"
            SELE 2
            topack=.T.
        ENDIF

** Check whether this is last reserve for a particular
** book/patron.  If so, change reserved flag.

        SET ORDER TO 2
        FIND &morder2
        IF .NOT. FOUND()
            SELE 3
            GOTO crecno
            REPLACE C->reserved with "F"
            SELE 2
            topack=.T.
        ENDIF

*     *** Wind things up

        SET ORDER TO 1
        SET DELETED OFF
        IF topack
            PACK
        ENDIF
        SELECT 1
    ENDIF
    CLOSE DATA
ENDDO
RETURN
```

Reserves List by Date

Printing a list of reserves by date is easy. While it could be done interactively, the tedium of setting up file relationships makes a short command file far more attractive:

```
** RSVBYDAT.PRG
CLEAR
answer=" "
@ 10,20 SAY "Send to printer as well as screen?
     ^^^^ (Y/N)" GET answer
READ
IF UPPER(answer)="Y"
    printspec=" TO PRINT"
ENDIF
USE reserves INDEX rsvdate
SELE 3
USE bib INDEX bibno
SELE 2
USE register INDEX regbornorn
SET RELATION TO reserves->bookno INTO bib
SELE 1
SET RELATION TO borrowerno INTO register
REPORT FORM rsvbydat
CLOSE DATA
RETURN
```

Here are the results of a run on a small sample file:

Page No.   1
08/23/86

                                Materials on Reserve
                                  Arranged by Date

Reserve   Title   Reserved for...
Date

** Reserve Date: 07/29/86
  07/29/86 Space   Summers, Blakely

** Reserve Date: 08/01/86
  08/01/86 Thinner   Smith, Fred

** Reserve Date: 08/08/86
  08/08/86 Thinner   Smith, Fred
  08/08/86 Space   Smith, Fred

** Reserve Date: 08/18/86
  08/18/86 BASIC Handbook   Summers, Blakely

```
** Reserve Date: 08/23/86
  08/23/86 Library Automation          Summers, Blakely
  08/23/86 Space                       Senter, Edward
```

Reserves Sorted by Borrower and Title

REPORT FORM doesn't lend itself to producing reports sorted by borrower name or title. To do that, another short command file is necessary. The key to making it work is the index file REGBYRSV.NDX. It arranges REGISTER.DBF first by the contents of the field RESERVED, placing all books on reserve within easy reach of one another, and then by the first ten characters of the last name.

The command file works its way down through the records corresponding to books on reserve. In processing each record, a search is done for all RESERVES.DBF entries corresponding to a given borrower number. Whether there is one book or fifty books on reserve for a given borrower, they will all come up this way.

Here is the command file to produce a list by borrower name:

```
** RSVBYBOR.PRG
CLEAR
answer=" "
@ 10,20 SAY "Send to printer as well as screen?
     ^^^^ (Y/N)" GET answer
READ
IF UPPER(answer)="Y"
    SET PRINT ON
ENDIF
SELE 3
USE bib INDEX bibno
SELE 2
USE reserves INDEX rsvborrn
SET RELATION TO bookno INTO bib
SELE 1
USE register INDEX regbyrsv
SET RELATION TO borrowerno INTO reserves

FIND T
CLEAR
DO WHILE reserved="T" .AND. .NOT. EOF()
    ? SPACE(30)+TRIM(lastname)+", "+TRIM(firstname)
    mborrower=borrowerno
```

```
      SELE 2
      DO WHILE borrowerno=mborrower
          ? SPACE(25)+DTOC(rsvdate)+"   "+TRIM(bib->title)
          SKIP
      ENDDO
      ?
      SELE 1
      SKIP
ENDDO
SET PRINT OFF
RETURN
```

It produces a list of reserves by borrower name like this:

```
                    Senter, Edward
          08/23/86  Space

                    Smith, Fred
          08/01/86  Thinner
          08/08/86  Thinner
          08/08/86  Space

                    Smith, Frances
          08/23/86  Winds of War

                    Summers, Blakely
          07/29/86  Space
          08/18/86  BASIC Handbook
          08/23/86  Library Automation
```

A parallel pattern can be used to produce a list by title of books on reserve:

```
** RSVBYTIL.PRG
CLEAR
answer=" "
@ 10,20 SAY "Send to printer as well as screen?
      ^^^^ (Y/N)" GET answer
READ
IF UPPER(answer)="Y"
    SET PRINT ON
ENDIF
SELE 3
USE register INDEX regborno
SELE 2
USE reserves INDEX rsvbibno
SET RELATION TO borrowerno INTO register
```

```
SELE 1
USE bib INDEX bibbyrsv
SET RELATION TO bookno INTO reserves

FIND T
CLEAR
DO WHILE reserved="T" .AND. .NOT. EOF()
    ? SPACE(30)+TRIM(title)
    mbibno=bookno
    SELE 2
    DO WHILE bookno=mbibno
        ? SPACE(25)+DTOC(rsvdate)+"  "+TRIM(register->
    ^^^^ lastname)+", "+TRIM(register->firstname)
        SKIP
    ENDDO
    ?
    SELE 1
    SKIP
ENDDO
SET PRINT OFF
RETURN
```

Here is the result:

```
                    BASIC Handbook
           08/18/86  Summers, Blakely

                    Library Automation
           08/23/86  Summers, Blakely

                    Space
           07/29/86  Summers, Blakely
           08/08/86  Smith, Fred
           08/23/86  Senter, Edward

                    Thinner
           08/08/86  Smith, Fred

                    Thinner
           08/01/86  Smith, Fred

                    Winds of War
           08/23/86  Smith, Frances
```

CIRCULATION

We've looked at patron registration files, overdues, and reserves. Now we'll add control of circulation transactions to come up with a complete, albeit rudimentary, circulation system using *dBase III+*.

Data Structure

The REGISTER.DBF, OVERDUE.DBF, and RESERVES.DBF files will be used without change. We will, however, have to create (CREATE) one new data file, CIRC.DBF, and add a circulation status field (INCIRC) to the bibliographic file, BIB.DBF. Here is the structure of the latter two files:

```
Structure for database: C:circ.dbf
Number of data records:        0
Date of last update   : 08/24/86
Field   Field Name  Type        Width     Dec
    1   BIBNO       Character       5
    2   BORROWERNO  Character       5
    3   DATEDUE     Date            8
** Total **                       19
```

```
Structure for database: a:bib.dbf
Number of data records:        7
Date of last update   : 08/08/86
Field   Field Name  Type        Width     Dec
    1   BOOKNO      Character       5
    2   TITLE       Character      50
    3   AUTHFIRST   Character      15
    4   AUTHLAST    Character      20
    5   COPYNO      Character       2
    6   CALLNO      Character      15
    7   RESERVED    Character       1
    8   INCIRC      Character       1
** Total **                      110
```

CIRC.DBF is a very small but indispensable file. DATEDUE is the only piece of original information it contains. BORROWERNO and BIBNO serve to connect other files and fields. The circulation file is just a bridge for connecting bibliographic and borrower information. As such, it is similar to RESERVES.DBF.

In general, transactions involving information from several large files are conveniently handled in the following fashion.

Check-Out

The process of checking out a book involves the following steps:

1. Prompt for the borrower's card number.
2. Check it against the registration file to make sure it is valid. Display corresponding name and ask for confirmation.
3. See if there are any overdues outstanding or any messages waiting for the borrower.
4. Prompt for each title number in turn. The number is input either by keyboard entry or a barcode wand connected in series with the keyboard.
5. Check to make sure the correct item is being checked out, and that there are no outstanding reserves on it. There shouldn't be if check-in procedures are working properly, but it's an imperfect world.
6. Store transactions in memory variables. When user indicates no more titles are to be entered, display all those to be checked out, give user last chance to abort transactions.
7. Add record to CIRC.DBF with BIBNO, BORROWERNO, and DATEDUE; change INCIRC to "T" in BIB.DBF.

The routine to accomplish these steps, CIRCOUT.PRG, is included below. Comments within the program file indicate which of the steps above is being accomplished in each section.

Let's look at what CIRCOUT.PRG does. An abbreviated, sample circulation file lists the following items as being in circulation:

```
. LIST
```

Record#	BIBNO	BORROWERNO	DATEDUE
1	00111	33228	09/03/86
2	11322	88832	09/05/86
3	23132	44328	08/30/86

A segment of the bibliographic file might list the following items in the collection:

```
. LIST bookno, incirc, TRIM(title)
```

Record#	bookno	incirc	TRIM(title)
1	00101	F	Space
2	00102	F	BASIC Handbook
3	00103	F	USA for Business Travelers
4	00104	F	Library Automation
5	00105	F	Thinner

```
6  00106  F     Thinner
7  00107  F     Winds of War
```

//
Checking Out Materials

Card number of borrower: [   ]

<RETURN> alone to exit check-out operations

//

The program comes back and asks for confirmation that the right borrower has been located in the registration file:

//

Borrower: Fred Smith   Card # 14422

<RETURN> if correct, (N)ot correct

//

The next screen suggests that the borrower be reminded of some overdue materials:

//

Borrower: Fred Smith   Card # 14422

Overdue Materials Reminder

08/08/86 Library Automation

07/31/86 Thinner
<RETURN> to continue, <ESC> to abort

//

The screen after that reports any messages that have been stored in MESSAGE.DBF (see section on registration for explanation of how the file works and what goes into it):

//

Borrower: Fred Smith   Card # 14422

                    MESSAGES:

Claims 5 books returned that we've never found.

    <RETURN> to continue, <ESC> to abort

//

Finally, we get around to checking out materials. An automatic check is made to see whether any title checked out is on reserve for someone else and has just slipped by in the check-in process. The second title number specified on the following screen was on reserve, and the library staff person had to decide whether to ignore the reserve and complete the circulation or put the book aside.

//

Borrower: Fred Smith   Card # 14422

               Check out of materials

       00103   USA for Business T

       00104   Reserves

                  Ignore? Y/N

      Press <ESC> to finish entering book numbers

//

The operator decided to check out the book anyway:

//

Borrower: Fred Smith   Card # 14422

Check out of materials

00103   USA for Business T

00104   Library Automation

Press <ESC> to finish entering book numbers

//

A final confirmation is required after pressing ESC to finish entering book numbers:

//

Borrower: Fred Smith   Card # 14422

Check out of materials

00103   USA for Business T

00104   Library Automation

CONFIRM TRANSACTION? (Y/N), <ESC> to abandon

//

This is how things look after running CIRCOUT.PRG and checking out a few books:

```
. LIST bookno, incirc, TRIM(title)
Record#  bookno incirc trim(title)
      1  00101  F      Space
      2  00102  F      BASIC Handbook
      3  00103  T      USA for Business Travelers
      4  00104  T      Library Automation
      5  00105  F      Thinner
```

```
         6  00106  F       Thinner
         7  00107  T       Winds of War

. USE circ
. LIST
Record#  BIBNO  BORROWERNO  DATEDUE
         1  00111  33228       09/03/86
         2  11322  88832       09/05/86
         3  23132  44328       08/30/86
         4  00103  00092       09/14/86
         5  00107  14422       09/14/86
         6  00104  14422       09/14/86
```

dBase III+ can be annoying in an application like this. Only fifteen files of all types may be open at any one time. CIRCOUT.PRG comes very close to butting up against this limitation. It would have, in fact, if the files in work areas 1 and 2 were not alternately opened and closed near the end of the program. Here's what the working environment looks like while the program is executing:

```
. DISPLAY STATUS
Currently Selected Database:
Select area:  2, Database in Use: C:register.dbf
      ^^^^ Alias: REGISTER
   Master index file: C:regborno.ndx  Key: borrowerno
   Related into: OVERDUE
   Relation: borrowerno

Select area:  3, Database in Use: C:overdue.dbf
      ^^^^ Alias: OVERDUE
   Master index file:  C:ovrborno.ndx   Key: borrowerno
   Related into: MESSAGES
   Relation: register->borrowerno

Select area:  4, Database in Use: C:messages.dbf
      ^^^^ Alias: MESSAGES
   Master index file:  C:msgborno.ndx  Key: borrowerno

Select area:  5, Database in Use: C:bib.dbf
      ^^^^ Alias: BIB
   Master index file:  C:bibno.ndx  Key: bookno
   Related into: RESERVES
   Relation: bookno

Select area:  6, Database in Use: C:reserves.dbf
      ^^^^ Alias: RESERVES
```

Master index file: C:rsvbibno.ndx Key: bookno

Purists will point out that files can be opened and closed during the course of program execution and stay well within the maximum. After all, lots of folks got along with the limitation of just two database files open simultaneously in *dBase II*. It is still a pain in the neck to have to worry about opening and closing files in the middle of a program. It is not only easier but more logical and understandable to open them at the outset and not worry about them until later.

Check-in Outline

Check-in will not be represented by a working model of program code. Instead, here is an outline for a check-in routine:

1. Request entry of book numbers one at a time. Display title, borrower, and due date.
2. Check to see if there are reserves. If so, enter reserves-processing routine.
3. Check to see if the book was overdue. If so, update overdues file.
4. Request user confirmation, then delete record from CIRC.DBF.

Check-out Program Listing

Here's the circulation check-out program:

```
** CIRCOUT.PRG
**    Circulation system check-out module

SELE 6
USE reserves INDEX rsvbibno
SELE 5
USE bib INDEX bibno
SET RELATION TO bookno INTO reserves
SELE 4
USE messages INDEX msgborno
SELE 3
USE overdue INDEX ovrborno
SELE 2
USE register INDEX regborno
SET RELATION TO borrowerno INTO overdue
SELE 3
SET RELATION TO register->borrowerno INTO messages
```

```
DO WHILE .T.
*    *** Prompt for the borrower's card number.
     SELE 1
     CLEAR
     mborrno=SPACE(5)
     @ 2,30 SAY "Checking Out Materials"
     @ 8,20 SAY "Card number of borrower: " GET mborrno
      ^^^^ PICTURE '99999'
     @ 22,30 SAY "<RETURN> alone to exit check-out
      ^^^^ operations"
     READ
     IF LEN(TRIM(mborrno))=0
         CLOSE DATA
         CLEAR
         EXIT
     ENDIF

*Check number against registration file to make sure it
*        exists, confirm it belongs to borrower at hand
     SELE 2
     FIND &mborrno
     IF .NOT. FOUND()
       CLEAR
       @ 10,40 SAY mborrno+" is not in registration file"
       @ 22,2 SAY " "
       WAIT
       LOOP
     ENDIF

     CLEAR
     @ 3,20 SAY "Borrower: "+TRIM(firstname)+"  "+
      ^^^^ TRIM(lastname)+SPACE (20)+"Card # "+borrowerno
     answer=" "
     @ 6,30 SAY "<RETURN> if correct, (N)ot correct "
      ^^^^ GET answer
     READ
     IF LEN(TRIM(answer))>0
         LOOP
     ENDIF
     @ 6,1

*See if there are any overdues outstanding or any
*     messages waiting for the borrower.
     SELE 3
     IF borrowerno=mborrno
         @ 6,30 SAY "Overdue Materials Reminder"
         mrow=row()+1
```

```
        ctr=1
        DO WHILE borrowerno=mborrno
            @ mrow+ctr,10 SAY DTOC(datedue)+"   "+
   ^^^^ TRIM(title)
            ctr=ctr+1
            SKIP
        ENDDO
        answer=" "
        @ 22,2 SAY "<RETURN> to continue, <ESC> to abort
   ^^^^ " GET                    answer
        READ
        IF READKEY()=12 .OR. READKEY()=268
            LOOP
        ENDIF
    ENDIF


    SELE 4
    IF borrowerno=mborrno
        @ 6,0 CLEAR
        @ 6,30 SAY "MESSAGES: "
        DO WHILE borrowerno=mborrno
            ?
            ? TRIM(message)
            SKIP
        ENDDO
        answer=" "
        @ 22,2 SAY "<RETURN> to continue, <ESC> to
   ^^^^ abort " GET
                answer
        READ
        IF READKEY()=12 .OR. READKEY()=268
            LOOP
        ENDIF
    ENDIF


*   *** Prompt for each title number in turn.  The
*       number is supplied either by keyboard entry or
*       a bar code wand connected in series with the
*       keyboard.
    SELE 5
    @ 6,0 CLEAR
    @ 6,30 SAY "Check out of materials"
    mrow=row()+1
    ctr=1
    mctr=1
    offset=0
    incremented = .F.
    DO WHILE .T.
        mbibno=SPACE(5)
```

```
        @ mrow+ctr,10+offset GET mbibno PICTURE '99999'
        @ 22,10 SAY "Press <ESC> to finish entering
^^^^ book numbers"
     READ
     IF READKEY()=12 .OR. READKEY()=268
        EXIT
     ENDIF
     IF LEN(TRIM(mbibno))<5
        LOOP
     ENDIF
     FIND &mbibno
     IF FOUND()

* Check whether a reserve on the book has slipped by
            IF bib->reserved="T"
                @ mrow+ctr,20+offset SAY "Reserves"
                answer=" "
                @ mrow+ctr+1,20 SAY "Ignore? Y/N"
^^^^ GET answer
                READ
                IF UPPER(answer)="Y"
                    @ mrow+ctr,20+offset
                    @ mrow+ctr+1,1
                ELSE
                    @ mrow+ctr,0
                    @ mrow+ctr+1,0
                    LOOP
                ENDIF
            ENDIF

*    *** Display book number, part of title
            @ mrow+ctr,10+offset SAY mbibno
            @ mrow+ctr,20+offset SAY SUBSTR(title,1,18)
            mitem="mitem"+IIF(mctr<10,STR(mctr,1),
^^^^ STR(mctr,2))
            &mitem=mbibno
            ctr=ctr+1
            mctr=mctr+1
     ELSE
            @ mrow+ctr,20+offset SAY "Not found"
            WAIT
            @ mrow+ctr,20+offset
            @ mrow+ctr+1,0
     ENDIF

*** Start a second column if more than 10 books to be
*       checked out.
```

```
            IF ctr>10 .AND. .NOT. incremented
                ctr=ctr-10
                offset=30
                incremented=.T.
            ENDIF
        ENDDO
        answer=" "


*    *** Confirm list of items to be checked out.
*        Start over if list is wrong
        DO WHILE answer<>"Y"
            @ 22,0
            @ 22,20 SAY "CONFIRM TRANSACTION? (Y/N),
    ^^^^ <ESC> to abandon" GET answer
            READ SAVE
            IF UPPER(answer)="Y"
                CLEAR GETS
                repctr=1


*    *** Set the in-circulation flag in BIB.DBF
                DO WHILE repctr<mctr
                    mitem="mitem"+IIF(repctr<10,
    ^^^^ STR(repctr,1),STR(repctr,2))
                    mbookno=&mitem
                    FIND &mbookno
                    REPLACE incirc WITH "T"
                    repctr=repctr+1
                ENDDO
                SELE 2
                USE


* Add new records to the circulation transaction file
                SELE 1
                USE circ
                repctr=1
                DO WHILE repctr<mctr
                    APPEND BLANK
                    mitem="mitem"+IIF(repctr<10,
    ^^^^ STR(repctr,1),STR(repctr,2))
                    mbookno=&mitem
                    REPLACE bibno WITH mbookno
                    REPLACE borrowerno WITH mborrno
                    REPLACE datedue WITH date()+21
                    repctr=repctr+1
                ENDDO


*** Swapping files around to keep under 15 file limit.
                USE
```

```
            SELE  2
            USE register INDEX regborno
            SET RELATION TO borrowerno INTO overdue
            EXIT
        ELSE
            EXIT
        ENDIF
    ENDDO

ENDDO
RETURN
```

STATISTICS

Electronic spreadsheets like *Lotus 1-2-3* and *VisiCalc* come to most people's minds when a need arises for doing financial and statistical calculations on a small computer. There is a good reason for that. Spreadsheets are easier to learn than any other type of software capable of dicing and slicing numerical values. They are easy because the row and column format continuously puts a maximum amount of data (as well as the relationships that have been defined among elements of the data) before the eyes of the user.

When one value changes, all others that are related to it immediately change as well. If the concepts don't all make sense at first, observe the results of commands on the values contained in the spreadsheet.

dBase does almost everything a good spreadsheet does and more. The problem is that *dBase* does numerical manipulations less obviously and in a different manner. With *dBase*, rows and columns are not on view all the time. The BROWSE mode can be used to gain a semblance of the effect, but it is only a clumsy half-effort.

Moreover, there are major differences in the way relationships are defined and dependent values calculated. A spreadsheet cell may contain a formula referring to the contents of other cells. The first cell's value is determined by the values in the cells to which it is connected by the formula. The relationship is permanent, although the actual value will change as those upon which it depends change. From the standpoint of *dBase III*, such calculated fields are redundant, unnecessary baggage. Why carry along fields in every record that contain values that could be constructed at any time with the appropriate command or report form formula?

With *dBase*, it is very easy to specify subsets of data over which calculations are to be made. Three or four field conditions connected with .AND., .OR., and .NOT. offer a powerful yet compact discriminatory capability.

Every library generates quantitative information pertaining to its support, services, and usage. When the calculation and presentation of statistics start to take a significant amount of working time, a small computer could reduce the workload.

Rather than construct a small dummy file of figures from some hypothetical library, we will use instead STATS.83, a database of statistics about public library operations in Maine during the year 1983. (1984 statistics are available, but haven't been loaded into *dBase* yet. 1985 may leapfrog them). Statistics for a single library for a series of years or months could be treated much the same way.

Structure

The data structure of STATS83.DBF contains a minimum of redundant data. There is no reason to carry fields for per capita circulation, turnover rate, and similar ratios. They can be generated on the fly with extremely modest effort.

There are two population figures in the structure below: LPOP and TPOP. The first is the library population served. Our practice is to consider that a particular library is serving the entire population of the community in which it is located, even if there are other public libraries in that community. All per capita figures are based on LPOP. Population totals for groups of libraries would be skewed, however, if the populations of communities with more than one library were counted more than once. Thus all summary calculations get population figures from the TPOP (town population field). TPOP is only filled in for what is judged the principal library in each town.

```
Structure for database: A:stats83.dbf
Number of data records:      227
Date of last update   : 06/13/86
Field   Field Name  Type        Width    Dec
   1    TOWN        Character      15
   2    DISTRICT    Character       1
   3    COUNTY      Character      15
   4    LPOP        Numeric         6
   5    TPOP        Numeric         6
   6    LIBRARY     Character      40
   7    HOURS       Character      10
   8    WHOURS      Numeric         2
   9    SHOURS      Numeric         2
  10    COLL        Numeric         7
  11    CIRC        Numeric         7
  12    SAL         Numeric        10       2
  13    BOOKS       Numeric        10       2
  14    TOWNAPP     Numeric        11       2
  15    TOTEXP      Numeric        11       2
  16    ILL         Numeric         6
** Total **                      160
```

The multiple figures for hours open to the public derive from the format in which the information was originally imported into *dBase III+*. Storing it temporarily as a text field gives us the time to work through the file and strip off figures for winter and summer hours and assign them to the proper numeric fields for use in calculations.

The contents of a typical data record look like this in EDIT mode:

```
//////////////////////////////////////////////////////
Record No.     225
TOWN           [Bangor          ]
DISTRICT       [N]
COUNTY         [Penobscot       ]
LPOP           [ 31643]
TPOP           [ 31643]
LIBRARY        [Bangor Public Library                    ]
HOURS          [ 68-W 50-S]
WHOURS         [68]
SHOURS         [50]
COLL           [ 477048]
CIRC           [ 469167]
SAL            [ 431779.00]
BOOKS          [ 153883.00]
TOWNAPP        [  304500.00]
TOTEXP         [  859954.00]
ILL            [       ]
//////////////////////////////////////////////////////
```

Let's make a list of libraries with a high per capita rate of circulation:

```
. USE STATS83 INDEX stattown
. LIST town, lpop, circ FOR circ/lpop>10
Record#   town                 lpop    circ
    225   Bangor              31643   469167
    168   Belfast              6243    75148
     49   Blue Hill            1644    92502
     50   Boothbay Harbor      2207    31359
      8   Bremen                598     6695
      9   Brooklin              619    14134
    121   Camden               4584    67040
*** INTERRUPTED ***
```

We forgot to specify display of the per capita rate. One touch of the up-arrow key enables us to retrieve the previous command and add that value, as well as suppressing the record number display and changing the cut-off to twelve circulations per capita rather than ten:

```
. LIST town, lpop, circ, circ/lpop FOR circ/lpop>12 OFF
town              lpop   circ   circ/lpop
Bangor           31643 469167     14.83
Belfast           6243  75148     12.04
Blue Hill         1644  92502     56.27
Boothbay Harbor   2207  31359     14.21
Brooklin           619  14134     22.83
Camden            4584  67040     14.62
*** INTERRUPTED ***
```

This time, we are only interested in towns in Knox or Waldo counties that meet our criteria:

```
. LIST town, lpop, circ, circ/lpop FOR circ/lpop>12
      ^^^^ .AND. (county="Knox" .OR. county="Waldo") OFF
town              lpop   circ   circ/lpop
Belfast           6243  75148     12.04
Camden            4584  67040     14.62
Isle Au Haut        57   1656     29.05
```

Notice the parentheses in the command line above. They ensure that records will be checked for county = "Waldo" or "Knox" before being checked for circulation per capita. Without parentheses, the precedence of .AND. over .OR. would result in retrieving all Waldo County libraries and just those from Knox County that had the high circulation rate:

```
. LIST town, lpop, circ, circ/lpop FOR circ/lpop>12
      ^^^^ .AND. county="Knox" .OR. county="Waldo" OFF
town              lpop   circ   circ/lpop
Belfast           6243  75148     12.04
Camden            4584  67040     14.62
Frankfort          783     59      0.08
Isle Au Haut        57   1656     29.05
Searsport         2309  10041      4.35
Winterport        2675   8365      3.13
```

Let's say we need some quick totals by county. It takes just a few minutes to do CREATE REPORT FORM STCTYSUM.FRM. We make a point to specify that records will be grouped by county. Only totals for the specified numeric fields (in this case all of them) will be printed.

Here's part of the report (artificially compressed to fit the page):

. USE STATS83 INDEX statcty

Page No.   1
08/26/86
    Summary of Maine Library Statistics By County
                            1983

Pop	Coll	Circ	Salaries	Books	Town Funds	Total Budget

** County: Androscoggin
** Subtotal **
90556 321205 362128 367294.00 107828.00 570714.00 675125.00

** County: Aroostook
** Subtotal **
62401 265252 356069 239345.00 86811.00 378879.00 447183.00

** County: Franklin
** Subtotal **
21983 134825 123990 50880.00 36529.00 59995.00 144662.00

*** INTERRUPTED ***

Unfortunately, averages and counts are not handled as simply. Here, we calculate a few statewide averages for circulation per capita, collection per capita, and collection turnover rate:

. USE stats83
. AVERAGE circ/lpop, coll/lpop, circ/coll
    227 records averaged
  circ/lpop   coll/lpop   circ/coll
       5.84   6.24   .44052E+98

Circulation and collection divided by library population served result in plausible results. But what is that foolishness under CIRC/COLL? Apparently, at least one of the libraries in the database failed to report a figure for collection size. Division of any number by zero results in an infinitely large result. Not being comfortable with infinity, *dBase* settles for 44052 followed by 93 zeroes.

A FOR condition eliminates from the average any record that has a zero value in any of the fields involved in the calculation. Notice the changes this brings to all three calculated values:

```
. AVERAGE circ/lpop, coll/lpop, circ/coll FOR circ>0
   ^^^^ .AND. coll>0 .AND. lpop>0
   217 records averaged
 circ/lpop    coll/lpop    circ/coll
    6.05         6.34         1.13
```

The moral here: Be sure you know what is being counted before relying on the figures resulting from any calculations. One last variation gives us a set of averages by district, rather than for the whole state.

```
. AVERAGE circ/lpop, coll/lpop, circ/coll FOR circ>0
   ^^^^ .AND. coll>0 .AND. lpop>0 .AND. district="N"
    85 records averaged
 circ/lpop    coll/lpop    circ/coll
    7.39         7.79         1.10
```

If a large number of counts, averages, and sums, each with its own set of qualifying conditions, is needed, a program file is far more efficient than entering queries one at a time. A word processor offering block copy and search-and-replace functions can be used to rapidly construct a long series of commands based on a few patterns.

Here, for example, is part of a program file to calculate circulation per capita and expenditures per capita by county and several community size ranges:

```
*   STATUTIL.PRG
use c:stats83
set print on
? 'ANDROSCOGGIN:'
average circ/lpop,totexp/lpop for county='Androscoggin'
     ^^^^ .AND. circ>0 .and. totexp>0 .and. lpop>999
     ^^^^ .and. lpop<2500
? 'AROOSTOOK:'
average circ/lpop, totexp/lpop for county='Aroostook'
     ^^^^ .AND. circ>0 .and. totexp>0 .and. lpop>999
     ^^^^ .and. lpop<2500
? 'CUMBERLAND:'
average circ/lpop, totexp/lpop for county='Cumberland'
     ^^^^ .AND. circ>0 .and. totexp>0 .and. lpop>999
     ^^^^ .and. lpop<2500
```

•
•
•

```
? 'ANDROSCOGGIN:'
average circ/lpop, totexp/lpop for county='Androscoggin'
      ^^^^ .AND. circ>0 .and. totexp>0 .and. lpop>2499
      ^^^^ .and. lpop<5000
? 'AROOSTOOK:'
average circ/lpop, totexp/lpop for county='Aroostook'
      ^^^^ .AND. circ>0 .and. totexp>0 .and. lpop>2499
      ^^^^ .and. lpop<5000
? 'CUMBERLAND:'
average circ/lpop, totexp/lpop for county='Cumberland'
      ^^^^ .AND. circ>0 .and. totexp>0 .and. lpop>2499
      ^^^^ .and. lpop<5000
```

•
•
•

SET PRINT OFF

While *dBase* lacks some of the statistical functions that can be found in a package like *SPSS*, it is awfully useful for the calculation of less demanding financial and statistical relationships.

An electronic spreadsheet is still accepted among the vast majority of computer users as the tool of choice for doing periodic financial reports. Nevertheless, *dBase* can be called upon if the data is already in *dBase* format. The formulas go into a report form rather than a spreadsheet cell. Year-to-date figures for each account might be represented by TOTEXP-(QUARTER1 + QUARTER2 + QUARTER3 + QUARTER4). It is a matter of personal preference rather than demonstrable fact, but it seems the quick *ad hoc* query from the command line is faster and easier than inserting, deleting, and generally adjusting columns and rows in a spreadsheet.

BULK LOANS

Many libraries make bulk loans of materials to schools, agencies, branch operations, and institutions of various types (including other libraries). Managing such a service involves more than plain vanilla circulation management, however. (Look to the chapter on circulation for suggestions on how to keep track of such loans.) A distinguishing feature of most bulk loans is the need to determine whether a particular item has ever been loaned to the same organization before.

We will concentrate here on examining the maintenance and use of a borrowing history file. For the sake of example, we will assume an operation in which one library makes bulk loans of large-type books to other libraries.

The borrowing history file comes into play in two day-to-day connections:

1. Given a group of books, we need to find out which of them haven't previously been sent to the recipient library.
2. Given a particular library, we need to make a list of books that have not been sent to it, in shelf order. This will facilitate shelf picking preparatory to making a loan.

The bulk loan system consists of the following files: BKLIBS.DBF--Name/address information for recipient institutions, i.e., a "registration" file; BKBIB.DBF--Bibliographic information representing materials in the collection from which bulk loans are made (for demonstration purposes, this file is artificially simplified to a small number of fields); BKCIRC.DBF--Record of materials currently on loan and what library has them; and BKHASHAD.DBF--Archive file recording what libraries have had which books.

These files are structured as follows:

```
Structure for database: C:bkbib.dbf
Number of data records:        9
Date of last update    : 08/18/86
Field  Field Name  Type       Width    Dec
    1  BOOKNO      Character       5
    2  CALLNO      Character      20
    3  TITLE       Character     100
    4  AUTHFIRST   Character      15
    5  AUTHLAST    Character      20
    6  PUBLISHER   Character      40
```

```
     7   DATE          Character     10
     8   CATEGORY      Character     25
** Total **                        236
```

```
Structure for database: C:bklib.dbf
Number of data records:        5
Date of last update   : 08/18/86
Field  Field Name  Type      Width    Dec
   1   LIBNO       Character      5
   2   LIBRARY     Character     30
   3   FIRSTNAME   Character     15
   4   LASTNAME    Character     20
   5   ADR2        Character     35
   6   ADR3        Character     35
   7   CITY        Character     15
   8   STATE       Character      2
   9   ZIP         Character      9
  10   PHONE       Character     15
** Total **                    182
```

```
Structure for database: C:bkhashad.dbf
Number of data records:       15
Date of last update   : 08/18/86
Field  Field Name  Type      Width    Dec
   1   LIBNO       Character      5
   2   BOOKNO      Character      5
** Total **                     11
```

```
Structure for database: C:bkcirc.dbf
Number of data records:        4
Date of last update   : 08/18/86
Field  Field Name  Type      Width    Dec
   1   LIBNO       Character      5
   2   BOOKNO      Character      5
   3   DATEDUE     Date          8
** Total **                     19
```

Book-by-Book Check of Borrowing History

Whether on a regular schedule or in response to a specific request, large-type books are to be sent to a recipient library. General subject categories may be specified (e.g., "twenty mysteries, ten romances, ten westerns, and twenty best-sellers"), or "any twenty-five we haven't had before" may be the request with which library staff deal every month. The key is easily determining whether a book has already been sent to the library.

One approach is to check the BKHASHAD file. To simplify and streamline the check, the shortest possible unique key should be used. We will assume a five-character book number is assigned to each large-type book as it is acquired.

The task, step-by-step, goes like this:

1. Open the BKHASHAD.DBF file with the BKHCOMBO.NDX in effect.
2. With a stack of books at hand, find the book number and find it (using FIND) in BKHASHAD.DBF. (Note that this is possible as a single step because the index file is based on a composite key (BOOKNO+LIBNO)).
3. Doing IF FOUND() will indicate that the library has already had the book. Display message to user indicating that book should be reshelved.
4. Doing IF .NOT. FOUND() will tell the user just that.
5. Offer opportunity to check it out in one keystroke.

These functions can be accomplished either by creative use of function keys or by devising a small program file. First, let's look at what can be done with function keys. The file BKTEMP.PRG can be run to redefine the meaning of F10, F9, and F8.

F10 opens files and asks for the library number. F9 asks for the book number while F8 checks to see whether it has already been borrowed by a particular library. F9 and F8 alternate until a different library is to be selected with F10. If an item is eligible for sending, F7 is a one-button check-out mechanism that updates the BKCIRC.DBF file.

Here are the definitions in a file that will set these function keys:

```
. SET FUNCTION 10 TO "SELECT 2;USE bkhashad INDEX
     ^^^^ bkhcombo;SELECT 1;USE bkcirc;ACCEPT 'Library
     ^^^^ Number: ' TO currlibno;"

. SET FUNCTION 9 TO "SELE bkhashad;RELEASE currbookno;
     ^^^^ ACCEPT 'Book Number: ' TO currbookno ;"

. SET FUNCTION 8 TO "key=currbookno+currlibno ;
     ^^^^ FIND &key; ? IIF(FOUND(), 'Do not send.
     ^^^^ Library has already had this book',
     ^^^^ 'Send it!');"

. SET FUNCTION 7 TO "SELE bkcirc; APPEND BLANK;
```

```
^^^^ REPLACE libno WITH currlibno, bookno WITH
^^^^ currbookno, datedue with date()+60;
^^^^ SELE bkhashad;"
```

Here's a sample session:

```
. DO bktemp
. DISPLAY STATUS
```

(first lines of display omitted)

```
Programmable function keys:
F2  - assist;
F3  - list;
F4  - dir;
F5  - display structure;
F6  - display status;
F7  - SELE bkcirc; APPEND BLANK; REPLACE libno WITH
        ^^^^ currlibno, bookno WITH curr
F8  - key=currbookno+currlibno ; FIND &key; ?
        ^^^^ IIF(FOUND(), 'Do not send.  Libra
F9  - SELE bkhashad;RELEASE currbookno;ACCEPT 'Book
        ^^^^ Number: '    TO currbookno ;
F10 - SELECT 2;USE bkhashad INDEX bkhcombo;SELECT 1;
        ^^^^ USE bkcirc;ACCEPT 'Library Number: ' TO currlibno
```

When F10 is pressed:

```
. SELECT 2
. USE bkhashad INDEX bkhcombo
. SELECT 1
. USE bkcirc
. ACCEPT 'Library Number: ' TO currlibno
Library Number: 10002
```

Let's look at the memory variable changed by F10.

```
. DISP memory
CURRLIBNO   pub   C  "10002"
    1 variables defined,        7 bytes used
  255 variables available,   3065 bytes available
```

Now comes F9:

```
. SELE bkhashad
. RELEASE currbookno
. ACCEPT 'Book Number: '    TO currbookno
```

Book Number: 20001
```
. key=currbookno+currlibno
. FIND &key
. ? IIF(FOUND(), 'Do not send.  Library has already
    ^^^^ had this book', 'Send it!')
```
Send it!

Now use F7 to check out the book:

```
. SELE bkcirc
. APPEND BLANK
. REPLACE libno WITH currlibno, bookno WITH
    ^^^^ currbookno, datedue with date()+60
. SELE bkhashad
. display status
```

Here's what memory looks like at this point:

```
. disp memo
CURRLIBNO    pub   C  "10002"
CURRBOOKNO   pub   C  "20003"
KEY          pub   C  "2000310002"
    3 variables defined,       26 bytes used
  253 variables available,   3046 bytes available
```

Here's what our abbreviated circulation file looks like, reflecting the most recent check-out.

```
. use bkcirc
. list
Record#   LIBNO BOOKNO DATEDUE
    1   10004 20006   10/12/86
    2   10004 20005   09/03/86
    3   10001 20007   09/08/86
    4   10003 20009   09/15/86
    5   10002 20004   10/17/86
    6   10002 20003   10/17/86
```

Basically the same steps are involved in BKHADCHK.PRG, though it is not necessary to remember which function key is which. It is nicer but longer.

```
** BKHADCHK.PRG
* Prompts for library number, book number, checks
* whether library had book before.
```

```
SELE 2
USE bkhashad INDEX bkhcombo
SELE 1
USE bkcirc
SELE 2
DO WHILE .T.
   CLEAR
   currlibno=SPACE(5)
   @ 10, 10 SAY "Library ID Number: " GET currlibno
   @ 22, 20 SAY "<RETURN> alone to exit"
   READ
   IF LEN(TRIM(currlibno))=0
      CLEAR
      EXIT
   ENDIF
   DO WHILE .T.
      CLEAR
      currbookno=SPACE(5)
      @ 10,10 SAY "Book Number? " GET currbookno
      @ 22,20 SAY "<RETURN> alone to exit number
   ^^^^ specification "
      READ
      IF LEN(TRIM(currbookno))=0
         EXIT
      ENDIF
      key=currbookno+currlibno
      FIND &key
      IF FOUND()
         @ 5,25 SAY "SHELVE IT!   Library has already
   ^^^^ had title."
         @ 23,1 SAY " "
         WAIT
        ELSE
         @ 5,25 SAY "SEND IT!!!   Not in hashad file"
         answer=" "
         @ 10,1 CLEAR
         @ 10,10 SAY "Want to check book out now? "
   ^^^^ GET answer
         READ
         IF UPPER(answer)="Y"
             SELE 1
             APPEND BLANK
             REPLACE bookno WITH currbookno
             REPLACE libno WITH currlibno
             REPLACE datedue WITH date()+60
             SELE 2
          ENDIF
```

```
        ENDIF
   ENDDO inner T
ENDDO outer T
```

The length of even this small and straightforward command file certainly casts the function key approach in a favorable light!

Producing a Picking List

Work flow considerations and usage patterns will determine whether it is more convenient to check whether a library has already received a particular book before or after it is taken from the shelves. In some circumstances, it may be easier to produce a list of acceptable books, in shelf order, to guide those who take materials off the shelf.

It may be worthwhile to qualify a listing by category, publication date, or some other characteristic of the bibliographic record in order to minimize the amount of processing necessary to come up with a list of acceptable titles of sufficient size.

The steps in this process are:

1. Open the BKBIB.DBF, indexed on CALLNO (or whatever other element dictates shelving order) and BKHASHAD.DBF, which indicates which libraries have received which books.
2. Get the library number of the library for whom the list is being developed. Relate the first into the second, using BOOKNO+LIBNO as the search key.
3. Use REPORT FORM (report name) FOR currlibno <> bkhashad->libno .AND. currlibno<>bkcirc->libno.

This is the program file to do the job:

```
** BKPICK.PRG
**    Generates picking list in shelf order for books not
**    in circulation and which haven't been borrowed by
**    library before

CLEAR
currlibno=SPACE(5)
@ 10,20 SAY "Library Number? " GET currlibno
READ

USE bkbib INDEX bkcallno
SELECT 3
USE bkcirc INDEX bkccombo
```

```
SELECT 2
USE bkhashad INDEX bkhcombo
SET RELATION TO bkbib->bookno+currlibno INTO bkcirc
SELECT 1
USE bkbib INDEX bkcallno
SET RELATION TO bookno+currlibno INTO bkhashad
REPORT FORM bkpick TO PRINT NOEJECT HEADING 'Library #
      ^^^^ &currlibno' FOR currlibno<>bkhashad->libno
      ^^^^ .AND. currlibno<>bkcirc->libno
```

A sample run looking for books that could be sent to library #10004 results in the following:

```
. DO bkpick
```

Page No.   1   Library # 10004
08/18/86
                     Books That Can Be Sent

   Call Number   Title

   620   Straw Giant
   654/0678h   Hypergrowth: The Rise and Fall
                            of Osborne Computer
                            Corporation
   W/FIC   Wagons Northwest
   W/Fic   Apache Trail

A Note of Humility

A librarian with a great deal of experience in bulk loans took one look at this scheme and said, "Well, that's nice but you don't have to do that on computer, you know. We have a manual method that is much faster." Large sheets of paper with sequential numbers corresponding to numbers on each book are kept for each borrowing library. As books are sent, the numbers that correspond to them are crossed off. If you want to know which books can be sent at any moment, take the sheets to the shelf with you. They constitute a default picking list.

Testimony, once again, that that which can be done and that which should be done are not necessarily the same.

INDEX